DAYS OF PERFECT HELL

PETER L. BELMONTE

DAYS OF PERFECT HELL

OCTOBER–NOVEMBER 1918

The U.S. 26th Infantry Regiment
in the Meuse-Argonne Offensive

Library of Congress Control Number: 2015937935

Designed by Matt Goodman

Type set in Agency, Interstate & Minion
ISBN: 978-0-7643-4921-8
Printed in China

Published by Schiffer Publishing, Ltd.
4880 Lower Valley Road
Atglen, PA 19310
Phone: (610) 593-1777; Fax: (610) 593-2002
E-mail: Info@schifferbooks.com

CONTENTS

Dedication

In honor of

PRIVATE LUIGI SANTELLI
(159th Depot Brigade, Camp Taylor, Kentucky, 1918)

&

PRIVATE BENEDETTO SICILIA
(158th Depot Brigade, Camp Sherman, Ohio, 1918),
who got me started,

&

PRIVATE ANTONIO GIORNO
(Company E, 26th Infantry Regiment),
who was there.

Acknowledgments

Records of the 26th Infantry Regiment, the 1st Division, the American Expeditionary Forces, and World War I soldiers in general are located in a number of places. Many researchers helped me find and copy those records. At the National Personnel Records Center, National Archives and Records Administration (NARA), at St. Louis, Missouri, Lori Berdak Miller found records and burial files of individual soldiers. Geoff Gentilini, Sim Smiley, Phyllis Goodnow, and Dennis Coryell found and copied very important records and documents at NARA in Washington, DC, and College Park, Maryland, and in the Library of Congress. At the Wisconsin Veterans Museum in Madison, Wisconsin, Russ Horton and Laura Farley found and sent copies of individual soldiers' records. Andrew Woods, at the Colonel Robert R. McCormick Research Center in the First Division Museum at Cantigny, in Wheaton, Illinois, sent me copies of rosters and scans of images that greatly improved the book. Andrew's help was indispensible.

Alan Tallis, United Kingdom, graciously gave me permission to use information about his relative, 2nd Lt. William Mansfield, that appears on his splendid tribute website. Janice Buchanan kindly allowed me to use information and photographs she provided about her cousin, Capt. Raymond D. Wortley. Patricia Fullerton Hamman braved a recalcitrant scanner and computer to send me copies of photographs and letters from her grandfather, 2nd Lt. Charles Bushnell Fullerton, regimental adjutant.

James Carl Nelson, author of two important books on World War I (*Five Lieutenants: The Heartbreaking Story of Five Harvard Men Who Led America to Victory in World War I*, St. Martin's Press, 2012, and *The Remains of Company D: A Story of the Great War*, St. Martin's Press, 2009), was a helpful mentor. He freely gave of his time and experiences, and he provided important tips on avenues of research. Jim encouraged me and very patiently answered my questions. His encouragement kept me going.

My family has been very supportive throughout the work on this book; many thanks to my wife Pam and my children Michael, Laura, Anna, Isaiah, and Domenic. My daughter, Heather Kaufman, and my son-in-law Andrew Kaufman, have also encouraged me greatly.

Introduction

Almost 100 years ago, on October 4, 1918, the cold, wet, cramped Doughboys of the 26th Infantry Regiment crept from their muddy foxholes and advanced through murderous shell fire to meet their destiny. As machine gun fire thinned their ranks that early October morning, they had no way of knowing that they were part of the final offensive that would end the war thirty-nine days later. The Meuse-Argonne Offensive, the American portion of the overall Allied strategy for a war-ending push in the autumn of 1918, would eventually see 1.2 million American soldiers in action. The ground over which the 26th fought had been occupied by the Germans since 1914, and they had fortified it well. The hills and woods were studded with machine gun nests with interlocking fields of fire, and artillery emplacements were dug into the many hills in the area. The 1st Division moved into an area where the rookie 35th Division had come to grief. The 35th, while making some modest gains, was eventually thrown back with terrible losses.

The 26th was one of about ninety American infantry regiments to see action in the Meuse-Argonne Offensive. Professional soldiers, eager volunteers, and draftees, both willing and unwilling, filled its ranks. Almost every background and social status was represented on the roster. Here, the son of a popular US president, prominent businessmen, and lawyers, shared the field with students, laborers, and immigrants who could barely understand the orders of their officers. This is the story of what the 26th Infantry Regiment accomplished in the dank woods and hostile hills so many years ago.

By the autumn of 1918 the 26th Infantry Regiment might be considered a typical American regiment. In the battle, it occupied the right flank of the 1st Division and served to guard that flank against heavy fire and counterattacks. The steadfastness of the regiment allowed the division to advance through the outlying portions of the Hindenburg Line, the Germans' vaunted line of defensive fortifications. They anchored the advance that permitted the out-flanking of the Argonne Forest itself; this, in turn, allowed the entire American line to advance. This book is an in-depth study of the regiment's role in this pivotal battle, a battle in which it lost more than 50% of its men as casualties.

It is not my intention here to re-hash events that have received a great deal of scholarly attention. Consequently I have not covered the history of the Great War, the American Expeditionary Forces (AEF), or the strategy of the various armies. Likewise, I do not delve too deeply into the history of the 1st Division, or into the history of the Meuse-Argonne Offensive as a whole. Other historians have written ably on these topics. My chief concern was to write a detailed history of one regiment during what was the largest battle in history to date. Thus I have not gone into detail to describe the actions of divisional units, such as artillery and engineer units, that supported the 26th Infantry. Nor have I found it necessary to report at length on the German order of battle facing the regiment. The forces facing the Doughboys were tough, professional, well-equipped troops who fought from fortified positions in terrain with which they were very familiar. In particular, I have avoided lengthy discussions of the pros and cons of AEF leadership and tactics. These topics have been thoroughly reviewed in recent scholarship, and interested readers should consult the Bibliographic Essay.

I used all available sources (company rosters for October and November 1918, the 1919 regimental history, and post-war monographs) to determine the ranks of individuals referred to herein. In the text, I use the rank a man held at the time of the events described; in the endnotes and bibliography, some of those same men are referred to by their post-war rank. I have also used standard 24-hour military time for all references to time of day; officers randomly used both twenty-four-hour time and twelve-hour a.m./p.m. time in their field messages. In 24-hour military time reckoning, the hours from 1 a.m. to 12 noon are designated 0100, 0200, and so on, to 1200. The hours from 1 p.m. to 11 p.m. are designated 1300, 1400, and so on, to 2300. Midnight is typically designated 2400 to signify the end of the day and 0000 to signify the beginning of the day. In original documents and papers, distance references were mostly metric; here I've converted them to standard yards and miles unless the original reference is in a quotation.

In quotations, I've retained the original spelling, grammar, and punctuation unless doing so would cause confusion; in such cases I've made minor corrections for clarification or used "*sic*." At the risk of being too cartographically heavy, I've included many maps of the areas of operations. Some maps are those hand-drawn by officers during the battle, usually on the reverse side of field message forms; these have grid reference numbers that helped to orient their sketches with the overall attack maps issued to regimental officers (a copy of which, via the 1st Division unit history, is in the author's possession). Other maps are those hand-drawn by officers attending post-war professional Army schools; all told, the maps herein will help to orient the reader and, it is hoped, give a feel for what junior officers experienced during the battle. Many of the books and papers I've consulted are available online. To enhance clarity, for online sources I've used the basic URL in endnotes and the bibliography, thereby avoiding lengthy and cumbersome URLs.

Although this is not a history of the Meuse-Argonne Offensive, a word or two about scope of the offensive is in order. In the summer of 1918, French Marshal Ferdinand Foch, Supreme Commander for the Allies, had decided upon a series of continuing offensives by the French, British, and American armies against the Germans. Foch had assigned Gen. John J. Pershing's First Army the role of attacking the German lines in the Meuse-Argonne area. This region, which the Germans had held and fortified since late 1914, stretched from the thick, tangled Argonne Forest in the west to the Meuse River in the east. The area was "a wasteland of shell holes and barbed wire."[1] German defenses consisted of three strong fortified lines stretching east-west across the whole area. Pershing's plan was for a rapid advance of seven to ten miles to the *Kriemhilde Stellung*, the second and strongest of these lines.[2]

The start of the offensive on September 26 found nine American divisions in line between the western border of the Argonne and the Meuse River. Initial gains looked favorable, but soon the Americans became bogged down; as the Germans retreated they also rushed reinforcements to the area. By October 1, the advance had stopped far short of the initial objective. The area into which the 1st Division moved had been fought over by the 35th Division. That division had not performed as well as had been hoped, and it had suffered terrible casualties. The American army continued their advance across the broad front, slowly forcing the Germans back by brute strength and flesh and blood.

The battle dwarfed anything the American military had ever experienced. Twenty-two American divisions, 840 airplanes, 324 tanks, and almost 2,400 artillery pieces took part. The forty-seven-day offensive "sucked in 1.2 million American soldiers, leaving 26,277 of them dead and 95,786 wounded."[3] In the end, the American army accomplished its strategic goal in the Meuse-Argonne Offensive, but at a tragic cost in lives, misery, and treasure. This, then, is the story of one regiment in that American army.

One:

OVERVIEW: THE 26TH INFANTRY REGIMENT FROM 1901 TO 1918

An American Division

The basic, self-contained fighting unit in the American army was the division. At this time, a division in the American army consisted of about 28,000 men, roughly double the number of men found in divisions in Allied or German armies. The main combat component of the division was infantry; each division had two brigades of infantry, with two infantry regiments in each brigade. There was one artillery brigade in the division; in it were three artillery regiments, two of which were equipped with 75mm cannons and one of which was equipped with larger, heavier 155mm cannons, and one trench mortar battery. The division also had one engineer regiment assigned to it, along with an engineer train that hauled supplies for the engineer regiment. Each division had three machine gun battalions assigned, one to each infantry brigade and one to the division at large. The division sanitary train included four ambulance companies and four field hospitals. Other support units included a supply train, which consisted of either animal-drawn wagons or motor trucks, an ammunition train to supply all elements of the division, military police troops, and signal troops. Smaller attached units included ordnance repair shops, bath and laundry units, a bakery company, and veterinary troops to care for the many horses and mules assigned to a World War I division. The headquarters troop consisted of the division commander and his staff, including administrative personnel. The brigades each had similar headquarters troops.

In the 1st Division, the infantry units were the 1st Infantry Brigade, consisting of the 16th and 18th Infantry Regiments, and the 2nd Infantry Brigade, consisting of the 26th and 28th Infantry Regiments. Supporting the infantry regiments were the 2nd Machine Gun Battalion (attached to the 1st Infantry Brigade) and the 3rd Machine Gun Battalion (attached to the 2nd Infantry Brigade). The 1st Machine Gun Battalion was attached to the division at large. The division's artillery was formed into the 1st Field Artillery Brigade, consisting of the 5th Field Artillery Regiment (equipped with 155mm howitzers) and the 6th and 7th Field Artillery Regiments (equipped with 75mm guns). Also attached was the 1st Trench Mortar Battery. The 1st Engineer Regiment provided engineer and, as we shall see, infantry support to the entire division.[1]

Upon arrival overseas, two or more divisions would be grouped into a corps (sometimes called an Army Corps). These corps were numbered and their composition changed as divisions and other support units were transferred into and out of them depending upon the tactical situation. Two or more corps were then assigned to an army. The First Army was formed, solely of American units, in August 1918; later the Second and Third Armies would be formed.

An American Infantry Regiment, 1918

Each infantry regiment consisted of twelve rifle companies divided into three battalions. The 1st Battalion consisted of Companies A, B, C, and D. The 2nd Battalion consisted of Companies E, F, G, and H. The 3rd Battalion consisted of Companies I, K, L, and M. Each battalion had a small headquarters staff. There was also a Machine Gun Company and a Supply Company in each regiment. The Headquarters Company consisted of the regimental commander and his staff, along with support platoons. These platoons consisted of support troops that would be assigned to various regimental units during an assault; they included the signal, trench mortar, 37mm (or one-pounder), pioneer, personnel, intelligence, and mess platoons. During combat, the men in these platoons would perform their various functions in support of the regiment at large or would be assigned to the battalions as necessary. Also the regimental band was in Headquarters Company; during combat these men often functioned as litter-bearers. A medical detachment rounded out each regiment.

By autumn 1918, each rifle company consisted of four platoons, each containing fifty-eight men – three sergeants, eight corporals, and forty-seven privates – led by a lieutenant. Each platoon consisted of a small headquarters and four sections. Each section within a platoon was led by a corporal or a sergeant, and each section was composed of one type of weapon specialty. There was a rifle section, automatic rifle section, rifle grenadier section, and hand grenade (also called hand bomber) section.[2]

Before discussing the weapons available to the Doughboys of the 26th, it is helpful to take an in-depth look at the typical attack formation of the 1st Division. The division's "normal formation" consisted of both brigades abreast; within each brigade front, both regiments formed abreast so that the entire division front consisted of the four regiments abreast. Each regiment formed in column of battalions. The first line battalion was the assault battalion; behind this battalion came the support battalion. The third line battalion was typically held in either division or brigade reserve, to be used at the division or brigade commander's discretion, respectively.

In each regiment's attack column, each battalion of four companies was formed with two companies abreast in the front line, and two companies abreast in the second line. Each company, in turn, placed two platoons abreast in the first line and two platoons in support, following at about fifty yards. Each platoon was formed in two lines with a half-platoon in each line and fifty yards between lines. Thus the very front of a regiment in assault usually consisted of two companies with four half-platoons abreast. Following the first line companies by 100-150 yards were the second line companies in the assault battalion; these second line companies were typically deployed in section or squad columns during the advance.[3]

An attached machine gun company followed the assault battalion by fifty yards; they were accompanied by Stokes mortars and a one-pounder, or 37mm, gun from the regimental Headquarters Company. Following this line by perhaps 500 yards was the support battalion, again deployed in much the same way as the assault battalion. The reserve battalion, arrayed in a similar manner, often followed the support battalion. Thus we can see that the advancing formation of three battalions in column gave great depth to the attack.

This formation had advantages and disadvantages. A formation of this depth would make it easier, in theory at least, to provide flank protection and liaison. If the lines maintained proper intervals, it would also lessen the chance of increased casualties due to enemy artillery. In combat, however, the natural tendency was for the lines to close up and merge, and this resulted in increased casualties. Also, a large number of men spread out over such a large area compounded problems of command and control. The limited number of officers and NCOs meant that, once under fire, elements of these formations often had to fend for themselves.

The US Army tactics of the time called for what was termed open warfare. This consisted of a reliance on a war of maneuver and mass whereby long lines of infantry, formed as indicated above, advanced against an enemy and, using primarily rifle fire and the bayonet, drove the enemy away or killed them. The complex realities of modern warfare, however, caused the Army to alter its tactics. Most of the change came from the lower level commands; platoon leaders, company commanders, and battalion commanders soon found out that advancing in long, straight lines against machine guns and artillery was a prescription for disaster.

Therefore, those small units in combat adapted their open warfare training to allow an increased reliance on support weapons such as machine guns and artillery. Instead of using a frontal assault against prepared positions, commanders learned to infiltrate forward in smaller groups; the men themselves, on the battlefield, learned to attack machine gun nests by outflanking them and by using rifles and grenades. Officers and enlisted men were, in many cases, slow to adapt to warfare as it existed on the Western Front; indeed, it had taken the other belligerents many years to come to the same conclusions. Still, in varying degrees in the AEF and with varying degrees of success, the units came to change their tactics to align more with the war into which they had been thrust.

1ST DIVISION TYPICAL ATTACK FORMATION, ASSAULT BATTALION

(Support Battalion Follows by approximately, 440 Yards)

Direction of Advance

ASSAULT COMPANIES

COMPANY A — 1ST PLATOON, 2ND PLATOON

COMPANY B — 1ST PLATOON, 2ND PLATOON

(25 YARDS)

(Assault platoons deployed as skirmishers)

3RD PLATOON, 4TH PLATOON, 3RD PLATOON, 4TH PLATOON

(Support platoons deployed in section or squad columns, follow assault platoons by 75 yards)

(300 YARDS)

SUPPORT COMPANIES

COMPANY C — 1ST PLATOON, 2ND PLATOON

COMPANY D — 1ST PLATOON, 2ND PLATOON

(75 YARDS)

3RD PLATOON, 4TH PLATOON, 3RD PLATOON, 4TH PLATOON

(All platoons in support companies deployed in section or squad columns)

(75 YARDS)

(machine guns, 37mm guns, trench mortars and Battalion HQ)

(Formation front approximately 600-800 yards wide)

American Weapons

The weapon in the hands of most riflemen of the 26th throughout the Meuse-Argonne Offensive was the Model 1903 Springfield rifle. The '03 Springfield was forty-five inches long with a twenty-four-inch barrel, and weighed eight pounds, eleven ounces. It was equipped with a sixteen-inch-long bayonet weighing one pound. The Springfield, modeled on the famous German Mauser rifle, was reliable and extremely accurate and had great range, "being sighted from 200 to 2,850 yards." It fired a .30 caliber bullet in clips of five, with a muzzle velocity of 2,700 feet per second. A rifleman going into combat would carry at least 100 rounds of rifle ammunition; usually they carried two extra bandoliers of ammo, each with sixty rounds.[4]

Officers and NCOs were armed with the Model 1911 Colt .45-caliber pistol. This reliable weapon used a seven-round clip. As an affectation of the times, many officers carried a cane into combat.

Each platoon was armed with four French Model 1915 Chauchat automatic rifles. Really a light machine gun, the .315-caliber Chauchat was fed by a twenty-round semi-circular magazine that was inserted in the underside of the gun; it weighed nineteen pounds and had a rate of fire of 240 rounds per minute. The gun was of questionable reliability; the magazines had "windows" through which the gunner could see how many rounds he had left in the magazine. Dirt and mud easily entered into the magazine through these apertures and soon lodged in the gun's mechanism, causing jams. A skilled gunner, however, could give the platoon an enormous amount of firepower. The Chauchat was crewed by three men, a gunner and two assistants/ ammunition carriers. Each man carried about twenty magazines, each one weighing two pounds.[5]

American soldiers with Hotchkiss machine guns, as used by machine gun units in the 1st Division. Note 25-round strips loaded into the guns. (Courtesy Colonel Robert R. McCormick Research Center.)

Firing Stokes mortars, 165th Infantry Regiment, 42nd Division. The 26th Infantry Regiment was equipped with this type of mortar. (Courtesy Colonel Robert R. McCormick Research Center.)

Each platoon also had hand grenade and rifle grenade sections. The so-called "hand bombers" threw standard fragmentation grenades. The rifle grenadiers affixed a cup to the end of their rifles, into which they inserted a grenade. Firing a blank cartridge caused the gas from the cartridge to eject the grenade toward the enemy. Both hand and rifle grenades were very effective tools in assaulting machine gun nests and positions located in ravines or on reverse slopes of hills.

On the march, the rifleman typically was laden with about seventy pounds of clothing, equipment, and weaponry. The auto-riflemen, due to the greater weight of the Chauchat and ammo, often carried about twenty pounds more than that. In combat, the men shed extra clothing and other items deemed non-essential to survival; the burden would be lessened to about 45-50 pounds.

Thus the platoon itself, deployed for combat in either half-platoons or by combat groups, could field forty-eight rifles and four Chauchat auto-rifles. It's important to keep in mind that, as the Doughboys of the 26th moved forward by platoons over the hills and through the ravines and woods, they carried, in varying configurations, rifles, auto-rifles, pistols, hand grenades, and rifle grenades. These were the primary tools with which each platoon confronted the enemy; their support weapons often followed close behind.

The machine gun was the primary portable support weapon. The 26th Infantry Regiment was supported by machine gun companies; one such company, the regimental Machine Gun Company, was organic to the regiment, and the others were part of separate machine gun battalions assigned to the brigades or division. Typically, one machine gun company would advance with and support each battalion. In the 1st

French 75mm artillery piece, the type used by the 6th and 7th Field Artillery Regiments in support of the 26th Infantry Regiment. (Courtesy Colonel Robert R. McCormick Research Center.)

Division during the Meuse-Argonne Offensive, all machine gun units used the Model 1914 Hotchkiss machine gun. This French-made was gas operated and air-cooled. The Hotchkiss had a rate of fire of 400 rounds per minute, and was fed using twenty-five-round metal strips. It fired a .315-caliber round and was very effective. The Hotchkiss was subject to some disadvantages. The gun itself weighed about fifty-two pounds and the tripod another fifty, making it difficult for the gunners carrying such a heavy load to keep up with the advancing infantry. Once set up, the gun's relatively high profile made it an easier target, and during rapid fire, it could overheat.[6]

The regimental Headquarters Company had a type of heavy weapons platoon consisting of six three-inch Stokes mortars and three 37mm guns. In the assault, two mortars and one 37mm cannon accompanied each battalion. The Stokes mortar fired an eleven-pound high explosive shell a maximum of about 875 yards. The mortar, consisting of the tube, bipod, and base plate, was quite heavy, weighing almost 110 pounds. It was very difficult for the crews to keep up with the riflemen during an advance; keeping the mortar supplied with ammunition was also a challenge. However, the mortar could be an effective weapon against troops or machine gun emplacements on the far side of hills or in ravines.[7]

The 37mm cannon, also known as a "one-pounder," fired a high-explosive shell that actually weighed about 1.5 pounds. Its maximum range was from 1,100 to 1,600 yards. The gun, being very accurate, was effective against machine gun nests and

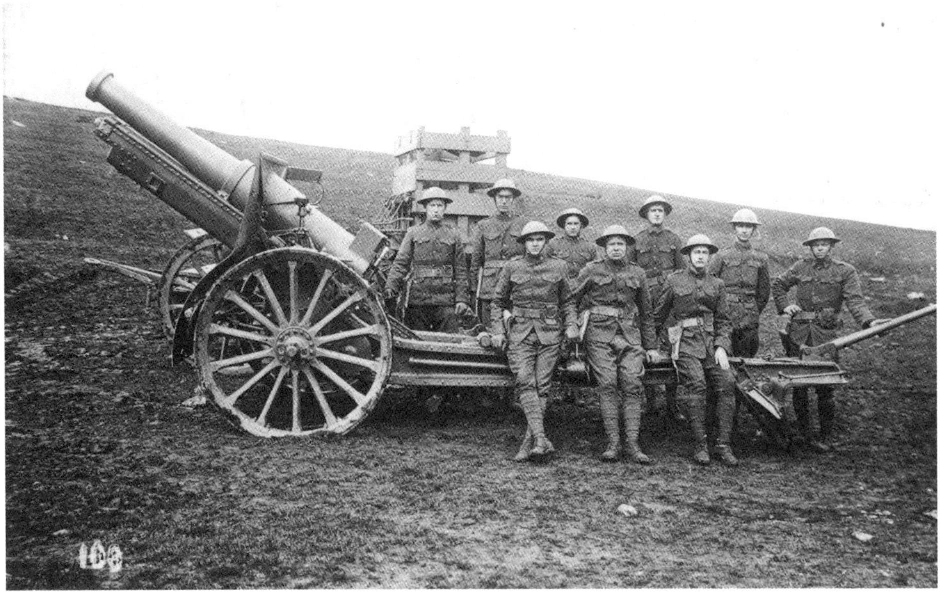

French 155mm artillery piece, the type used by the 5th Field Artillery Regiment in support of the 26th Infantry Regiment. (Courtesy Colonel Robert R. McCormick Research Center.)

other strongpoints. One type of shell could pierce armor almost one inch thick at 2,500 yards. It could also fire a shrapnel shell, "which formed a cone-shaped pattern that was effective against personnel at seventy-five yards." A skilled three-man crew could fire 28-35 rounds per minute. The gun and its carriage weighed 170 pounds.[8]

The 26th was supported by the artillery of the 1st Field Artillery Brigade. The 5th Field Artillery Regiment was equipped with 155mm howitzers. During the Meuse-Argonne Offensive, it provided support to the entire division at large. The 6th and 7th Field Artillery Regiments were equipped with the lighter 75mm gun. The 7th Regiment supported the 26th Infantry during the battle. Also assigned to the artillery brigade was the 1st Trench Mortar Battery, equipped with six-inch Newton mortars.

The ubiquitous French-made 75mm gun was a reliable workhorse that could fire 15-20 rounds per minute in the hands of a good crew. The 75mm could fire either a 16-pound shrapnel shell or a 12.3-pound high explosive shell "to ranges of 9,100 yards and 9,846 yards, respectively."[9] The 5th Artillery used the French made 155mm howitzer. This gun, an excellent counter-battery weapon, was extremely accurate. It could deliver shells weighing 95-99 pounds to distances exceeding 21,000 yards.[10]

German Weapons

The Doughboys of the 26th, armed with and supported by the weapons mentioned above, advanced against skilled veteran soldiers using similar weapons against them. While still crouching in their foxholes, and indeed, even well behind the lines, the Doughboys were subject to artillery bombardment. The Germans used a 77mm gun that fired shrapnel, high explosive, and gas shells. These weapons were feared, deadly, and accurate. The shells from Austrian 88mm guns fired on a flat trajectory moved so fast that they detonated before the report of the gun was heard; the men called these types of shells "whiz-bangs." Long-range mortars included a 210mm behemoth that was very effective and in use against the 26th during the offensive.

German *minenwerfers* (trench mortars or "mine throwers") came in a variety of calibers: 76mm, 170mm, and 250mm. These weapons could be used "with pinpoint accuracy" against American positions comparatively close to German lines. The mortars could fire further, too. The Model 1916 76mm mortar could, for example, throw a ten-pound shell 1,422 yards.[11]

One of the most fearsome weapons used against Americans was the German Maxim machine gun. Actually two types of Maxims were in use, the heavy and light models. Each one fired .311-caliber rounds at an astonishing 600 to 700 rounds per minute rate. The machine guns were "[h]ated and feared more than any other weapon in the war ... no one ever doubted the bravery of the gun crews, few of which were ever taken prisoner. As the advancing waves rolled over them, the guns were fired until the last." These guns mowed down waves of attacking Doughboys like wheat.[12]

During an assault, those Doughboys who survived the rain of shrapnel, high explosives, and gas from German artillery, and the scything fire of the German machine guns, then had to contend with German rifles and grenades. The German riflemen were typically armed with the Mauser, which fired a .311 caliber bullet and was sighted from 440 to 2,600 yards. It was also equipped with a "rapier-like bayonet."[13] German snipers, using the Mauser with a telescopic sight, were very successful, preying upon unwary Americans who showed themselves carelessly.

Almost all soldiers who fought in World War I had to contend with poison gas. The two main types encountered by the 26th during the Meuse-Argonne Offensive were mustard and phosgene, but chlorine gas was also common.[14] The normal delivery method was by artillery shell, however many men were exposed when they passed over, or dug into, ground that had been previously saturated with gas. Exposure to poison gas was not always fatal. However, gas caused painful, frightening, debilitating wounds that often affected a person for life. Mustard gas was the most feared. It caused no immediate problems, but a few hours after a soldier was exposed he would "develop extremely painful blisters, especially on uncovered parts of his body, under his arms, and in his crotch. Then the eyes would burn and swell shut, causing temporary and sometimes permanent blindness." If a soldier inhaled mustard gas, the final stages were painful: his lungs would develop blisters and bleed; the mucous membranes would dissolve, "usually leading to a lingering, agonizing death." Phosgene, too, if inhaled, eventually dissolved the soldier's lungs.[15] Both sides had and used effective gas masks and trained in gas discipline.

Gas produced desired effects. Soldiers had to don and wear gas masks for a prolonged period of time; these masks, while effectively protecting the wearer from gas, made many wearers claustrophobic. The eyepieces fogged up and breathing was difficult. Soldiers wearing these devices in the midst of battle were quickly fatigued and dehydrated. Men would more easily become disoriented and confused, and difficulties in command and control were magnified. At night, rest would be difficult if not impossible.

In addition to gas shells, both sides used high explosive (HE) and shrapnel shells. High explosive shells were of varying calibers and explosive power. The shells could be fused to explode just before impact with the ground, upon impact, or just after impact. Upon explosion, HE shells sprayed the area with deadly shards of jagged metal. The concussive power of these shells was astonishing. Explosions could suck the air from men's lungs and crush internal organs. After every heavy bombardment, some men were found dead but without any marks on their body. Prolonged exposure to severe bombardment, such as that delivered before the assault at St. Mihiel and earlier in the Somme Offensive, could drive men mad. The relentless pounding jangled nerves and dulled men's sensibilities. It made some men who survived the ordeal unfit for further active service. Still, during even the most savage, prolonged bombardment, enough men survived in dugouts to exact a very dear toll on the assaulting forces. Shrapnel shells contained dozens of lead balls. Timed to explode in the air above infantrymen, the shells were like huge shotgun shells and caused fearful wounds.[16]

The 26th Infantry Regiment, 1901-1918

The 26th Infantry Regiment was formed as part of the Regular Army on February 2, 1901. A month later, the regiment transferred to the Philippines where it saw active service against rebel Filipinos. In July 1903, the regiment transferred back to the US where it assumed duties in Texas. In May 1907, the 26th returned to the Philippines for another two-year stint; this was followed by a four-year tour in the cold expanses of Michigan and, in 1913, a transfer to Texas. Upon orders from the War Department, in August 1915, the regiment began patrols along the Rio Grande River and along the St. Louis, Brownsville, and Mexico Railroad.[17]

When the United States declared war on Germany on April 6, 1917, the US Army had no tactical unit as large as a division. President Woodrow Wilson chose Gen. John Pershing to command the first troops to be sent to France, and he gave Pershing the authority to select which units would make up this first contingent. The 26th Infantry Regiment was still engaged in patrol duty, stationed at San Benito, Texas, when it received the call for overseas duty. The regiment left San Benito on June 3, 1917, bound for the port of embarkation. On June 13, the 26th boarded the transports *San Jacinto*, *Momus*, and *Lenape*, bound for France. After an uneventful crossing, the regiment arrived safely at St. Nazaire on June 27.[18] Thus the initial cadre of the 26th consisted of regulars who had been in the Army before the declaration of war, augmented by a large number of men who enlisted in the Army after April 6. Later this composition would change as replacements from the National Army, draftees, began to arrive.

At this time, General Headquarters (GHQ) of the American Expeditionary Forces (AEF) planned for a 16-week, six-phase training period in France for newly arriving divisions. The first two phases, to last seven weeks, provided for training small units, from squad to battalion, in tactics and weapons then in use on the Western Front. The next two phases, lasting six weeks, were devoted to training regiments and

Officers of the 26th Infantry Regiment, Gondrecourt, France, October, 1917. Lieutenant Colonel Theodore Roosevelt, Jr., future commander of the regiment, is kneeling in the front row, third from the right. Others in the photograph include Captains Lyman S. Frasier, Paul N. Starlings, and Barnwell R. Legge, all of whom figured in the fighting one year later. (SC-111, WWI Signal Corps Photo #80071, National Archives.)

brigades. The fifth phase was to train the division and lasted three weeks. The sixth and final phase continued with division training and culminated in an inspection by the corps commander to determine whether the division was combat ready.[19] To begin their training the 26th moved to the Gondrecourt area in mid-July and came under the tutelage of French instructors from the elite Alpine Chasseurs. The men were instructed in hand grenades and Chauchat automatic rifles, and they built trenches and laid barbed wire defenses. The men of the 26th were being introduced to the methods and tactics of modern war.[20]

By October, training had progressed enough to permit the 1st Battalion to enter the trenches in the Luneville Sector. Per the AEF training plan, each company had a short stint in the front lines, learning more of the intricacies of trench warfare. After ten days, the 2nd Battalion relieved the 1st, and the 3rd in turn relieved the 2nd. On October 13, Company I had the distinction of suffering the 26th's first combat casualties as three men were killed and five others wounded by shellfire. Upon relief from the trenches, each battalion underwent more training.[21]

In November the regiment received its first influx of reserve officers, fresh from training in the US and France. It then "entered upon a period of training the severity of which had probably never before been experienced by American soldiers."[22] The men trained in both trench and open warfare. Building up from platoon to battalion, then regiment, and finally brigade level exercises, the men honed the skills they'd soon need in the front lines. In early January 1918, the entire division participated in maneuvers.

On March 2, the regiment began movement to Rambucourt, preparatory to entering the front lines near Toul. Germans on Mont Sec, a large hill to the regiment's front, had perfect observation of the Americans. As was common throughout the war, this necessitated a nocturnal existence in the trenches; men slept by the light of day and worked in the gloom of night. The area was considered a rest sector; the French and Germans here had adopted a live-and-let-live attitude. However, in the mud and slush, the regiment conducted trench raids and learned still more of the intricacies of trench warfare and trench life. In due course the regiment bagged its first enemy prisoner. Perhaps most importantly, the men were subject to three gas bombardments. They were becoming familiar with the milieu of the modern battlefield, and they learned to function while wearing an uncomfortable gas mask. On April 1, the 26th was relieved from the line. During this period, the regiment suffered 101 casualties.[23]

While the 26th lived in the mud of the trenches in front of Mont Sec, the Germans, on March 21, began a great offensive, another attempt to push on to Paris. The 26th, after a brief rest at Bois L'Eveque near Toul, moved northwest to Picardy to help stem the German tide. Before being committed to the line, however, the regiment was pleased to enjoy pleasant spring days in nice surroundings, a wonderful change from the misery of living in sodden trenches while under observation by the enemy. On April 24, the 1st Brigade (16th and 18th Infantry Regiments) went into line to relieve a French unit while the 2nd Brigade (26th and 28th Infantry Regiments) waited in reserve near Froissy.[24]

On the night of May 15-16 the 26th Infantry relieved the 16th Infantry in the Broyes Sector. Although the relief went well, on May 16 the regiment suffered its first casualties in the sector, "and from that date almost until the end of our tour, scarcely a day passed without its toll."[25] The division was at the point of the most advanced German salient; the 26th fought skirmishes almost every day until mid-June. The men were subjected to gas and high explosive bombardment and trench raids. They lost their first prisoner during a series of raids on their lines on May 27; the regiment, however, didn't lose any ground.

The 1st Division entered into history on May 28 when the 28th Infantry attacked and took the village of Cantigny after an artillery bombardment. The 26th was to the right of the 28th, ready to lend support if necessary; the 1st Battalion of the 26th helped to repulse two counterattacks from the right flank. The taking and holding of Cantigny, although a comparatively minor affair, was of great significance. It provided a brake to the German onslaught, halting their momentum.

After Cantigny the regiment once again settled down to life in the trenches. Each night there was ample work to do improving trenches, stringing wire, and patrolling no-man's land. The 26th conducted trench raids and captured prisoners. On July 7, the regiment was relieved by French infantry; it retired to Haudivillers where it remained for two days before the 2nd Brigade was called to act as corps reserve for the French in Campremy. The 26th remained there for five days. Upon relief, the regiment moved to Ermenonville, about nineteen miles northeast of Paris. The weary men enjoyed "the beautiful surroundings and luxurious billets" for only two days before boarding trucks destined for the front once again.[26] The 1st Division, now under Maj.Gen. Charles P. Summerall, who would command the division through October 12, was tasked with helping to stop the renewed German drive toward Paris.

The 2nd Battalion went into line on the night of July 16, relieving a Moroccan division near Soissons; the 3rd Battalion moved up in support while the 1st Battalion was in brigade reserve. The regiment faced rolling terrain "which concealed hundreds of machine gun nests and fortified heights." The Germans were confident and bent

Major General Charles P. Summerall, commander of the 1st Division from the start of the offensive until October 12, 1918, in an early post-war photograph. (Courtesy Colonel Robert R. McCormick Research Center.)

on taking Paris; the combined American and French lines were equally determined to stop them.

On the morning of July 18, the Doughboys attacked simultaneously with the start of a rolling barrage. For the next five days the 26th fought desperately through the French countryside and destroyed villages. Their ranks were thinned by machine gun and shellfire as they steadily pushed the Germans back. The French-American victory here "marked the turning point in that great German offensive which began early in March and had continued almost without interruption."[27]

They were finally relieved by Scottish troops on July 22. The regiment suffered a tragic loss of 1,560 enlisted men killed and wounded; the officers lost twenty killed and forty-two wounded. Among the dead were the regimental commander, Col. Hamilton A. Smith, and the assistant commander, Lt.Col. Clark R. Elliott. By July 24 the weary Doughboys arrived in the area around Orry-le-Ville for a much needed rest.[28]

St. Mihiel

The 1st Division was to be a key part of the first offensive action by the newly formed American First Army under Gen. Pershing. The Americans were given the task of reducing the St. Mihiel salient, a large triangular-shaped area bulging into the American lines between Verdun in the north and Pont-a-Mousson in the southeast. Each of the legs of the triangle that faced the allies was about sixteen miles long. The Germans had occupied this area since their September 1914, offensive. The salient had served to complicate Allied transportation lines in the area, and it afforded the Germans with a wonderful observation post atop Mont Sec, which dominated the whole area.[29] The 1st Division's zone was along the southern face of the salient, between Marvosin on the left and Seicheprey on the right. The 26th occupied the right flank of the line, with its right flank resting on Seicheprey.

The 26th moved to Pont-a-Mousson in the Saizerais Sector where they received about 1,500 replacements from such units as the 4th Depot Division (formerly the 85th Division). These men filled ranks greatly depleted by the terrible combat at Soissons. While in this relatively quiet sector, the new men had to quickly blend into the veteran regiment and learn from the experienced men. For training, they engaged in limited patrolling in the thick woods and manned listening posts day and night. For recreation, the men tended gardens left by their predecessors in the sector; also, the divisional engineers had dammed a creek in the area, creating a swimming hole which saw "hundred[s] of doughboys splashing about" from time to time. On August 22, the 26th left the sector and trucked to Uruffe.[30]

With the arrival of so many new men, mostly draftees, the complexion of the regiment changed, but the spirit did not. Many of them had been drafted at the end of May and were now in an active, if not particularly dangerous, sector. Just over two months had passed since they had been civilians; much of their time thus far in the Army had been taken up with administrative issues and travel. This illustrates the precarious position that replacements found themselves in. Men who had been drafted in the spring and summer of 1918 and sent as replacements to combat units rarely had more than two or three months of service before being sent to a sector; what usually followed quickly enough was actual combat. Men who had been drafted or enlisted earlier had the luxury of being able to absorb much more training, to include training that gradually exposed them to active sectors and operations. The new men also had the unenviable task of trying to blend into a cohesive unit with longer-serving veterans who had formed bonds during combat. Since the roster of the regiment in late August was roughly the same as it was during the Meuse-Argonne Offensive, it is worth examining the St. Mihiel Offensive in some detail.

At Uruffe, the men underwent a ten-day training schedule that included terrain exercises with tanks and artillery rumbling in the background.[31] On September 8, the regiment marched to Reine Woods. The going was miserable with knee-deep mud and vehicles of every description blocking the boggy roads. On September 11, the infantry began to move into position for the start of the St. Mihiel Offensive. The 26th Infantry Regiment occupied a front of 660 yards on the right of the 1st Division line. Once again the men were in front of the German observation posts on the imposing Mont Sec, just to the left of the division's sector. The veterans in the group could well remember the barbed wire positions and guns that awaited them. So good was the view from the hill that "observers on Mont Sec could tell what we had for breakfast. There was never a better example of the enemy being able to look down your throat."[32]

Jump-off was scheduled for 0500 on September 12. The assault, to be led by the 3rd Battalion on the 26th's front, with the 2nd Battalion in support, was preceded by a four-hour bombardment of the enemy's lines. When it let loose, the men watched in awe of the powerful barrage sent over to the Germans. The "preparatory fire of the artillery was imposing and awe inspiring to a degree. If the Hun had been undecided about moving out of the salient there was little doubt left in his mind a few minutes after the bombardment started. He shot up every rocket he could lay hands on, and a lot we had never seen before."[33]

At precisely 0550, the men went over the top. Things went like clockwork; the initial resistance of occasional shellfire and machine gun fire was less than expected. The regiment reached its first objective before 0600, and then moved to the second. "The most serious resistance of the day was encountered between the 2nd and 3rd objectives at the southern edge of the Quart de Reserve," through which woods the enemy's main line of resistance ran. By attacking and flanking this area, the 26th was able to move on. At the third objective, the 2nd Battalion leapfrogged the 3rd and resumed the assault. At 1100, following behind a rolling barrage, the infantry reached the day's objective; at noon the men eagerly consumed their rations of hard bread and "bully-beef" (canned beef). The regiment was ordered to continue its advance; by the end of the day, they had advanced a total of five miles while suffering relatively light casualties.[34]

At 1730 the 1st Division was ordered forward to cut the Vigneulles-St. Benoit road, a thoroughfare vital to the safe evacuation of German forces. With the 2nd Battalion leading, the 26th moved forward into Bois de Vigneulles. Company E, deployed as skirmishers, was sent ahead to cut the road and the adjacent railroad line. As darkness fell, the advance in the thick woods slowed as men became confused and squads began to separate from platoons. During each halt, tired men fell asleep and could not be roused. Soon Maj. William C. Whitener, commander of the 2nd Battalion, determined that he had only remnants of his battalion left; the others were lost, wandering in the woods. Moving forward through the tangled woods and bushes, Whitener managed to collect about forty-five men; these he placed under Capt. Rice Youell, commander of Company E. Youell and his men went forward to cut the road, along which traffic could be heard in the distance.[35]

By 0500, Youell and his small detachment managed to cut a secondary road and in the process bag almost 200 prisoners and destroy three enemy machine guns. An hour and a half later, the primary road and an adjacent railroad line was cut by elements of the 3rd Battalion.[36]

On September 13, the 2nd Battalion now leading, the regiment again advanced against fading opposition. Later that day, elements of the 1st Division moving north met up with elements of the 26th Division coming from the west, and the St. Mihiel salient was effectively cut off. The 1st Division was pulled back into reserve. It had advanced nine miles as the crow flies. The 26th Infantry Regiment suffered six killed and ninety-six wounded. It had captured 350 prisoners.[37]

Participation in this successful battle helped the unit cohesion of the 26th. It served to make the new men more at ease with active campaigning, and it instilled confidence in the officers and enlisted men. Captain Walter R. McClure, commander of Company M, recalled that a, "successful attack without heavy losses is the best training that green troops can have. Every man in the 1st Division felt that he was a hardened veteran and that he belonged to an outfit that was at the height of battle efficiency."[38] This self-confidence and esprit was vitally important to the 26th Infantry Regiment as it marched forth to participate in what was to be the largest and bloodiest battle fought by American troops to date.

In the final months of 1918, the Allied high command had planned a concerted effort to drive the German armies back along all fronts. On September 26, the AEF's portion of the final Allied thrust of 1918 was scheduled to begin. First Army's role in the Meuse-Argonne Offensive was to attack, generally northward, on a broad front. The eastern limit of this front was the Meuse River, and the western limit, the vast stretches of the almost impenetrable Argonne Forest. The monumental task of moving 600,000 men of the First Army from thc St. Mihiel battlefield northwest to the Meuse-Argonne area in ten days was accomplished despite logistical and transportation obstacles. The 26th Infantry Regiment was part of this great move to the northwest.

Following the St. Mihiel Offensive, on September 21, the regiment rode all night on French trucks to Neuville, where they spent two uncomfortable days bivouacked in the woods. Later they proceeded to Bulainville where they received a small number of replacements and participated in such training as night marches through the woods and small unit tactics.[39]

The 1st Division, and the 26th Infantry Regiment, were on the eve of participating in the greatest battle ever fought by American forces.

Two:

"GRUELING DAYS," SEPTEMBER 26 THROUGH OCTOBER 3

September 26 to September 29

On September 26, the 1st Division was assigned to III Corps, in the east near Verdun, and was designated as First Army reserve. On September 29, the division was assigned to I Corps in the west and ordered to move that night. The division moved by truck to Neuvilly, and on the 30th, Maj.Gen. Summerall was ordered to relieve the 35th Division by 0500 the next day. Most of the area designated for the American attack, including the 1st Division's assigned area, was covered by a series of hills with wooded heights and intervening ravines filled with tangled, thick woods. In short, it was an area ideal for defense but a nightmare for attacking troops.

The 35th Division occupied the sector east of the Argonne Forest proper; they had jumped off on September 26 and had suffered badly. They had achieved some initial success, but in the process, like many of the American divisions in the initial advance, they had become disorganized and tired. The "1st Division came into line with orders to continue the First Army attack immediately upon completion of the relief."[1] With the disorganization of the 35th Division, however, the relief was more difficult than anticipated. Therefore, the attack orders were canceled on the night of the 30th. The renewed attack was scheduled to jump off on October 4.

September 30 to October 3

For the start of this phase of the Meuse-Argonne Offensive, Col. Hjalmar Erickson, "a fine troop leader and a powerful man physically," who had joined the regiment just after the St. Mihiel Offensive, was the commander of the 26th Infantry Regiment.[2] Major Barnwell R. Legge, a twenty-seven-year old South Carolinian, commanded the 1st Battalion. Captain Raymond Wortley, a twenty-six-year old native Kansan who had come up through the enlisted ranks in the California National Guard, commanded the 2nd Battalion. Major Lyman S. Frasier, a twenty-six-year old native New Yorker, commanded the 3rd Battalion.[3]

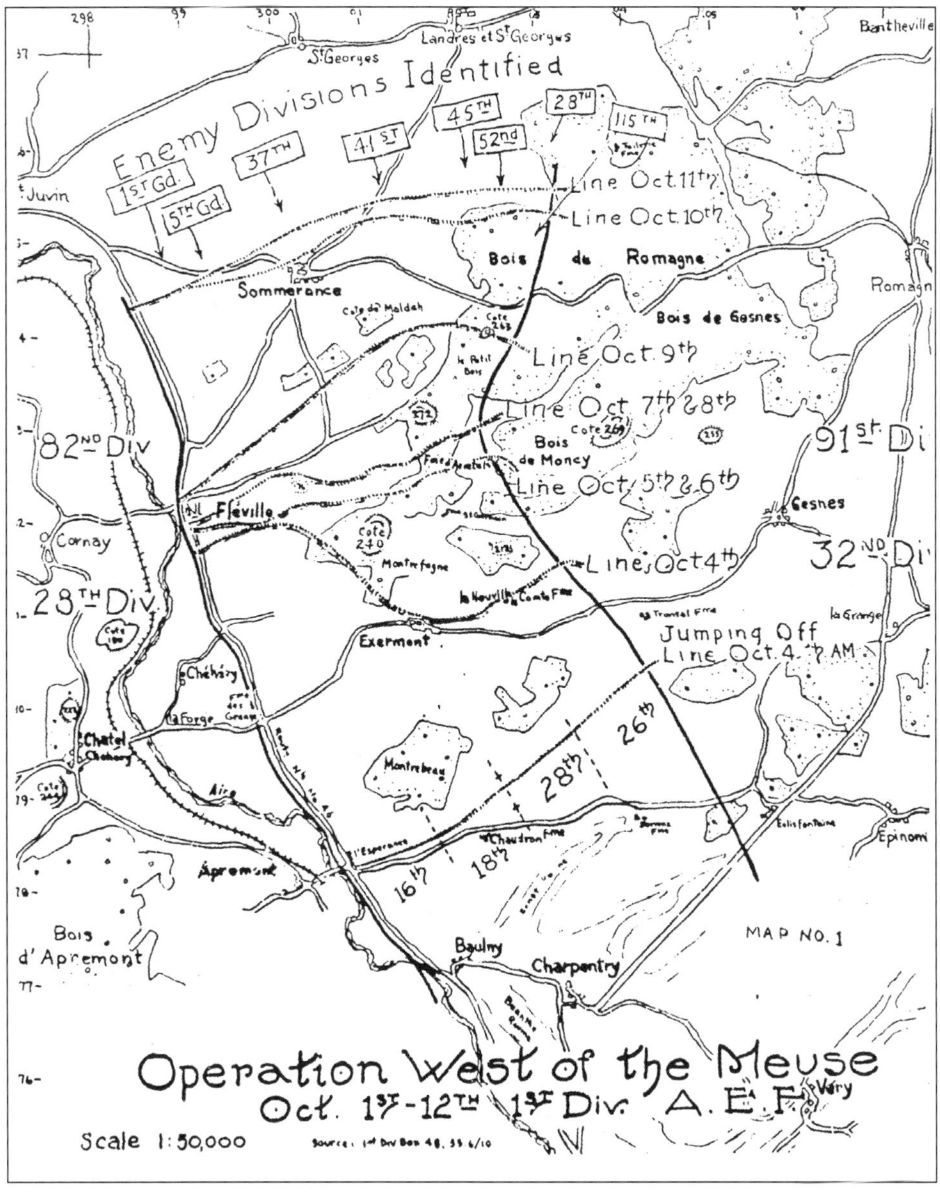

Map showing the 1st Division area of operations, October 4 through 12, 1918. (Cochran, "The 1st Division Along the Meuse.")

The 1st Division was to go into line, from left to right, 16th Infantry Regiment, 18th Infantry Regiment (these regiments comprising the 1st Brigade), 28th Infantry Regiment, and 26th Infantry Regiment (these regiments comprising the 2nd Brigade). The 26th arrived at the Post of Command (PC) of the 35th Division at Cheppy by the evening of September 30. According to Maj. Frasier, "no definite line existed on the right of the 35th Division where the 2nd Brigade was to make its relief. No one could be found who knew where the enemy was except that he was in a northerly direction."[4] The regiment moved up through Very by midnight and effectively relieved their portion of the 35th Division.[5] Very, once a thriving community, was now in ruins. The men moved cautiously over ground that had been fought over by the 35th Division; the muddy ground was marked by huge shell holes, some large enough to hold a small house. Advancing in the dark, the men had to contend with barbed wire, wrecked machine gun nests, dead, bloated horses, and the miscellaneous filthy detritus of war. Some units moved through mine fields.[6]

Second Lieutenant Clarence Crossland, adjutant of the 3rd Battalion, recalled what greeted his first glimpse of the area: "Splintered trees machine-gunned knee high and dead bodies of fallen Germans and horses." Years later he still remembered: "Many younger Germans had been killed, while older ones with families had to fight the losing battle – a touching sight to see – the fallen, brave men with pictures of their families."[7] Adding to the eeriness and misery, the weather was gloomy and rainy, both September 29 and 30 being dreary and cold.[8]

The 26th moved into position in the order in which they were to form for the pending attack. The 1st Battalion, scheduled to lead the assault, marched along the Very-Epionville road until it was due south of its assigned sector, at which point it faced left and advanced north, in a narrow column of twos led by the battalion commander, until it was in place on the northern slope of Ravin de Mollevaux, just south of the line Serieux Farm-Eclisfontaine.[9] The 2nd Battalion followed, heading north until reaching the ravine running northeast from Charpentry, where they dug in. They would be the support battalion for the attack. The 3rd Battalion, scheduled to be in reserve, moved off the road where they found shelter alongside a road on the northern slope of Rau de Baronvaux. Thus the 26th was located in three parallel ravines behind the jump-off line. At Very, the divisional engineers, the 1st Engineer Regiment, had issued entrenching tools to the infantrymen; in the darkness, on unfamiliar ground and with no specific idea of where the enemy was, the tired Doughboys of the 26th dug foxholes and settled in for the night.[10]

The 26th's front was about 1,000 yards wide, facing roughly northwest. The immediate front was "a series of high ridges with outstanding peaks, deep valleys and ravines. The valleys as a rule were clear of vegetation but the ridges and hills were covered with patches of woods. The slopes of the ravines are steep and difficult to climb."[11]

Exermont Ravine was about 1,000 yards to the front of the regiment. This ravine was about 200 yards wide and 120 feet deep, and it ran roughly east-west. Branching off from Exermont Ravine, near the western boundary of the regiment's zone and running diagonally roughly southeast-northwest, was Rau de Mayache, another

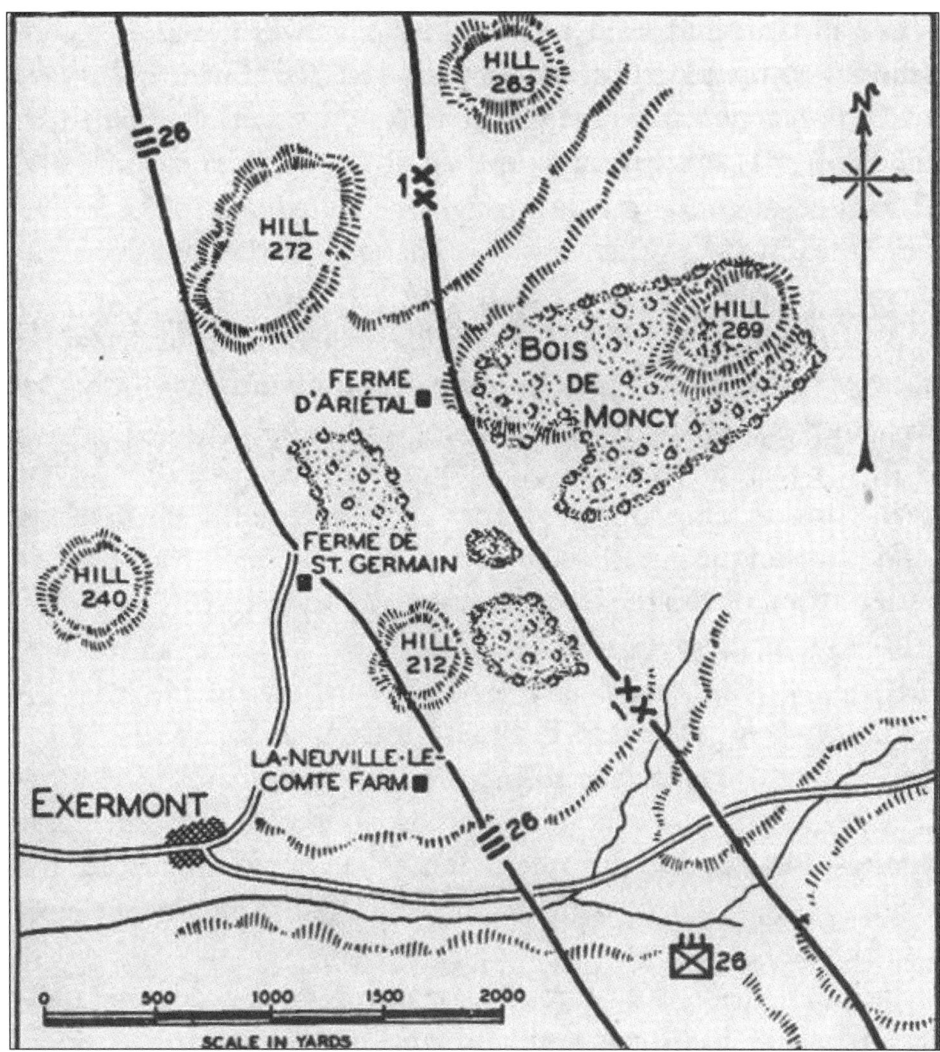

Map showing the 26th Infantry Regiment area of operations, October 1 through 12, 1918. (Courtesy Colonel Robert R. McCormick Research Center.)

steep ravine. This ravine was about 120 feet deep; its west/southwest slope was slightly wooded. The high ground between Rau de Mayache and Exermont Ravine formed a triangular knoll with Tronsol Farm at its base to the east, and its rounded apex near the 26th's western boundary.[12] Facing the 26th Infantry Regiment was the German 52nd Division, rated "effective and excellent." The woods in front of the 26th teemed with "machine guns and supporting troops."[13]

The plan was for the 1st Battalion, supported by the regimental Machine Gun Company, to lead the attack; the 2nd Battalion would follow in support with Company B, 3rd Machine Gun Battalion. Following in reserve was the 3rd Battalion and Company A, 3rd Machine Gun Battalion.[14] The Machine Gun Company, which was to advance with the 1st Battalion, was a part of the 26th Infantry, while the 3rd

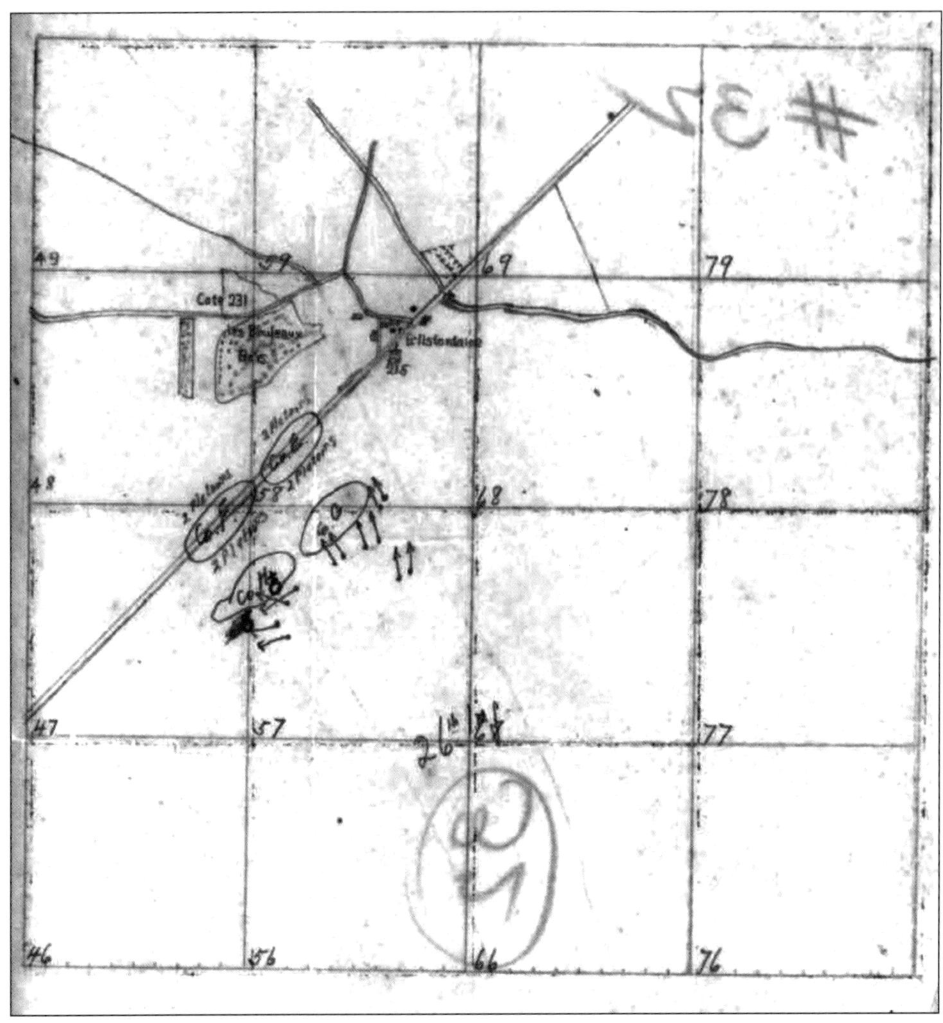

Captain Raymond D. Wortley's sketch of 2nd Battalion positions, October 1-3, 1918. (National Archives, Record Group 120, Field Messages.)

Machine Gun Battalion was assigned to the 2nd Infantry Brigade. The pairing of machine gun companies with rifle battalions followed during the Meuse-Argonne Offensive was the same that had been followed during other engagements.

By 0600, October 1, the 1st Battalion had established liaison with the 28th Infantry Regiment on its left and was organizing near their assigned line. The battalion had received "considerable scattering fire" from German 77s and was still trying to establish liaison with elements of the 91st Division on their right. The 1st Battalion had Companies D and A (left to right) in the front line, with Companies C and B (left to right) in the second line.[15] The infantrymen were deployed in combat groups, which were sections of platoons. The regimental Machine Gun Company and the battalion command post were in position behind the second line companies. The total depth of the battalion was about 500 yards.[16] Soon thereafter, Col. Erickson

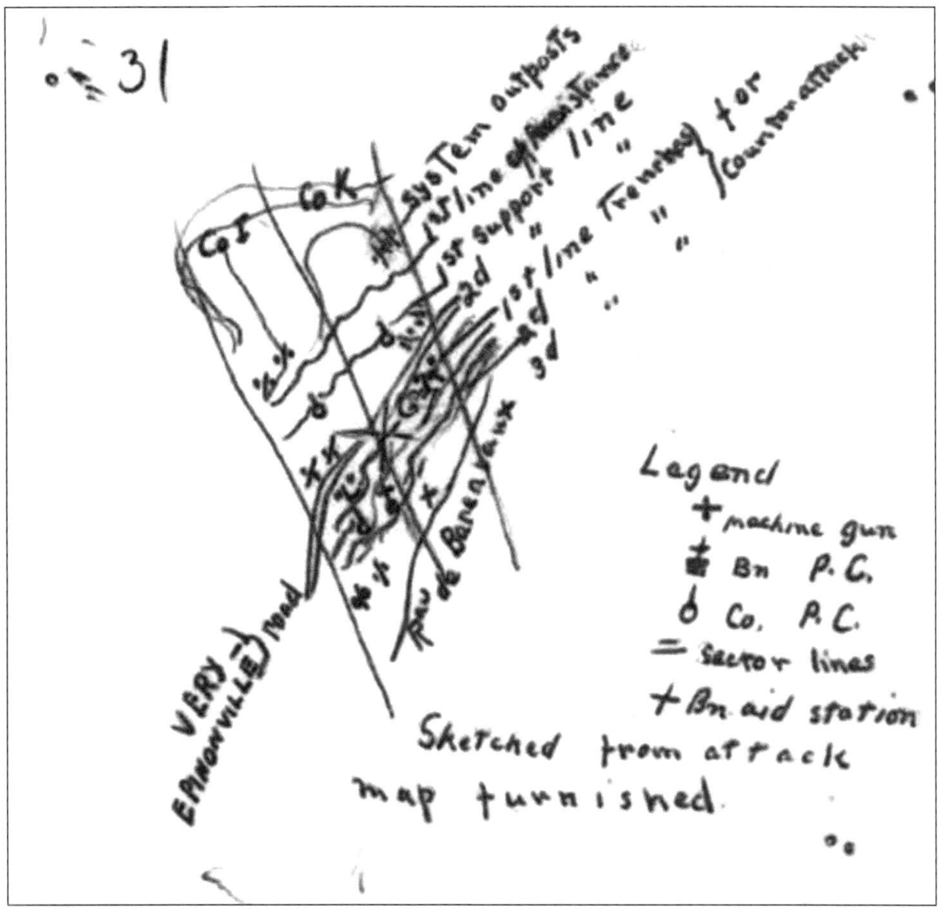

Major Lyman S. Frasier's sketch of 3rd Battalion positions, October 1-3, 1918. (National Archives, Record Group 120, Field Messages.)

sent messages to the battalions requesting sketches of their precise location and inquiring about liaison on their right.[17]

Second Lieutenant Willis C. Conover, a platoon leader in Company C, later claimed that Company C was in the front line on October 1, on the north slope of Ravin de Mollevaux, about 700 yards south of Serieux Farm. The position indicated by Conover on a map, however, is slightly outside of the 26th Infantry's zone, just inside the zone of the 28th Infantry to the left.[18] Conover also stated that, on the morning of October 2, his company "moved forward about 100 yards and to the right about 200 yards," in order to close the gap with the neighboring 91st Division on the right. This might be in accord with a later field message sent by Maj. Legge stating that, upon initially moving into position, his battalion had stopped just short of their assigned positions.[19]

The 2nd Battalion was in position with Companies F and E (left to right) along the Charpentry-Eclisfontaine Road, with two platoons each north of the road and two platoons each south of the road. In support were Companies H and G (left to right); behind them were the machine guns of Company B, 3rd Machine Gun Battalion, commanded by Capt. Charles W. Yuill. Yuill placed four machine guns facing west/northwest behind Company H and eight machine guns facing north/northwest behind Company G. The battalion PC was near Company H.[20]

By 0800, the 3rd Battalion was in position, with Companies I and K (left to right) in three lines north of the Very-Epionville Road and Companies L and M (left to right) in three lines south of the road. The machine guns of their supporting machine gun company were interspersed among the lines. They had deployed a line of out-guards to their front and had sent liaison patrols to their flanks, but without result. The battalion PC was in the rear of the right flank of Company L; the battalion aid station was in the rear of the left flank of Company M. While moving into and preparing their positions, the 3rd Battalion suffered one man killed and seven wounded by shellfire.[21]

Throughout the morning and afternoon the men settled in, and the officers developed liaison and strengthened their positions. At daybreak, Maj. Legge had determined that his battalion had ended up just short of their assigned position and had sent out two patrols of ten men each, armed with some Chauchat automatic rifles, to provide a screen near the Serieux Farm-Bouleaux Road. By 0925 the 1st Battalion had established contact with both the 28th Infantry on their left and the 363rd Infantry, 91st Division, on their right. Shortly thereafter, Maj. Legge reported one man killed and several wounded by shellfire and mustard gas being used against Company D. About this time, 1030, the 363rd Infantry advanced about one mile; although they were now farther advanced than the 1st Battalion, Maj. Legge still maintained a mixed liaison post with the 363rd. At 1330, Maj. Frasier reported establishing liaison with the 316th Engineer Regiment, 91st Division, on his right. Thus, with the 26th Infantry deploying in depth, they strengthened their liaison in depth with the units to their left and right.[22]

At 1600 Maj. Legge deployed a line of out-guards some 200 yards in front of the battalion. This group consisted of three squads and one sergeant from each company, for a total of twelve squads, under the command of 1st Lt. Thomas L. Cornell of Company A. The patrol first moved to the northeast, taking advantage of cover provided by the high ground to their north, then slipping into the western edge of le Bouleaux Bois before turning back to the north. Heading north, the patrol moved into position just south of Rau de Mayache; the patrol was "heavily shelled, losing about fifteen men." Cornell sent small patrols across Rau de Mayache to maintain liaison with the 363rd Infantry Regiment of the 91st Division at Tronsol Farm on the right. While in this forward position, the men rescued a wounded soldier from the 35th Division. The position was so far advanced that Germans in the woods to their right rear "threw flares beyond our lines" that night. Although at 2300 the patrols were ordered to retire to the area south of Rau de Mayache, at least part of this group remained in their forward position until the attack on October 4 when they joined the advancing waves that jumped off from their position.[23]

Other elements of the regiment set up in position among the roads, woods, and valleys north of Very. "The rolling kitchens of the regiment were in the valley northeast

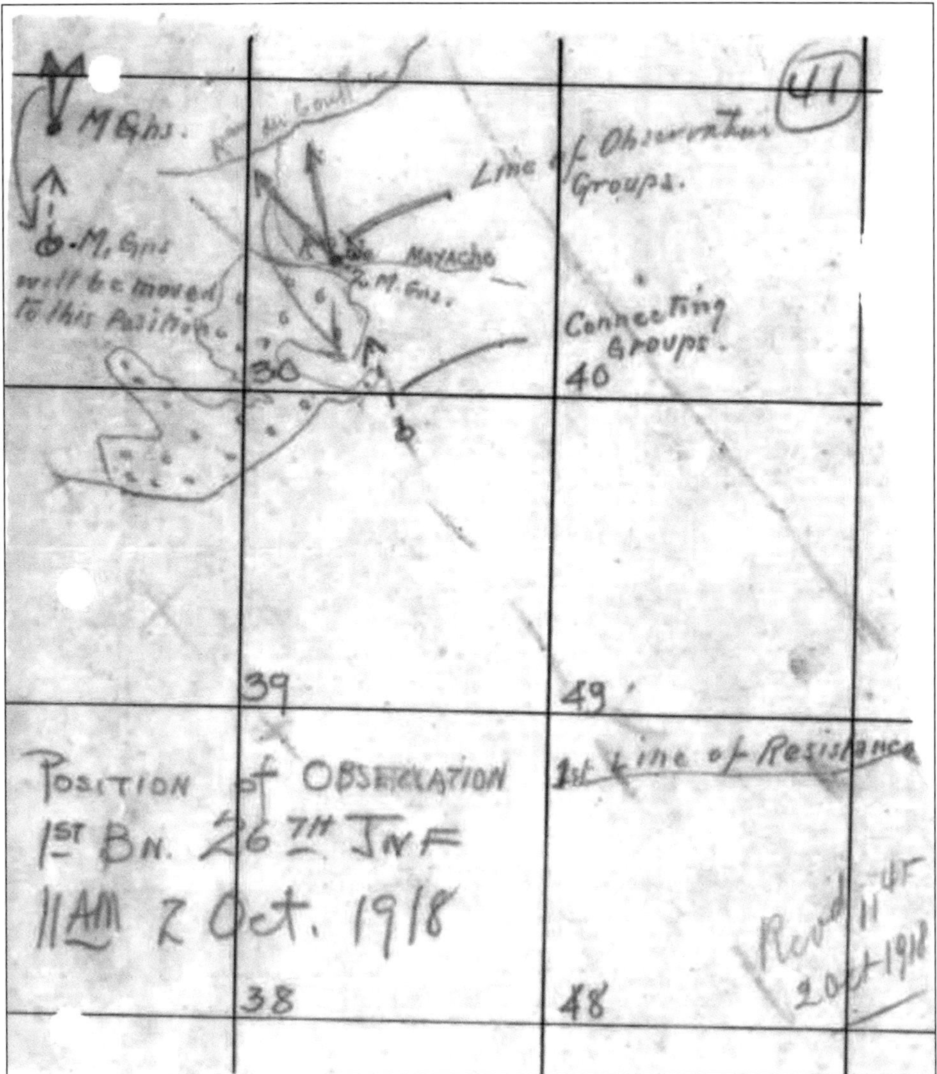

Major Barnwell R. Legge's sketch of out-guards for the 1st Battalion, October 2, 1918. Note main line of battalion's position near grid number 48. (National Archives, Record Group 120, Field Messages.)

of Very [probably near the 3rd Battalion's location]. Food and supplies were sent up nightly by wagon, the food in marmite cans."[24] Some of the other logistics of warfare during the Great War were also being worked out. Although Maj. Frasier of the 3rd Battalion was preparing to send food forward to the 1st Battalion, he inquired of regimental headquarters as to who would supply the chow carts necessary to transport the food forward. He reported that he was, however, ready to send forward two carts of chlorinated water by 1900.[25]

The period from October 1 through 3 was a very trying time for the entire division. The men of the 26th suffered badly, "Both the First and Third Battalions were heavily shelled at frequent intervals. The ravine occupied by the Second Battalion was being constantly gassed."[26] The 1st Battalion, while moving into position on the night of September 30/October 1, had come under "sharp machine gun fire" as it approached its position. The 3rd Battalion was subjected to artillery bombardment from its front and right front, day and night. In addition, the 3rd Battalion, and probably the others, was strafed by German aircraft, although very few men were injured by them. The aircraft did succeed, however, in destroying one of the battalion's kitchens just before dusk on October 3; this kitchen had steaming food ready for delivery to the men in line as soon as darkness should descend. Another kitchen had been destroyed by artillery fire earlier.[27] Interestingly, according to Maj. Frasier, 3rd Battalion commander, "throughout the Meuse-Argonne Offensive we had been forbidden to fire upon aircraft because of the possibility that we might fire upon friendly craft as well as hostile, as we had done once before. Incidentally we met with far greater success in bringing down allied aircraft than German."[28] Still, a German aircraft was indeed shot down in the regimental zone at 1000 on October 2; how the aircraft was brought down is a mystery.[29]

Even in the best of conditions, remaining motionless in cold, wet foxholes for three days would be a trying, incapacitating experience. When shellfire and poison gas is added, it is easy to see why Maj. Frasier stated that these were "grueling days [that] tested the endurance of the men to the extreme."[30] To alleviate muscle cramps and keep the men from hypothermia, the 3rd Battalion resorted to exercising their men in-place by night, giving them silent setting up exercises and even double-timing them. They were also "required to keep shaved and to keep their arms spotlessly clean. … It seems like irony now to think that we required these things of men, all of whom were so soon to struggle to the point of utter exhaustion and many of whom were living their last days on this earth." Still, these measures kept the men in good condition and bolstered their discipline for the violent days ahead.[31] It's not known if the other two battalions, located closer to the enemy, engaged in these exercises during this waiting period.

Second Lieutenant William A. Mansfield, a twenty-five-year old platoon leader from Rochester, New York, in Company E in the 2nd Battalion, recalled that he had "managed to shave, bathe, and clean my teeth all with a precious half canteen of extremely scarce water." The men of Company E had dug "roofless homes … hand fashioned, about four feet deep, within whispering distance of good neighbors." His own foxhole had a view of Exermont ahead. Captain Rice M. Youell, a twenty-seven-year old native Virginian and commander of Company E, covered his foxhole, located about twenty yards in advance of his company just beyond the edge of a road, with tree limbs.[32]

The division field hospital records show that the 1st Division gas casualties for October 1-2 total 469; the 26th Infantry Regiment had fifty-two men gassed during that time. Some men became ill when they passed over or dug into ground that had been previously saturated with gas. In such cases, the exposure happened too quickly for the men to don their masks. The division gas officer reported that, for October 2-3, there were 409 gas casualties, all from mustard gas, in the area occupied by the 26th. In total, it appears that during the three-day wait for the resumption of the

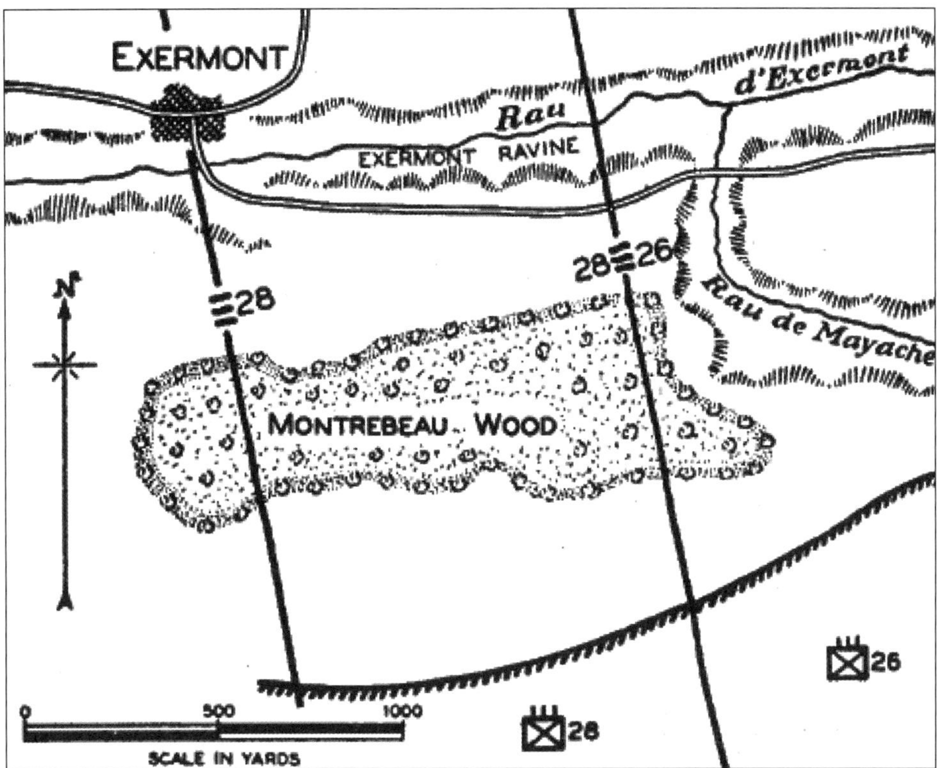

A map showing the zone in front of the 28th Infantry Regiment, center, and part of the zone in front of the 26th Infantry Regiment, right, depicting the ravines through which the 26th fought on October 4, 1918. (*Infantry in Battle*, The Infantry Journal, Incorporated, Washington, D.C., 1939.)

attack, the 1st Division suffered "almost 1,500 casualties, of which over 900 were caused by gas."[33] This is not surprising given that the ground had been saturated with gas during previous attacks and that the 1st and 2nd Battalions were held in ravines that could be considered "natural gas traps."[34] Although gas was not always fatal, exposure could produce debilitating and frightening effects. Typical of 26th Infantry gas casualties was Pvt. Eugene Strasbaugh of Company I. Sometime during the battle Strasbaugh was gassed; afterwards he was evacuated. Speechless for four weeks and sightless for two, he remained in hospitals in France for almost three months.[35]

Although the 1st Battalion had been in contact with enemy patrols the moment they moved into the area, the exact location of the enemy's main line was not known. Based upon a French report that the Germans had withdrawn, I Corps ordered the 1st Division to send out combat patrols to determine the Germans' defensive positions. Colonel Erickson therefore ordered the 1st Battalion to conduct such a patrol, and well before dawn on October 2, the weary men assembled for action. The patrol was led by 2nd Lt. Thomas D. Amory and consisted of another officer, 1st Lt. David E. Meeker, and seventy-seven men. The battalion commander also added a corporal and a private from the regimental signal detachment; these two men, equipped with a breast reel of wire and a telephone, were to see to it that the patrol would remain

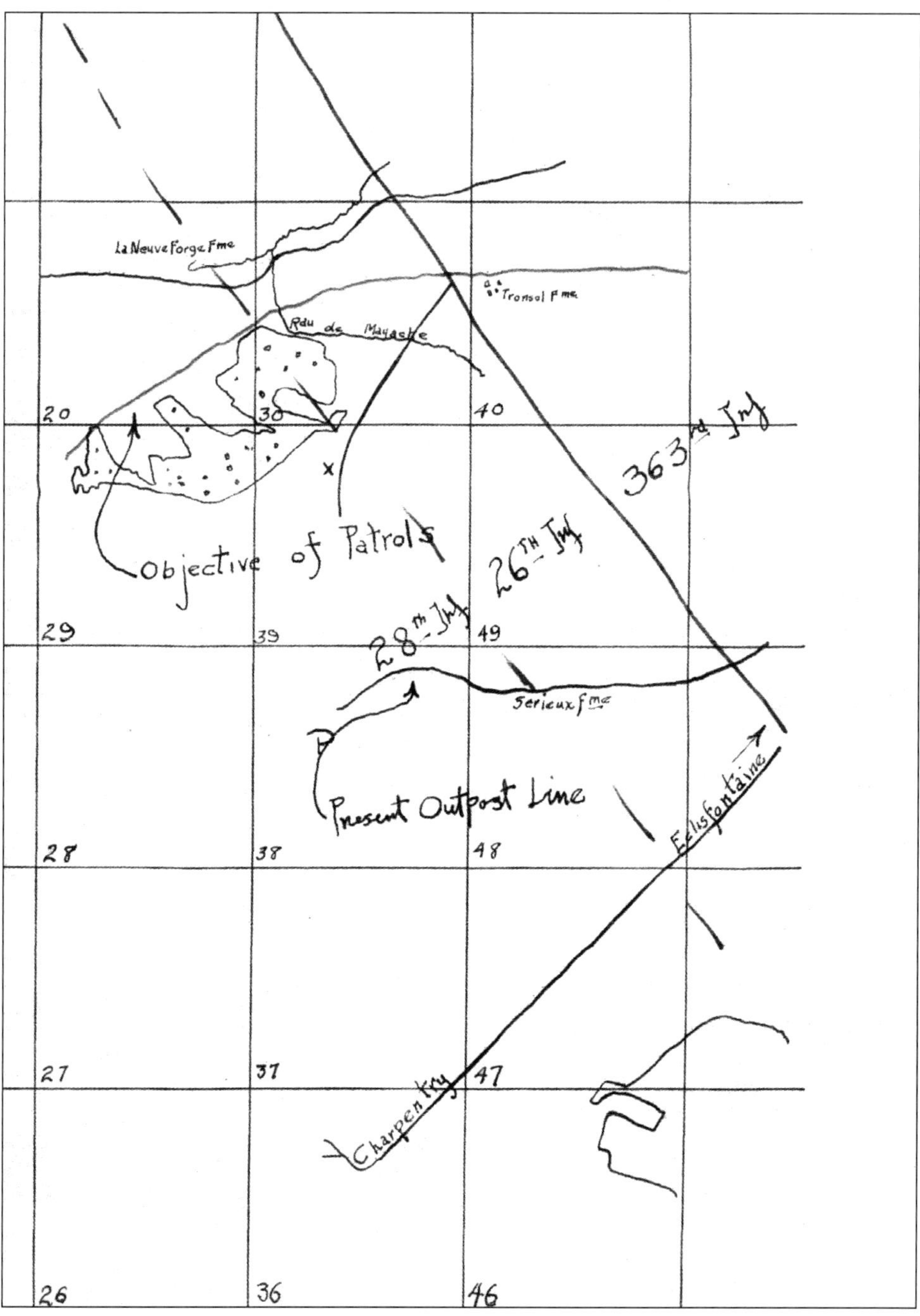

A sketched map showing the area of the 1st Battalion's patrol on October 2, 1918. Note positions of neighboring units' patrols. (National Archives, Record Group 120, Field Messages.)

in contact with battalion headquarters. The objective of the patrol was to advance to the ridge between Rau de Mayache and Exermont Ravine while determining enemy positions.[36]

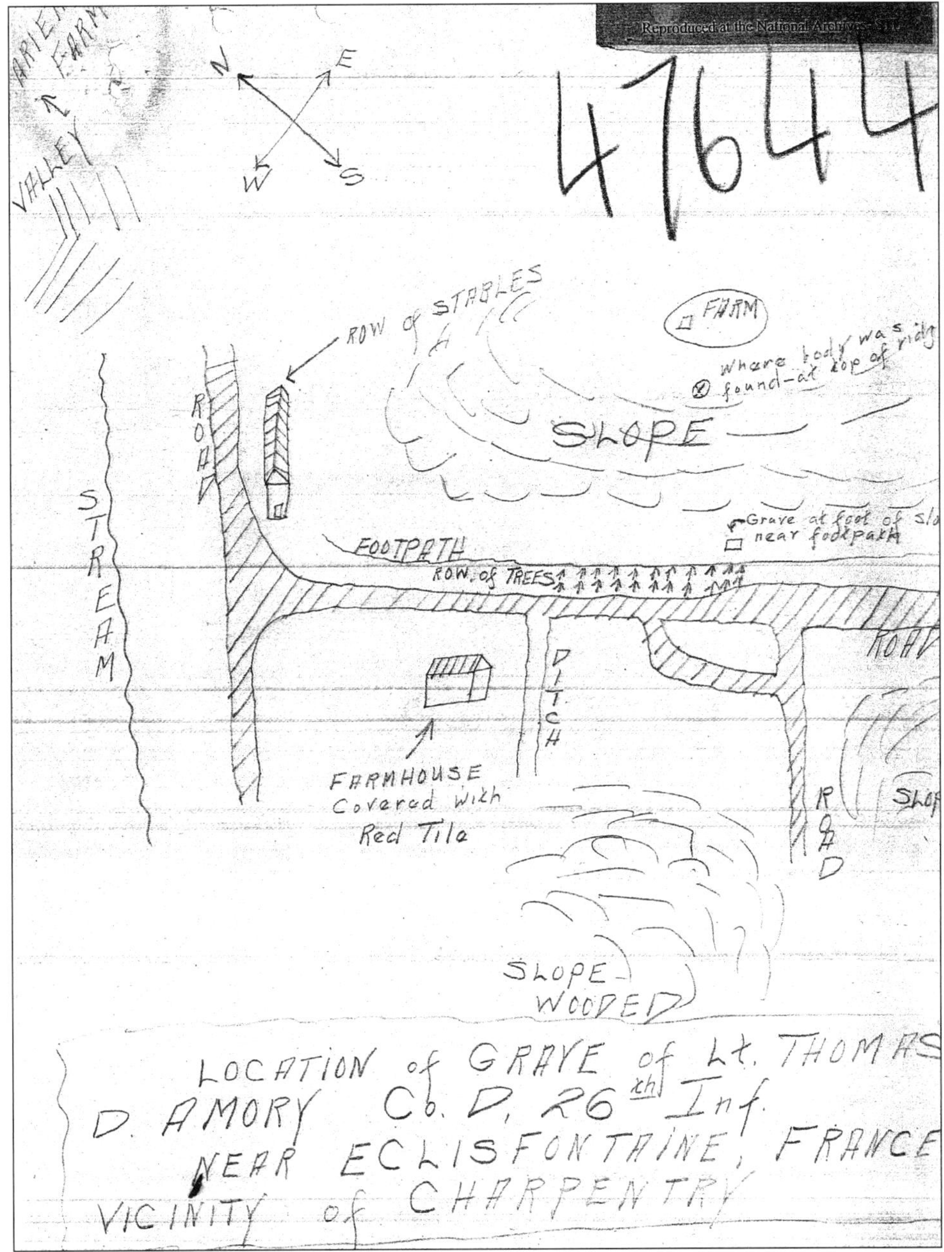

A post-war map sketched by Sergeant Charles W. O'Connor of Company D. O'Connor sketched the map in order to show where Lieutenant Amory's body was buried. The sketch also shows detail of the area in which the ill-fated patrol fought. (National Archives, Record Group 92, Thomas Amory Burial Information File.)

The reported number of men on the patrol differs among the various accounts, however, Lt. Meeker, who was a participant, reported seventy-seven men on the patrol. The patrol consisted of one platoon from Company D and four squads from Company A. Meeker also stated the patrol left battalion headquarters at 0300, but

Second Lieutenant Thomas D. Amory, Company D, 26th Infantry Regiment, killed in action October 2, 1918; awarded the Distinguished Service Cross. (findagrave.com)

field messages and the regimental operations report state that the patrol departed at 0540. Probably the men began assembling at 0300 and left the line of outposts closer to 0540.[37]

About an hour before dawn, the patrol moved out in a double file. In the mist the men crept past the out-guards and deployed in two waves. The first wave was a line of skirmishers, and the second wave was a column of squads following at fifty feet; the officers took up positions between the two waves. When the patrol had advanced about a half kilometer it was raked by machine gun fire from Montrebeau Woods to the left. Lieutenant Amory immediately ordered the men to double time to Rau de Mayache just ahead. The survivors plunged into the ravine and part way up the ridge on the far side. The patrol, unable to see enemy targets, remained under fire from the left, left-rear, and from across Exermont Ravine to its front. Several machine gun nests, some as near as forty yards away, opened fire on the patrol; Lt. Amory advanced with three men in an attempt to silence the nests. The men knocked out one nest and killed its crew; at about 0615, as they advanced on another gun, located in a house about ten yards away, Lt. Amory was killed by machine gun fire, his last words being, "We will take that nest or die trying." One of the signalmen was relaying messages to Maj. Legge on the telephone, giving him a real-time account of the battle, reporting, "They are firing on us from three sides. I believe we are surrounded. … Lieutenant Amory has just been shot through the head and killed." Several men attempted to advance against the nest and they, too, were gunned down. Eventually the nest was silenced, and two Germans killed. The patrol continued to suffer casualties from the heavy fire, and they dug in on the hillside. For his actions, Lt. Amory was posthumously awarded the Distinguished Service Cross (DSC), the nation's second highest award for valor.[38]

The precarious position of the patrol is evident in the field messages that morning. At 0730 Maj. Legge sent a message to regimental headquarters: "Lieutenant Meeker … reports that eight machine guns are firing on him. His right and left flanks are being played on heavily. He is also being fired on from his left rear. The wood in

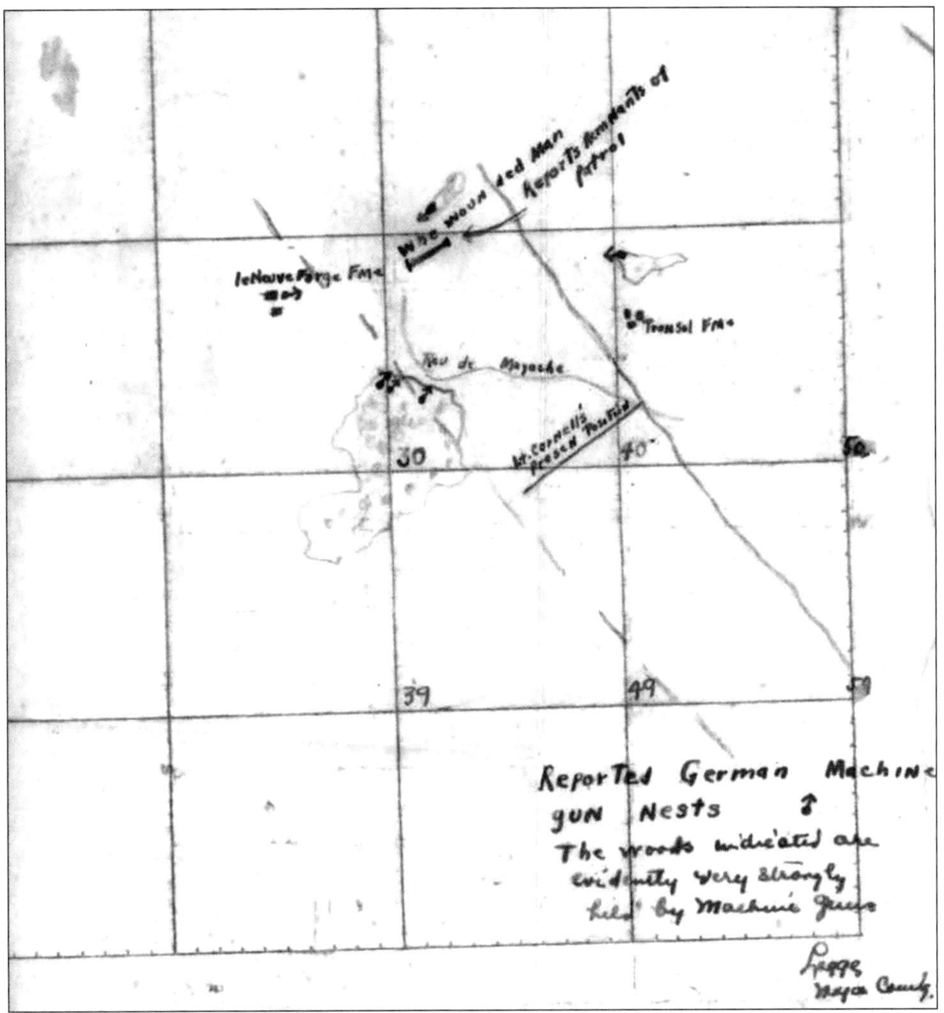

Major Legge's sketched map showing the situation after the 1st Battalion's patrol of October 2, 1918. Note the position of Lieutenant Cornell's earlier patrol and the remnant of the main patrol to the north. (National Archives, Record Group 120, Field Messages.)

front of 1st objective appears to be held heavily with machine guns." At the same time, Lt. Meeker sent a message to Maj. Legge stating, "thirty-five casualties, being shelled very heavily, small hostile infantry column to left front, am still holding. Amory killed."[39]

Private Eugene McEntee, one of the signalmen from Headquarters Company who accompanied the patrol, although shot in the ankle, refused to be evacuated. Instead, Pvt. McEntee advanced about 1,400 yards under heavy fire repairing the telephone line. Lieutenant Meeker, now in command of the patrol, was able to use the telephone to contact Maj. Legge who ordered him to hold the patrol in position. Meeker then ordered a corporal and six men to maneuver against the machine guns in the woods to the left-rear; these men succeeded in knocking out one light machine gun, and they confirmed that there were many Germans in the woods. About thirty Germans infiltrated from the woods to the rear of the patrol. Part of the patrol faced the rear and confronted these Germans. Just then, support from the main body of the 1st Battalion came forward, and the intervening Germans withdrew. The patrol had only about twenty men remaining, deployed along a 200-yard front, when at 0740 they were ordered to withdraw.

Only twelve survivors were able to return to the out-guards where Lt. Meeker delivered his report to Maj. Legge, who later said "although the cost was great, the patrol had accomplished their mission: information was now available to lay the barrage for the initial attack." Thirteen years later, Capt. George R.F. Cornish, who commanded Headquarters Company of the 26th during this operation, sounded a slightly less positive note when he wrote, "This patrol found out what was previously known, that the enemy was in strength in front of the Twenty Sixth Infantry." Some of the survivors of the patrol were trapped outside the lines, and not until the 1st Battalion advanced two days later were they found and rescued. Among these survivors was Pvt. Arthur H. Vogel. Vogel, his "stomach riddled with bullets and part of his hip shot away," lay among the dead and wounded without water or attention until they were rescued during the general advance.[40] For gallantry in action "in the face of terrific machine gun and artillery fire," Lt. Meeker was awarded a Silver Star. Private McEntee, one of the signalmen, was awarded a Distinguished Service Cross for his effort that enabled the patrol to maintain telephone contact with headquarters.[41]

By 1100 the patrol had withdrawn but had left some men in observation posts with machine guns at the edge of Rau de Mayache and in the woods to the west. The original out-guards from Company A were still in place just to the south, ahead of the main line of resistance on Serieux Farm Road.[42] At 1230, Maj. Legge, observing American artillery fire against the positions his men had uncovered, sent a message to Capt. Shipley Thomas, regimental intelligence officer, requesting to adjust the artillery fire. Legge asked that the "artillery that is firing in small oblong shaped woods directly in front and on right of 1st objective lengthen range seventy-five yards and pound hell out of the woods. Machine gun nests are located there."[43] The next night, despite his harrowing experiences of the day before, Lt. Meeker again took out a patrol of eight men as far as the knoll between Rau de Mayache and Exermont Ravine. The patrol returned to battalion headquarters at midnight, having found no friendly or enemy troops during their excursion.[44]

In the ensuing days the battalion commanders made adjustments to their positions. Captain Wortley's handwritten note on a sketch of the 2nd Battalion's positions betrays his frustration at efforts at proper liaison and positioning. "Incorrect positions caused by improper locations of units on our right and left. To be corrected at dusk," he wrote. Also, referring to the 1st Battalion of the neighboring 363rd Infantry, Wortley wrote, "These people change their positions every few hours." The battalion in question was in position just northwest of Eclisfontaine, slightly ahead and to the right of the 26th's own 1st Battalion.[45]

From October 1 through 3, the battalion commanders met daily with the regimental commander to discuss plans and contingencies. At 2300 on October 3, Col. Erickson

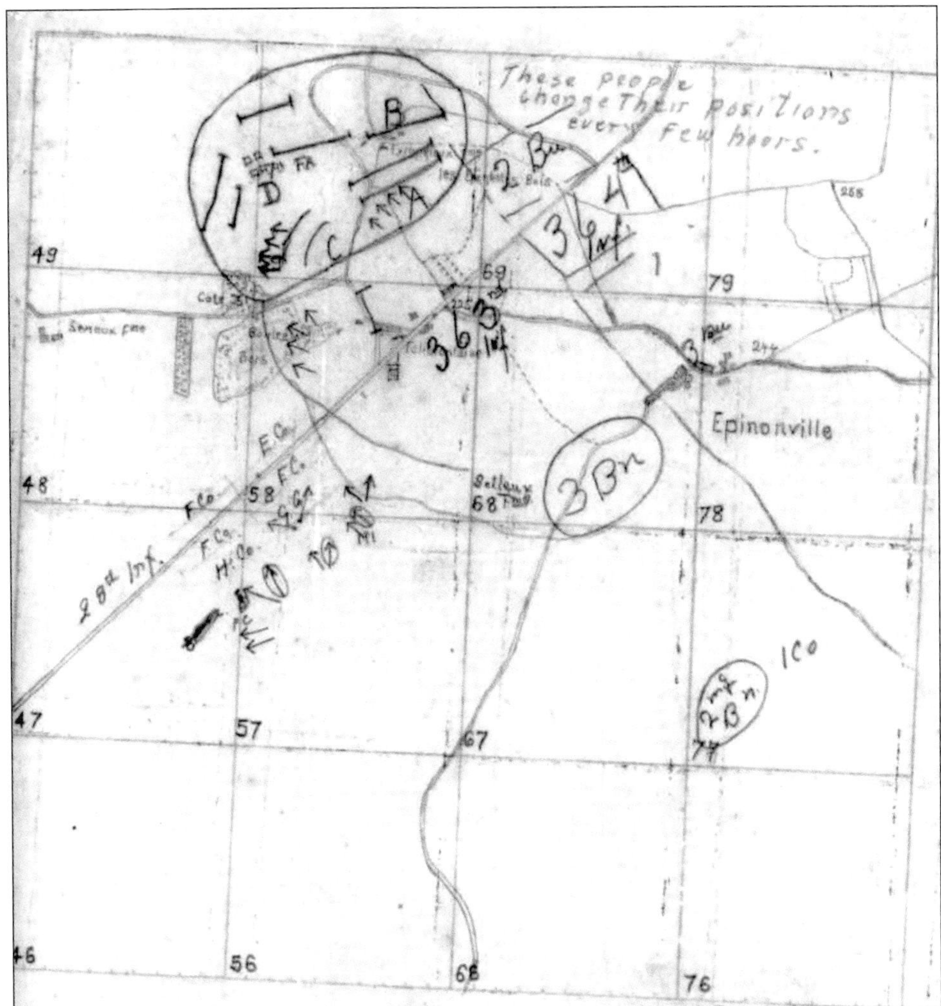

Captain Wortley's sketch showing the position of his 2nd Battalion and the position of the neighboring unit, 363rd Infantry Regiment, 91st Division. This illustrates the efforts of officers to maintain liaison and grasp situational awareness. (National Archives, Record Group 120, Field Messages.)

delivered verbal orders to the battalion commanders for the attack the next day. The order was an explanation of the divisional order with specific assignments given to the battalions and support forces. Each commander was issued a 1:20,000 scale map marked with zones of action and objectives.

The 1st Division's mission was to drive northward in an effort to clear the enemy out of the area to the immediate east of the Aire River, thereby out-flanking the Germans in the Argonne Forest and allowing the entire American line to move northward. Accordingly, the division assigned a series of three objectives for its regiments. The first objective was a line passing along the north edge of Montrebeau Woods. The barrage would stand here for thirty minutes in an effort to pound the enemy on the crests of Exermont Ravine and to allow the infantry to reorganize after passing through the Woods (although there was only a small portion of this wood in the 26th's zone); the second objective was a line along the northern base of Montrefagne Woods and Hill 240. Here, too, the barrage would halt for thirty minutes to allow the troops to regroup. The final objective was a line passing just north of Fleville. Here the barrage would stand for twenty minutes and then stop altogether.[46]

Crouching in filthy, gas-soaked funk holes in the rain and cold while under artillery fire for three days, the men were more than ready to resume the advance. On the afternoon of October 3, the men of Company E, "had observed an allied fleet of planes numbering more than 100 in a large group fly over the enemy line and harass the enemy reserves." This no doubt at least cheered the waiting men and gave them hope.[47] On the evening of October 3, non-commissioned officers (NCO) made final checks of the men and their equipment; men ate one last meal before jump-off. The commander of the 2nd Battalion, Capt. Wortley, had a cup of coffee and a tin of beans with a regimental chaplain; this was the last meal of Capt. Wortley's life.[48]

On the eve of battle, the 26th Infantry Regiment was suffering from a lack of experienced officers. According to the February 1918 AEF Table of Organization, each regimental rifle company should have six officers: one captain, three first lieutenants, and two second lieutenants. The captain would command the regiment with the senior first lieutenant as second in command; the first and fourth platoons would be commanded by first lieutenants, and the second and third platoons would be commanded by second lieutenants. The table below shows how many officers, and the highest rank, that each rifle company of the 26th had at the start of the next phase of operations:[49]

COMPANY	NUMBER OF OFFICERS	HIGHEST RANK
A	4	Captain
B	3	First Lieutenant
C	4	Second Lieutenant
D	3	Captain
E	4	Captain
F	3	Captain
G	3	Captain
H	4	First Lieutenant
I	4	Captain
K	3	Second Lieutenant
L	2	First Lieutenant
M	4	Captain

Three:

"THE FIRE IN FRONT WAS WITHERING," OCTOBER 4

Well before dawn on October 4, weary platoon sergeants made the rounds of their foxholes quietly awakening their men. Tired soldiers rubbed their stiff joints and aching muscles prior to making their bedrolls. At 0200, Lt. Mansfield of Company E walked among his platoon, ensuring that the men were carrying extra ammunition. He also delivered some good news to one of his platoon's NCOs: the man had been selected to attend Officer Training School and was to report to regimental headquarters. The sergeant, identified only as "Sergeant O," wasted no time leaving his foxhole, no doubt happy to be missing the impending battle, but depriving the regiment of an experienced NCO at a crucial time. The 2nd Battalion at this time was under a gas alarm, and the men, deprived of rest right up to the last minute, were wearing their gas masks. Enemy artillery had been shelling the 2nd Battalion all night, although in Lt. Mansfield's area the shells had been landing about fifty yards to his rear.[1] This shelling continued intermittently; but at 0330 Lt. Mansfield recalled that it was "near noiseless." He watched two French Renault tanks move down the road in the company's front; one tank turned off the road near Capt. Youell's foxhole and moved toward the front while the other tank continued down the road. Soon a French-crewed 75mm field gun came down the road and, also turning off near Capt. Youell's precariously located foxhole, moved toward the assault battalion. This gun was apparently slated to accompany the 2nd Battalion as they advanced. These additional weapons added "improvement to our superior morale." The gas alarm had by now ceased, and the men removed their masks and placed them at alert, ready for use. Lt. Mansfield reported to Capt. Youell that his platoon was ready for jump-off.[2]

Captain Youell decided to have his company file through a gap in the wire in front of their position even before the American barrage began. He knew that the Germans would send over a retaliatory barrage against his company's foxholes; it would be better if the men had already moved forward when that happened. At about 0400 Youell requested squad columns, and the men of Company E arose and left their foxholes, filing through the wire, with Youell leading them and Mansfield bringing up the rear. Nearby the French gun crew sat on their horses and caissons, observing as the Doughboys filed past.[3] By 0430, the 2nd and 3rd Battalions sent out files of scouts to the battalion in their front, the 1st and 2nd Battalions, respectively. These files would assist in keeping spacing during the attack. With the darkness and thick fog that hugged the ground on this morning, the scouts would be vital.[4]

Men in the other battalions followed suit. They checked weapons, gear, ammunition, and grenades. Machine gunners, such as Cpl. John Crabtree and Pvt. Giovanni Filice of Machine Gun Company, checked and rechecked their equipment. Crabtree and Filice, an Italian immigrant from Connecticut, knew well that the infantry would need the firepower of their machine guns during the assault. Second Lieutenant Samuel C. Gholson, one of the machine gunners' platoon leaders, was a twenty-two-year old recent officer replacement. So recently had Gholson, a native Mississippian, joined the 26th that he still wore insignia from his old unit, the Machine Gun Company of the 168th Infantry Regiment, 42nd Division. Another platoon leader in the Machine Gun Company was 2nd Lt. George A. Reed. Reed had been a school superintendent in South Dakota when he joined the Army – "He enlisted, he wouldn't let them draft him," wrote his mother, Eliza, later.[5]

For the assault on October 4, the 1st Battalion would lead, with the 2nd in support. The 3rd Battalion, in divisional reserve, was ordered to follow behind the 2nd Battalion. Major Legge rearranged the 1st Battalion formation so that the first line consisted of Companies A and B (left to right) and the second line consisted of Companies D and C (left to right). The assault platoons were deployed as skirmishers and the follow-on platoons were in column of squads, with fifty yards between waves and 100-150 yards between platoons. The second line companies followed at 200 yards. The regimental Machine Gun Company, 37mm gun, and Stokes mortars, along with the battalion PC, followed behind the second wave companies.[6] First Lieutenant George J. Forster, the 37mm gun platoon commander, accompanied the gun with the assault battalion. The gun followed "immediately in rear of battalion runners and telephone men." The gunners pulled the 37mm gun using hand ropes and hand-carrying "all the ammunition we could manage."[7] A combat liaison patrol was sent to the right flank to keep contact with the neighboring 32nd Division that had relieved the 91st Division just prior to the attack. The patrol was under the command of 2nd Lt. Eric H. Cummings, a twenty-seven-year old Kansan. Cummings had enlisted in the Army two weeks after the declaration of war; he had been sent to France and was promoted to corporal before being selected to attend an AEF officer candidate school. A fairly recent officer replacement, he was now part of a vital link in the first wave.[8] Lieutenant Meeker, of Company D, later recalled that Companies B and C (left to right) were in the front line, and Companies D and A

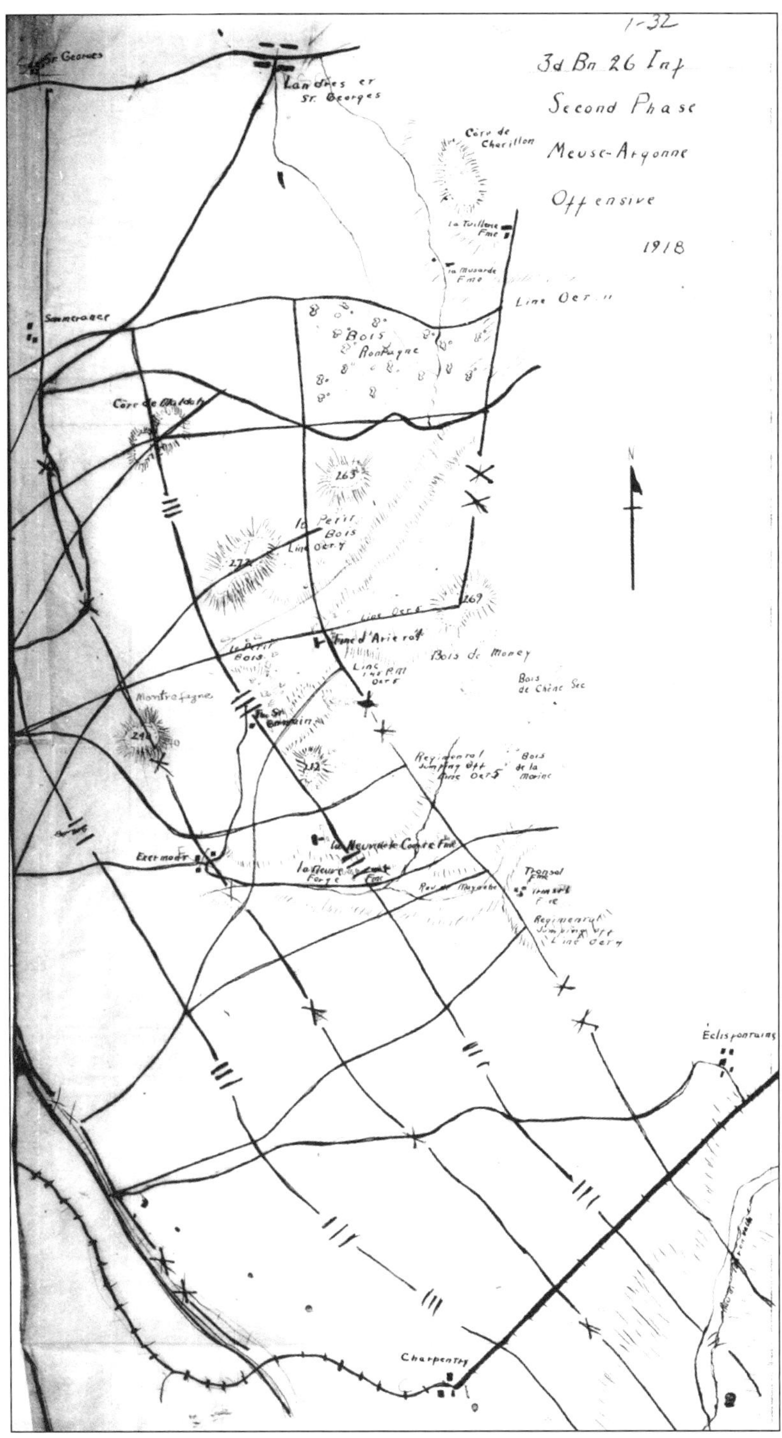

Post-war sketched map by Major Lyman S. Frasier, commander of the 3rd Battalion, 26th Infantry Regiment, showing the area of operations of the 1st Division. The 26th advanced along the far right lane. (Captain Lyman S. Frasier, "Operations of the Third Battalion.")

(left to right) were in the second line. Probably the first configuration, reported by Maj. Legge, is the correct one.[9]

The 2nd Battalion formed behind the 1st Battalion with Companies F and E (left to right) in the assault wave and Companies H and G (left to right) in support.[10] Company E formed up with two platoons in the assault position, one commanded by Lt. Mansfield and the other by 2nd Lt. Levis R. Bune. The support platoon was commanded by 2nd Lt. Gordon B. Knowles.[11] Although there were normally four platoons per each company, Lt. Mansfield mentioned only three platoons in the assault; perhaps a shortage of officers or enlisted men, or both, caused Company E to form in three platoons.

At 0525 on October 4, the American artillery began their barrage of the area to be covered in the infantry advance, about 200 yards ahead of the jump-off line. Lieutenant Mansfield, in Company E, recalled that "the heavens opened up and the roar was deafening. Brilliant blasts of fire, smoke and dust rose in clouds just a few hundred yards ahead. … Smiles could be distinguished underneath steel helmets as we were aware of the uncomfortable position the enemy was in right now." The men of the 2nd Battalion, lying flat on the ground, watched red star shells, indicating an attack and calling for a barrage, rise from the German lines. These reminded Mansfield of "pretty colored roman candles and 4th of July fireworks."[12] Five minutes later, the barrage began to creep northward while the infantry jumped off. In darkness and a thick fog, the 26th Infantry Regiment jumped off with the 1st Battalion leading and the 2nd Battalion in support.

Enemy artillery responded, and a 75mm artillery gun of the 7th Field Artillery Regiment, accompanying the assault wave, was immediately put out of action, resulting in the loss of nine out of thirteen men, and eleven out of twelve horses.[13] In the 2nd Battalion, Lt. Mansfield of Company E, recalling the French-crewed gun that was supposed to advance with their wave, suspected that the "Frenchmen, their guns and horses never lived after the enemy barrage dropped."[14] The infantry was met with waves of machine gun fire from the north, northeast, and east; artillery also played on the advancing men. The infantrymen passed over many dead Americans of the 35th Division; some of these men had had their wounds dressed indicating that the Germans had left them to die where they had fallen. The right flank liaison patrol was "annihilated at jump-off." Second Lieutenant Cummings, the patrol leader, was among those killed.[15] Private Axel C. Lundegard of the regimental medical detachment became aware of the location of a man who had been wounded in the ill-fated patrol of October 2; the man had lain in enemy territory for almost two days. Lundegard advanced alone and unarmed to retrieve the man and bring him to safety. For his actions, Pvt. Lundegard was awarded the Distinguished Service Cross.[16]

Soon after jump-off, Company A slowed down. Its commander, Capt. Hamilton K. Foster, a twenty-two-year old "curly-headed boy" from New York, was young for a company commander. Foster went forward with Sgt. Al Stallings to check on the situation. As he neared the front of the assault line near a farm on what the men called Dead Man's Hill, he was "killed instantly by an explosive bullet between the

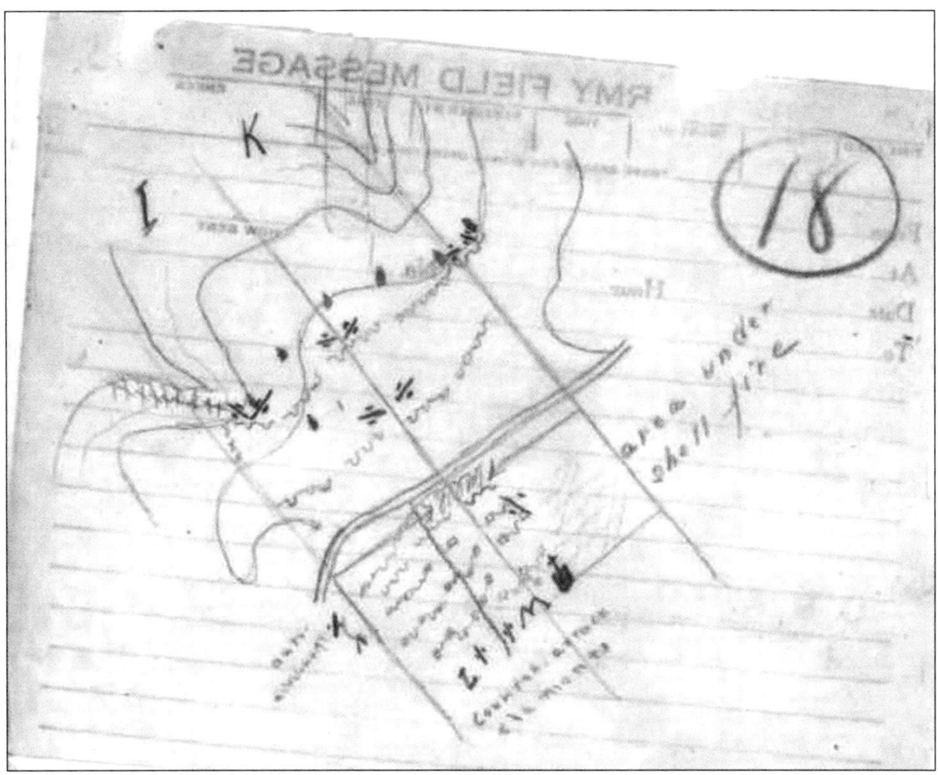

Major Frasier's map sketched on the reverse side of a field message slip, showing the position of his 3rd Battalion prior to jump-off. (National Archives, Record Group 120, Field Messages.)

eyes." Sgt. Stallings, too, was killed by his side. A brave man and a good leader, Foster had already been awarded the Distinguished Service Cross and the Italian *Croce al Merito di Guerre* for gallantry in action.[17]

On the right of the assault line, 1st Lt. Stuart A. Baxter, a twenty-two-year old Michigander, led Company B forward. Baxter was soon wounded, but he continued to advance through the machine gun and artillery fire until the company could go no farther. For his actions on this day, Baxter was awarded the Distinguished Service Cross.[18] Lieutenant Forster, with his men hauling the 37mm gun at the rear of the battalion, recalled that Company B, the right flank assault company, received most of its fire from the right flank and was "badly shot up."[19] As the 1st Battalion descended into Rau de Mayache, the 37mm gun crew, following behind, was met by a "sheet of machine gun fire." The gunners hit the ground for protection. Soon a runner came from the front asking for the one-pounder to be brought up; Lt. Forster and his crew, however, could not manage to get the gun down into the ravine at this point. It would be an hour and a half later before he caught up with the battalion commander.[20]

The 2nd Battalion, about 500 yards behind the 1st Battalion, moved forward; it presented to Lt. Mansfield an impressive sight: "As far as vision permitted right and left, a wave of khaki clothed men with bayonets at the 'high carry' were moving forward as on maneuvers."[21] Right away the battalion ran into a buzz saw as enemy artillery and machine gun fire tore into it; Capt. James A. Edgarton, commander of Company F, recalled that, "a murderous barrage caught us about southwest of Tronsol Farm."[22] The commander of Company H, 1st Lt. Walter A. Sands, was killed by high explosive shellfire within 100 yards of the jump off, and within a couple hours Company H had lost all its officers.[23] Lieutenant Mansfield picked up a discarded steel shovel as he advanced. This he held in front of his face as a shield "against which resounded shell fragments, dirt and rock splinters." The 2nd Battalion halted on a reverse slope of a small hill. The fire at this point was described as "withering." Mansfield watched as one tank rumbled over the crest; "It lasted two minutes. A direct hit by enemy artillery had made it spin around and halt." The second tank got slightly further before it, too, was destroyed. These tanks were part of Company C, 345th Tank Battalion, 1st Tank Brigade, which supported the 26th on October 4 and 5.[24]

The platoon leaders in the 3rd Battalion had also been up early, checking on their men and offering words of exhortation. Second Lieutenant Bayard Brown of Company K was no stranger to combat. The twenty-seven-year old native of Genoa, Illinois, had graduated from the University of Illinois in 1916 and had been working in agriculture in Libertyville, Illinois, when he entered the Second Officers Training Camp at Fort Sheridan, Illinois, in 1917. After his graduation and commissioning he had been sent overseas and eventually was assigned to the 26th Infantry Regiment. Brown had already been wounded twice and awarded the French *Croix de Guerre*, and once again he was preparing for a tremendous test of his leadership.

Company I's 2nd Lt. Morgan M. Anderson was typical of the platoon leaders in the 26th, young men just starting out in life. Anderson, a twenty-seven-year old native of Milwaukee and graduate of the University of Wisconsin, was preparing to enter the practice of law when he, too, entered the Second Officer Training Camp at Fort Sheridan. Like Brown, he was sent overseas and, after additional training, was sent to the 26th as a platoon leader.

The 3rd Battalion, following the 2nd Battalion, moved forward very slowly. Owing to the darkness and fog, the battalion advanced by compass bearing; visibility was less than fifty yards. Formation was preserved only by use of the connecting files of scouts. For the 3rd Battalion, Companies I and K (left to right) were in the first line and Companies L and M (left to right) followed in the second line; the machine gun company followed. Due to heavy shellfire, the men formed in column of squads. A platoon from Company K protected the right flank of the battalion.[25]

To the west (left), the 1st Brigade (16th and 18th Infantry Regiments) suffered heavy casualties but managed to reach their first objective, the northern edge of Montrebeau Woods, approaching Exermont Ravine, by 0700.[26] The assault waves of the 2nd Brigade (28th and 26th Infantry Regiments) struggled to reach and traverse Rau de Mayache and Exermont Ravine. A battery of German 77s located near La Neuville le Comte Farm, to the west and just north of Exermont Ravine, opened fire on them at less than 800 yards; small groups of men from both regiments worked their way forward and killed the crews of these guns. The 1st Battalion of the 26th became bogged down in Rau de Mayache that was being enfiladed by both machine gun and artillery fire. The regimental Machine Gun Company, supporting the 1st

Battalion, moved to Montrebeau Woods and provided overhead covering fire. The machine gunners came under high explosives fire as they advanced to support the infantry. Corporal Crabtree watched as his friend Pvt. Filice was hit by a high explosive shell that shattered his head. Filice, who was cited in division orders for gallantry in action, had been wearing a gold signet ring bearing his initials; that ring was one of the means of identifying his remains upon disinterment after the war.

Sergeant Clinton G. Allen of the Machine Gun Company watched in horror as platoon leader 2nd Lt. Samuel Gholson was hit by shrapnel in the legs and body. Both his legs were blown off, and he was killed instantly. Second Lieutenant George Reed, Gholson's fellow platoon leader in the Machine Gun Company, was also struck by shrapnel in both legs; Reed was evacuated to a hospital where he died the next day.[27]

The 1st Battalion, maneuvering in Rau de Mayache, "practically lost all its officers and suffered about 50% casualties."[28] The 2nd Battalion was halted on the brow of Rau de Mayache in anticipation of a German counterattack.[29] While the 1st and 2nd Battalions were being raked by enemy fire from the front and right, the 3rd Battalion suffered fewer casualties. Experienced squad leaders could tell when the noise of an incoming shell indicated that it would impact nearby, and they then ordered their men to hit the dirt, thus saving many lives. By 0750, as the assault and support battalions struggled in the ravines ahead, the fog began to clear. The 3rd Battalion, at that time, had advanced to the high ground about 1,000 yards northwest of their jump-off positions. Now they came under direct enemy observation, and artillery fire became heavier. Without the darkness and fog, control became easier, and the men began to use the natural cover of the ground in their advance. By noon the 3rd Battalion reached a ravine south of les Bouleaux Bois.[30]

In Rau de Mayache, the 1st Battalion fought its way through the gulch and up the steep, unprotected slope. The battalion became badly disorganized, and its companies merged. At one point, a patrol commanded by Sgt. Lain Dobbs and consisting of Cpl. Theodore E. Crist, Pvt. Peter A. Victor, and four others, all from Company B, attacked an area of woods protected by machine guns. Soon, the small patrol was surrounded by about fifty Germans; the men fought savagely and beat back the enemy, killing and wounding many of them. Sergeant Dobbs, although gassed, fought on until he was seriously wounded by shellfire. For his bravery in action, Sgt. Dobbs was awarded the Distinguished Service Cross while Cpl. Crist and Pvt. Victor were awarded Silver Stars. With all of Company B's officers out of action, Pvt. Mark C. Lindsay assisted in reorganizing the survivors; for his actions, he was awarded the Silver Star. Sergeant Lubomir Pusitz of Machine Gun Company, in support of the 1st Battalion, led his men against German positions in the woods and high ground. Although he had been badly gassed, Sgt. Pusitz refused evacuation. He, too, was awarded the Silver Star for his actions.[31]

At 0840, Col. Erickson, greatly concerned about the progress of the 1st Battalion and still worried about his right flank, sent a message to Capt. Wortley, commander of the 2nd Battalion, telling him that if the 1st Battalion was disorganized he was to "assist [the 1st Battalion] to first objective and leapfrog. Be sure to protect your flank."[32] Lieutenant Forster recalled that Wortley, in response to this message, went forward to converse with Maj. Legge. Legge, in turn, replied to Col. Erickson at 1000, telling him that he was on a "ridge across ravine where original first objective was and are delayed by machine gun nest in woods at bottom ... Request that artillery immediately place heavy fire on these woods."[33] At this time, Legge was in position on the ridge between Rau de Mayache to the south and the Exermont Ravine to the north.

At 1000 the machine gun nest referred to by Maj. Legge stopped Company C with frontal fire. Second Lieutenant Harry Dillon, commander of Company C, a twenty-eight-year old native of Mondovi, Wisconsin, had been working on a family farm when he entered the Second Officers Training Camp at Fort Sheridan in 1917. Now far from his Wisconsin farm, Dillon, already a twice-wounded and decorated veteran, once again felt the dread weight of responsibility as he pondered his company's dilemma. With one platoon, Dillon moved ahead, instructing the remaining men to await his signal for the go-ahead once the machine guns were cleared out. Dillon and his men moved forward toward the machine gun nests as the rest of the company waited. The watched-for signal never came. As the small attack group moved against the machine guns, the Germans opened fire. Dillon was instantly killed by a burst of machine gun fire; his men fought ferociously for their lives, and only fourteen men made it back to the company out of the approximately fifty-eight who had gone forward with the lieutenant. Later, after the company had succeeded in eliminating the machine gun nests, they moved forward, and one of the privates found "Lieutenant Dillon with a machine gun bullet through his forehead." Second Lieutenant Glen Brody then assumed command of Company C. Dillon had been "respected and loved" by his men; his battalion commander, Maj. Legge, also paid him tribute, saying, "I can personally testify to his gallantry in the battle of the Argonne Forest." So popular was Lt. Dillon among his men that one of the privates in his company took it upon himself to write to Dillon's alma mater, the University of Wisconsin (class of 1913), to tell about the circumstances of his death. The letter was only the second that the man had ever written.[34]

Around this time, according to Pvt. Carmine Ferritto of Company C, "about 150 men got over 2,000 yards ahead of the American barrage and lost many of our men whittling down to a number of about thirty-five men. ... We had about twelve men left by the time that the main body got caught up to us."[35]

As the 1st Battalion fought in Rau de Mayache and the ridge to its north, the 2nd Battalion continued to take heavy fire from the right flank. At 1000, 1st Lt. Andrew Van Lopik, the 2nd Battalion adjutant, sent a message to Maj. Frasier, commanding the 3rd Battalion in reserve, informing him that both the 1st and 2nd Battalions had been held up. The 1st Battalion, Lt. Van Lopik said, had suffered heavy casualties. He closed with the plea, "send us some help."[36] Lieutenant Van Lopik was later wounded during the drive.[37]

At 1100, Col. Erickson, by this time with the 3rd Battalion PC, replied to Maj. Legge via runner, telling him that he had relayed his request for artillery fire to the artillery regiments. Legge's message had taken a long time to reach Col. Erickson, and the colonel considered that it was possible that the 1st Battalion had already overcome the resistance. Erickson told Legge, "if you still need help call me on telephone and send runner." He ended his message with a plea to "make your messages clearer."[38] At 1135, Col. Erickson's concern about his right flank led him to send a message to the commander of the 64th Infantry Brigade of the 32nd Division, the unit on the 26th's immediate right, requesting "information as to whereabouts of Regiment on my right, supposed to be 127th Inf."[39] The 26th continued to be hit by fire from that zone and continued to devote manpower to protect that flank. Officers in the 32nd Division felt that the meeting point of the 32nd Division and the 26th Infantry "was the hot spot of the entire line and continued to be during the next few days." Indeed, the whole area at the juncture of the two divisions consisted of a string of "obstinate German detachments."[40]

And that right flank was on Maj. Legge's mind as he pondered whether to continue the advance considering his battalion's disorganized condition, or whether to ask for help from the 2nd Battalion in support. Captain Wortley, commander of the 2nd Battalion, on the telephone with Col. Erickson while coming forward to converse with Legge, was mortally wounded by two machine gun bullets in his chest; Capt. Edgarton "commanded the battalion for about five minutes until Capt. Youell [commander of Company E, and the senior captain] could be found." Youell then assumed command of the 2nd Battalion although he himself had already sustained a painful wound.[41]

Captain Youell had previously declined a promotion to major in order to allow Capt. Wortley to continue as battalion commander. "A real man, officer, and gentleman was Captain Y," recalled Lt. Mansfield. As Youell moved forward to converse with Legge, Lt. Levis R. Bune, a twenty-eight-year old teacher from Wisconsin, assumed command of Company E.[42] The fire that mortally wounded Wortley also knocked out the 2nd Battalion's assigned 37mm gun and killed and wounded most of its crew. Thus the regiment was deprived of one-third of its allocation of an effective weapon.[43]

As it turned out, Youell was the perfect man to lead the 2nd Battalion through the savage fighting of the next eight days. He had been a star athlete in Virginia Military Institute's Class of 1914 and a "First Captain" of its Corps of Cadets. Once, 2nd Lt. Charles Ridgely, also of the 26th, came upon Youell as he was making observations of the enemy positions; soon shells started falling all around them, and Ridgely dove for cover in a shell hole. Youell, however, calmly continued his observations. "He has nerves of iron," said Lt. Ridgely later.[44]

Both the 1st and 2nd Battalion commanders were very concerned about the exposed right flank, and both men agreed that the 2nd Battalion should pass through the lines of the 1st Battalion and continue the assault. Colonel Erickson was notified via telephone, and he approved the plan; indeed, he had been considering such a move since his 0840 message to the 2nd Battalion. This decision was reached shortly after noon. It was deemed too important to wait for the artillery called for earlier, so the artillery request was cancelled; the men would have to overcome the machine gun nests with rifles, grenades, and a 37mm gun. In the meantime, Capt. Wortley was carried to the rear in a blanket. Eventually he was taken to Evacuation Hospital 11 where he died two days later. He was posthumously cited for gallantry in action in AEF General Orders.[45]

According to Capt. Edgarton, the 1st Battalion "had been more or less broken up by a big machine gun nest which lay in a small woods" on the brow of Exermont Ravine, just to the west of the north-south running Rau du Gouffre.[46] With the 1st Battalion pinned down and disorganized on the high ground between Rau de Mayache and Exermont Ravine, the 2nd Battalion "came forward in squad columns widely deployed, crossed the exposed ground by infiltration, reformed in the ravine, and passed the remnants of the First Battalion on the ridge south of Exermont Ravine, by rushes of small groups and fought their way abreast of the 28th [on the left]."[47] The 2nd Battalion's one-pounder having been destroyed, Lt. Forster's gun and crew joined the 2nd Battalion as it passed through the 1st Battalion. The surviving gunners from the 2nd Battalion gun brought up all the ammunition they had for the use of the remaining gun.[48]

With his 2nd Battalion now spearheading the 26th's assault, Youell came forward with a map to try to pinpoint the German machine gun nests and artillery positions for his own artillery to bombard. Youell called for the 37mm gun that was now attached to Company E. With a large chew of tobacco in his cheek, Youell knelt on one knee while placing the map on his other knee. While under heavy machine gun, rifle, and artillery fire, he directed the shots of the 37mm gunners.[49] Lieutenant Forster found it difficult to find cover for his gun and crew. They "finally crawled out into a shell hole dragging the trails and gun by the pulling ropes and took with us some brush for cover." The targets, four German machine guns, were about 800 yards to their right front. Lieutenant Forster with three men crewed the gun. Forster described the action in words that reveal his, and the gun crew's, excitement and zeal: "I fired the first three rounds and was induced to give way to the pleading of the gunner who got on the target in about six rounds and then pumped two boxes at them."[50]

Some of the rifleman of the 2nd Battalion were "lying flat on the ground with no cover" in vicinity of the gun. Other men, being naturally curious about the 37mm gun and its effect on the enemy positions, exposed themselves to watch the firing. The riflemen as well as the gunners involuntarily flinched at the sharp bark of the 37mm with each shot. As might have been expected, the one-pounder's firing brought down German retaliation in the form of 77mm artillery fire. The riflemen in the area suffered as the shells exploded on the high ground where the 37mm was firing. Lt. Forster remembered that, "one platoon commander lying close to our position kept complaining while we were firing that in a little while we would bring down a barrage and get them all killed and it looked like he was about to be right." In short order, the Germans in the target area left the edge of the woods "and beat it to their rear." American artillery then found the range and began to hit the area. Recalling the incoming 77mm fire, Forster said, "The experience in the face of that German 77 firing direct was no laughing matter. Actually the shell would burst before we would hear the report of the gun."[51] But resistance in the front of the 2nd and 1st Battalions wasn't gone; more Germans came into the area while the battalions were engaged in the delicate passage of lines.

Around 1400, Capt. Youell gave the order to assault German machine gun positions located at the edge of a woods about 1,000 yards in front of the 2nd Battalion. Youell placed Companies E and F in the assault wave with Companies G and H in support. Lieutenant Bune, commander of Company E, placed his 1st and 3rd platoons in assault and the 2nd platoon in support. Lieutenant Mansfield, commanding the 3rd platoon, once again made the rounds of his men, checking ammunition. Companies E and F were on the high ground south of Exermont Ravine. The fighting to this point had been severe; as Lt. Mansfield recalled, "not too many men in Lt M's Platoon now." Waiting for the order to start the assault, "some of the men [of Company E] from their positions on the reverse slope smoked their cigarettes and would not be present at roll call tomorrow morning."[52]

At H-hour, 1500, the order to move forward came; the men went "over the crest, down the slope, running men falling, shells bursting" as they approached a creek at the bottom of Exermont Ravine. There was a bridge crossing the creek; Lt. Mansfield immediately ascertained that this "enemy-made crossing" was certainly zeroed in by multiple machine guns. The lieutenant shouted to his men to avoid the bridge. Half of the 3rd platoon reached the creek and began to re-form, still under severe fire from Germans within 100 yards of them. The men began a heavy return fire. One Company E rifle grenadier at the creek had only two rifle grenades left; with these he made direct hits, and the enemy firing eased up a bit after these "cool, well-directed shots." Mansfield led his men into the creek as some men from Company F, to the right, began a bayonet charge against the Germans on the far side of the creek in their sector. The next thing Lt. Mansfield remembered was being on a French hospital train on his way to the rear with a severe bullet wound in his leg. For his actions on this day, Mansfield received the Silver Star.[53] Capt. Youell, for his extraordinary heroism during this action and some later actions, received the Distinguished Service Cross.[54]

Without a preparatory artillery barrage, the 2nd Battalion pressed forward up the north slope of Exermont Ravine and into the woods which contained the twelve-gun machine gun nest on the brow of the ravine. It was Capt. Edgarton's impression that the Germans fought a strong rear-guard action, abandoning the position just before the Americans got to it. But there were other guns and other nests still active in the area. Due to the heavy fire, it had taken from about 1500 to 1700 for the 2nd Battalion to pass the 1st Battalion and assault Exermont Ravine.[55]

Enemy machine gun nests still infested the woods confronting the 2nd Battalion. Corporal Thomas J. O'Keefe of Company H moved alone into the woods to destroy one of these nests. Engaging eight Germans in a pistol duel, Cpl. O'Keefe killed four of the enemy before he was killed. For his extraordinary heroism, he was posthumously awarded the Distinguished Service Cross. Soon the line became hung up again; Cpl. Byron C. Echols of Company B, 3rd Machine Gun Battalion, supporting the 2nd Battalion, led his crew ahead of the infantry line. Exposed to heavy artillery and machine gun fire, Cpl. Echols fired upon two machine guns and silenced them, allowing the infantry to resume their advance. Later, as he led his men in an advance against another machine gun nest, Echols was severely wounded. For extraordinary heroism in action, Cpl. Echols received the Distinguished Service Cross.[56]

By 1500, the 3rd Battalion, following in reserve, had reached the area west of the Bois Communal de Baulny, where the 1st Battalion had jumped-off about nine and a half hours earlier, a stark indication of just how much resistance the assault and support battalions had encountered in their terrific struggle in the ravines ahead. Now the 3rd Battalion became embroiled in their own battle. Here the men came under artillery, machine gun, and rifle fire from Tronsol Farm, just outside the 1st Division sector, in the 32nd Division's sector to the right. Some elements of the 32nd attacked this position, while a 37mm gun from the 26th Infantry fired on the position. Company A, 3rd Machine Gun Battalion, supporting the 3rd Battalion, moved into les Bouleaux Bois to the south. The commander dispatched a platoon of machine guns to work with the 37mm gun against the enemy at Tronsol Farm. This enabled the troops from the 32nd Division to occupy the farm, however, German artillery soon drove those troops back out.[57]

Up ahead, the 2nd Battalion came under renewed artillery fire from north of Exermont, and machine gun fire from Le Comte Farm. And both the assault and support battalions were raked by fire coming from the east, outside of the division's sector; the 32nd Division had failed to advance in line with the 26th thereby allowing the enemy in the woods to the right of the 26th to inflict damage on their attacking line. Thermite shells fired by the 1st Gas Regiment, supporting the 1st Division's attack that morning, and the advance of the 28th Infantry Regiment helped silence the guns to the west of the 26th; then the 26th advanced against enemy positions in the woods to the east, on the high ground north of Exermont Ravine.[58] The enemy in the woods showed no inclination to surrender, and, as a consequence, "there was some lively hand to hand fighting." To wipe out these machine gun nests in the woods required teamwork; it was painstaking and extremely hazardous work. The men had to flank these nests and attack them with Stokes mortars, hand grenades, and rifle grenades.[59] As the 2nd Battalion advanced north of Exermont Ravine, Lt. Forster and his gun crew passed the area they had fired on earlier in the afternoon; Forster found "three abandoned enemy machine guns and four dead Germans." The Germans' bodies being "badly torn," Lt. Forster knew that American artillery had caused some of the carnage; although he made no close inspection, he was "satisfied that we [the 37mm gun] did assist in overcoming their stubborn stand."[60] The 1st Battalion, now in support behind the 2nd Battalion, closed up with the 2nd and occupied almost the same ground.

The end of the day found the regiment dug in on the wooded high ground north of Exermont Ravine, between Le Comte Farm on the left, and the edge of Bois de la Morine on the right; they had advanced a little over one mile under heavy fire that day.[61] The companies of the 1st Battalion, in Exermont Ravine were close together, taking advantage of the cover in the ravine. The front line, consisting of the 2nd and 1st Battalions, refused their right flank to protect from counterattack from that sector.[62] In the second line, the 3rd Battalion, still in reserve and now occupying the ground near the morning's jump-off for the 1st Battalion, also sought to protect the right flank; the battalion commander faced a platoon of Company M to the right, and one platoon of machine guns also covered that area. The other machine guns supporting that battalion prepared to fire overhead at the crests to the battalion's front.[63] The 2nd and 1st Battalions continued to receive harassing artillery fire in the early evening, but Lt. Forster remembered that the troops "had a good night's rest." Captain Youell sent out patrols to determine the location of the enemy.

At 2200, Col. Erickson came to the 2nd Battalion PC and met with all three battalion commanders and most officers of the 2nd and 1st Battalions. The men discussed plans for the next day's attack. Colonel Erickson decided that the 1st Battalion would lead the assault the next day, advancing through the 2nd Battalion at jump-off. Accordingly, wire-cutting details went forward at midnight to cut passages through the wire in front of Hill 212, the next day's objective.[64]

According to Capt. George R.F. Cornish, Headquarters Company commander, the regimental PC had started the day in a ravine south of les Bouleaux Bois (probably near the 2nd Battalion jump-off line); it moved up to high ground northeast of Serieux Farm, and then ended the day on the north slope of Exermont Ravine, "where it remained for the greater part of the operation." Major Frasier stated that, by 0300 on October 5, the PC was in a "little valley that opened into Rau de Mayache southwest of Tronsol Farm."[65]

For the first day of the advance, "the regiment lost 188.4 [men] per thousand ... or about 565 officers and men."[66] The toll on the 2nd Battalion had been heavy. Writing of Company F, Capt. Edgarton recalled that, "I started with about two hundred men. After arriving on the Exermont Ravine I had ninety. The other companies [of the 2nd Battalion] had sixty apiece."[67] The 2nd Battalion commander and one company commander, Lt. Sands of Company H, had been killed. The hostile fire was so severe that even the reserve battalion suffered many casualties. For example, the 3rd Battalion aid station, which had made three successive moves throughout the day, "taking advantage of such cover as had been dug by the troops preceding [them]," had lost all their medical personnel, killed or wounded.[68] In the 1st Battalion, two company commanders, Capt. Hamilton K. Foster of Company A and Lt. Harry A. Dillon of Company B, had been killed. Also in the 1st Battalion, 2nd Lt. Willis C. Conover, a platoon leader in Company C, was wounded and gassed and evacuated to a hospital.[69] Second Lieutenants Reed and Gholson, platoon leaders in the regimental Machine Gun Company, were killed, thus severely crippling that company's leadership at the outset of battle.[70]

Major Legge, commander of the 1st Battalion, was awarded the Distinguished Service Cross for extraordinary heroism in action, inspiring "his men by his courage, cutting his way through entanglements and directing the attacks against three different strong points."[71] Indeed, all three battalion commanders would eventually earn the DSC for their actions during this battle. Of Legge, Lt.Col. Theodore Roosevelt Jr., commander of the 26th immediately after this phase of the battle, would later say, "I have seen him under all circumstances. He was always cool and decided. No mission was too difficult for him to undertake. His ability as a troop leader was of the highest order. In my opinion no man of his age has a better war record."[72]

It is appropriate to pause here to examine some of the logistics of battle that, although unsung, are quite often keys to victory or defeat. Of prime importance was liaison and communications.

A company commander, for example, had to have communications established with his subordinate units, the platoons, and with his superior unit, the battalion. The battalion commander, for his part, needed to have adequate communications with each of his companies, with the other battalions, and with the regimental commander. Likewise, all units had to establish liaison with whatever units happened to be on their flanks. Communication up and down the chain of command was typically handled via telephone, when available, and with runners, men who were assigned to carry verbal and written orders to the next level of command. Liaison could be handled via runner, or more often via a liaison platoon assigned to the task.

So vital was communications to success in battle that Col. Erickson had impressed upon the battalion commanders that their first duty was to advance, and their next most important duty was to stay in contact with regimental headquarters.[73] Typically the assault battalion commander was responsible to maintain communications back to the support battalion; the support battalion commander was responsible to maintain communications back to regimental headquarters. The reserve battalion would, in this case, maintain communications with division headquarters until such time as it was released to the regiment.

For telephone communications, the method adopted in the 26th was to use a telephone with a ladder line that consisted of two parallel lines of twisted pair wires running up to the battalions; at intervals the parallel lines were bridged by connecting wires. Telephone operators at battalion headquarters "cut in" on the lines when necessary, to establish contact with regiment. Since these wires were easily cut by any number of means, not the least of which was hostile artillery, the two parallel lines and the bridging connectors helped to increase the odds of maintaining communications during the advance. The parallel lines were laid close enough together so that a patrolling lineman could observe breaks in either line easily; typically the distance was about ten yards. Men assigned to bridge the wires used test sets to ensure connectivity. Patrols and guards were assigned so that one man patrolled about 500 yards of the line; this was kept up day and night. The linemen were mostly from the regimental signal detachment, but sometimes riflemen from the line companies had to be detailed to do this work.[74]

Major Frasier, 3rd Battalion commander, later determined that, for this phase of the Meuse-Argonne Offensive, maintaining the lines of communications in this manner cost the battalion seventy-four men in killed and wounded. Yet he declared that, had communications been allowed to falter because of lack of dedicated patrols and repairmen, the cost to the battalion would have been perhaps ten times as much.[75] Up to this stage in the battle, at least, the 1st Battalion commander felt that communications, via phone and via runner, were satisfactory.[76] During the next nine days, the adjutant of the 1st Battalion, 1st Lt. Donald H. Grant, would volunteer to carry messages from Maj. Legge to his company commanders under "intense enemy fire." For his bravery during this campaign he was awarded the Distinguished Service Cross.[77]

Runners, men detailed to carry messages, were used exclusively for communications between companies; mounted messengers and runners were used for communications between the battalion and regimental headquarters when the telephone wasn't available. This system, as with the telephone line, cost the companies in manpower. Important messages were often sent via two separate runners leaving at different times. The runners bore some distinguishing mark and carried their messages in a similar place so that if anyone came upon a dead or wounded runner, they could easily recognize him as such and also retrieve the message for delivery. If a distinguishing mark was not used, the runners had to pin the message to themselves in a conspicuous place.[78] Often an armband or brassard identified runners; such distinguishing marks also served to indicate to military police and others that the runner had legitimate business behind the lines and was not straggling.

A first-hand account of the hazards a runner faced is given by Pvt. Ernest L. Wrentmore, who lied about his age and enlisted at the age of twelve years, ten months in 1917. Wrentmore, who served as a runner in Company I, 60th Infantry Regiment, 5th Division, recalled that:

> A "runner," carrying messages up and down the front lines ... meeting each situation as it came along – such as giving aid to his buddies in hand-to-hand combat with the enemy, or unexpectedly finding it necessary to fight it out alone *en route* to his destination, was exposed to continual danger, carrying out his orders in the face of death-dealing gas attacks across bullet-swept "No-Man's Land," while his every movement brought a rain of fire to halt his progress. A runner's sole duty, and objective, was to deliver the message, despite the weather, the darkness of night, or the exposure to enemy cross fire in the daytime.[79]

During the first day of the battle, runners were used exclusively to carry field messages "until almost six hours after the battle started."[80]

Ammunition for the regiment's Hotchkiss machine guns and Springfield rifles was brought forward from the supply dumps in machine gun carts that belonged to the various machine gun companies. The carts, pulled by horses or mules, had to traverse rugged terrain at night, under shellfire, bringing loads of ammunition from as far as Rau de Mayache, where the regimental infantry ammunition dump was located as of October 5. Often, on return trips to the rear, these carts would haul back wounded men in what was undoubtedly a terrifyingly uncomfortable ride. The carts could hold only one man at a time, so not many men were evacuated by this method. Later, rations were brought forward using the same carts.[81]

During active fighting such as that experienced by the 26th in the Meuse-Argonne Offensive, feeding the troops was very difficult. Kitchens had to be kept to the rear, under cover and generally beyond the reach of any hostile fire except for larger caliber artillery. According to Lt. Forster, a "hot meal would come up at dusk and details [from the rifle companies] were sent several hundred yards behind the front lines to get it. ... Another meal would come up between two and three o'clock in the morning. There were no meals between 3:00 a.m. and 5:00 p.m."[82] As will be seen, the 26th experienced trouble in getting meals forward to the infantrymen.

It was also something of an ordeal for the men to get fresh water, so vital during combat. Once halted for the day, as the men dug in and sought whatever cover they could find, details from each platoon went in search of water. According to Lt. Forster, "two men with as many as twenty canteens strung on a pole would go for water." This was, of course, often extremely difficult to do; men had to search in the dark, over shell-torn and gas-soaked ground; the chance encounter with an enemy patrol was always a possibility, and the area was still subject to machine gun and artillery fire. And if the details found water, there was no guarantee that it was fit to drink. Lieutenant Forster related that, "water details frequently drew water from streams which were contaminated. Fifty per cent of our troops were complaining of disentary [*sic*] for a period of five days after we left the lines."[83]

Major Barnwell R. Legge, Commander, 1st Battalion, 26th Infantry Regiment, shown as a Brigadier General during World War II, awarded the Distinguished Service Cross. (http://en.wikipedia.org/wiki/Barnwell_R._Legge)

Captain Raymond D. Wortley, Commander, 2nd Battalion, 26th Infantry Regiment, shown here as an enlisted man in the California National Guard, c. 1910, killed in action, October 4, 1918; awarded the Silver Star. (Courtesy Janice Buchanan.)

Major Rice M. Youell, Commander, Company E and 2nd Battalion, 26th Infantry Regiment, shown here as a cadet at Virginia Military Institute, c. 1912, awarded the Distinguished Service Cross. (http://www.fanbase.com/member/nailboys/photo/1169247?n=15)

Second Lieutenant William A. Mansfield, Company E, 26th Infantry Regiment. Wounded in action, October 4, 1918; awarded the Silver Star. (Courtesy Alan Tallis, "Diary of a Shavetail.")

General John J. Pershing presents the Distinguished Service Cross to Private Axel C. Lundegard, Medical Detachment, 26th Infantry Regiment, for his heroism on October 4, 1918. Ceremony March 14, 1919, Germany. (SC-111, WWI Signal Corps Photo #155650, National Archives.)

Scene near Cheppy, October 1, 1918. (Courtesy Colonel Robert R. McCormick Research Center.)

Dead horses and destroyed caisson, near Exermont, October 5, 1918. (Courtesy Colonel Robert R. McCormick Research Center.)

Destroyed heavy gun, 56th Artillery Regiment, Coast Artillery Corps, near Charpentry. (Courtesy Colonel Robert R. McCormick Research Center.)

A French-built Renault tank of the type that supported the 26th Infantry Regiment, October 4 and 5, 1918. (Courtesy Colonel Robert R. McCormick Research Center.)

1st Division Headquarters, near Apremont, early October, 1918. (Courtesy Colonel Robert R. McCormick Research Center.)

Wounded 1st Division soldier receiving first aide, near Exermont, October 5, 1918. (Courtesy Colonel Robert R. McCormick Research Center.)

An example of the appalling road conditions encountered by American troops in the Meuse-Argonne Offensive. (Courtesy Colonel Robert R. McCormick Research Center.)

Company B, 803rd Pioneer Infantry Regiment, digging trenches near Cheppy, October, 1918. Although given basic infantry training, Pioneer Infantry Regiments normally performed engineer tasks behind the lines. (Courtesy Colonel Robert R. McCormick Research Center.)

Traffic jam in the area the 26th Infantry passed through, near Neuvilly, October 3, 1918. (Courtesy Colonel Robert R. McCormick Research Center.)

Quartermaster ration dump, October 4, 1918. From points such as this, regimental supply companies hauled rations forward for distribution to the battalions and companies. (Courtesy Colonel Robert R. McCormick Research Center.)

Four:

"VICIOUS IN THE EXTREME," OCTOBER 5

The original division attack plan had envisioned that the 1st Brigade, on the left, would run into more resistance and have a harder time advancing than the 2nd Brigade on the right. Actually, it turned out that the 16th Infantry, on the division's left flank, was the only regiment to come near to the corps' objective by the end of the day, that regiment having advanced to Fleville, just short of the objective. On the right flank, the 2nd Brigade had only been able to reach the day's first objective, having advanced to a line just north of Exermont Ravine. This was due largely to the crippling enemy fire coming from the right flank, outside the division's zone, which fell upon the 26th Infantry. The 18th Infantry ended the day facing northeast, connecting the right flank of the 16th Infantry and the left flank of the 28th Infantry. The 32nd Division, on the right of the 26th Infantry, had failed to keep pace in its advance. The 26th's right flank, indeed the right flank of the 1st Division, was thus "up in the air," with no friendly troops in that direction.

The division's order for the advance on October 5 was in two phases. The first phase was for the 2nd Brigade and the 18th Infantry to advance to a line running along "the northern edge of the woods on Hill 212 to the crest of Hill 240."[1] Here the assault waves were to halt for two hours to reorganize, while the divisional artillery laid heavy concentrations on the enemy located in the zone ahead, including shelling Bois de Moncy, to the right of the 26th, with shrapnel. Afterward the assault wave would continue the advance so that the entire line would come abreast of the 16th Infantry, with the 26th Infantry occupying the crest of Hill 272. Once again there would be a halt of two hours to allow the units to reorganize. Following this the entire line was to advance to the original corps objective along a line about a half-mile north of Fleville to the area north of Hill 272.[2]

Hill 272 was to prove a tough nut to crack for the 26th Infantry. Its commanding heights afforded "unobstructed observation and field of fire" to the south, southeast, and southwest. On its eastern slope were the thick woods of the far reaches of le Petit Bois; other parts of the hill were dotted with patches of woods, except for the steep southern slope, which was bare. The Germans had "fortified its crest, slopes and flanks with machine guns and direct fire 77mm guns." Later, officers estimated that fifty machine guns and many *minenwerfers* had defended Hill 272.[3] At 0300, the 3rd Battalion commander reported to regimental headquarters to receive the final attack orders; a regimental staff officer brought the orders to the 1st Battalion, in the lead, at 0400. The 2nd Battalion, in very close support, probably also received the orders via a staff officer.[4]

The attack was to start at 0630, H-hour. Fifteen minutes prior to H-hour the artillery was to bombard the area immediately in front of the 1st Battalion up to and including the first objective. At H-hour the artillery would switch to a rolling barrage laid down 200 yards in front of the 1st Battalion and advancing at the rate of 100 yards in four minutes.[5] The 1st Battalion was to seize the territory southwest of Bois de Moncy, including Hill 212. At that point, the 3rd Battalion, which had been given back to the 26th's regimental commander for use in this assault, was to leapfrog both the 1st and 2nd Battalions and capture Hill 272 and Cote de Maldah to the north.[6] At this point, the regiment was to send the 1st Battalion at right angles to the line of attack, with the goal of clearing the enemy out of Bois de Moncy and "the west slopes of Hill 269, securing the right flank of the Division."[7]

On the first day of the assault, the leading waves had trouble following the rolling barrage closely enough. Therefore the division commander passed control of artillery fire to the brigade and regimental commanders. Artillery liaison officers were with the 1st Battalion and with the regimental commander; an officer from the 7th Field Artillery Regiment, supporting the 26th, reported to the 3rd Battalion, along with a horse-drawn 75mm field piece, at 0600. This gun was to accompany the battalion during the advance. A similar gun with the 1st Battalion, it will be recalled, met with disaster during the first day.[8]

Six tanks were to accompany the 1st Battalion in the assault. These passed through the 3rd Battalion, on their way forward, at about 0600. Not a single one of the tanks made it to the assault battalion, all falling victim to German artillery firing from Hill 240 in the 18th Infantry Regiment's sector. Three tanks were hit on the high ground northeast of le Neuville le Comte Farm; one was hit as it came out of the woods in front of Hill 212; two others were destroyed by thermite shells east of St. Germain.[9] At least two of these locations, as reported by the 3rd Battalion commander, appear to be beyond the jump-off position of the 1st Battalion; it is possible that the tanks could not reach the jump-off line by H-hour and the surviving tanks never caught up to the assault battalion. In any event, this shows the skill of the German gunners and the inviting targets that tanks made; likewise, it shows the importance of mutual support in the attack since the hostile guns were in other regiments' zones.

It will be recalled that, on October 4, the 2nd Battalion had leap-frogged the 1st and had continued the assault, with the 1st following closely behind. The 2nd Battalion assaulted and captured the high ground and woods just east of le Neuville le Comte Farm, and at the end of the day the battalions were occupying almost the same ground, with the right flank refused and the 1st Battalion taking cover in Exermont Ravine, just behind the 2nd Battalion.[10]

The 1st Battalion, having been disorganized during the first day's advance, was realigned for the renewal of the assault. In the first line were, left to right, Company C and Company A. In the second line were, left to right, Company B and Company D. The supporting machine gun company followed the second line company at fifty yards, with the Stokes mortars and the 37mm gun immediately behind the machine guns. The troops were deployed in the same formation as the previous day, with the first line as skirmishers and the following lines in squad columns. The total depth of the 1st Battalion was about 400 yards.

The regiment's zone was still about 800 yards wide; the attack formation covered only a portion of this. The terrain that would confront the 1st Battalion as they passed through the 2nd was open, with a hill, Hill 200, to the right front. North of that hill, the ground became more wooded. To the left front, the ground then rose until it culminated in the peak of Hill 212, about 700-800 yards from the jump-off line. Beyond Hill 212, the wooded ground descended gradually into a little valley or ravine about 600 yards to the north; St. Germain Farm was situated in the west part of this valley. In the east part of the zone, the valley curved to the north and culminated at Arietal Farm. From there the terrain rose more sharply before descending again, the resultant wooded knoll resembling a little bump in the valley between Hill 212 to the south and Hill 272 to the north. North of this knoll the ground descended into le Petit Bois, the wooded valley in front of Hill 272. It was about 800 yards from the knoll to the peak of Hill 272. Hill 240, to the west in the 18th Infantry's zone, offered excellent observation and firing positions for the Germans.

At 0630, the rolling barrage fell 200 yards in front of the assault troops, and all three battalions moved out into a dense fog.[11] By 0700 the fog cleared, permitting direct observation of the 26th's line by the Germans. At once the regiment was rocked by enfilading machine gun and artillery fire from the right flank. Periodically an enemy battery in Bois de la Morine, off the right flank, bombarded the 3rd Battalion with "very severe and deadly" three-minute bursts.[12] About this time the field piece accompanying the 3rd Battalion was destroyed; the commander of the piece and most of the crew were killed.[13] The 3rd Battalion had to advance rapidly through this fire; the battalion thus advanced in squad columns. Due to heavy casualties, the 3rd Battalion extended their front to 700 yards while expanding their depth to 600 yards. Even with this expanded formation, officers were able to maintain adequate control because of improved visibility and the absence of thick woods.[14]

The 1st Battalion continued its advance against wired areas in the woods in front of and on Hill 212. At one point, Company A was held up by a machine gun nest. Lieutenant Thomas L. Cornell, who had become company commander upon the death of Capt. Foster on the first day, moved to a captured German machine gun and, turning the gun on its former owners, fired the gun himself. After expending a belt of ammunition, Lt. Cornell led a charge that captured the position. As losses mounted, more junior men had to take command. One section of Company A lost all its NCOs; Pvt. Frank Dugan then assumed command of the section and led an attack against a

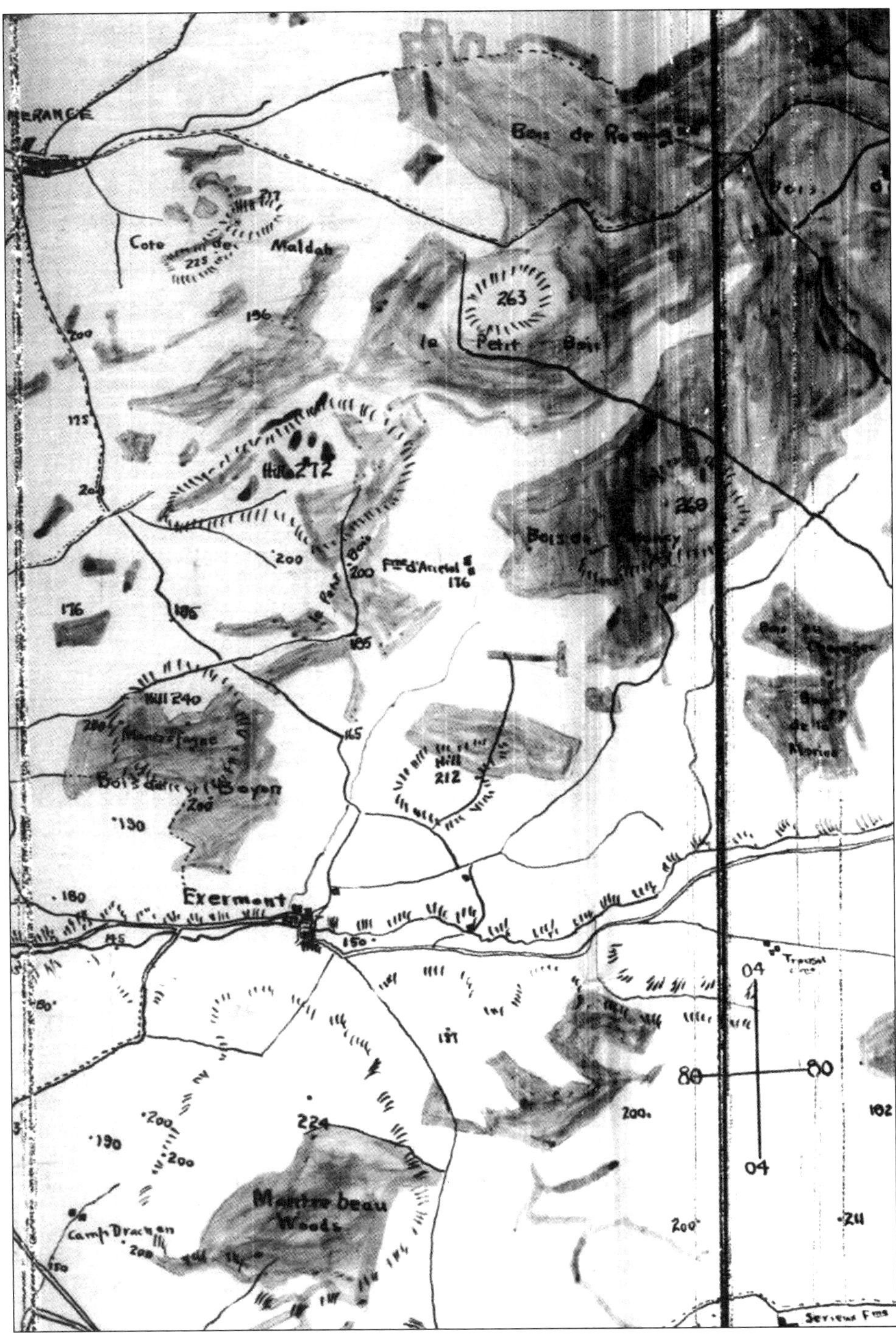

Post-war hand-drawn map showing the area of operations of the 26th Infantry Regiment, October 4 through 12, 1918; note the area around Hill 212 and Hill 272.(Captain Albert B. Helsley, "Operations of the Machine Gun Company, 16th Infantry.")

machine gun nest. The men captured several prisoners and three machine guns, but Pvt. Dugan was seriously wounded in the action. He continued to lead his men until he fell exhausted from blood loss. Lieutenant Cornell and Pvt. Dugan both earned the Distinguished Service Cross for their heroism.[15] As Cpl. Abraham Birnbaum led his platoon forward he saw his friend Pvt. John Rosplock go down. Later, as he herded German prisoners back to the rear, Birnbaum "returned to the spot where [Rosplock] fell with some prisoners in the hope that he might have been wounded. He was dead, having been shot through the heart with a machine gun bullet."[16]

At 0825, Maj. Legge informed Col. Erickson via runner that he was "on my objective [Hill 212] and organizing." He reported that the battalion had "killed a number of Germans and captured some material." Encouragingly, he stated that his losses had been light, and he requested that the 3rd Battalion advance as soon as possible. Legge also reported sniping "in the woods in right rear of us." He was attempting to clear that area out.[17] By 0830, Maj. Frasier was on his way forward to confer with Maj. Legge in anticipation of taking the lead in the resumption of the advance.[18] After the meeting, Frasier quickly returned to his battalion.

Lieutenant Cornell later claimed that "Maj. Legge gave me command of what was left of [Companies] A, B, and C" and that he drove from a position on the northern slope of Hill 212 across the valley to the south slope of Hill 272. This advance started in the morning and culminated in the afternoon, according to Cornell. In light of reports from other officers, it is possible that Cornell, reporting almost nine years after the battle, placed his advance farther to the north than was the actual case. Then again, there are several draws, wooded areas, and hills between Hills 212 and 272, and it's also possible that Cornell was correct in his recollection.[19]

The 1st Battalion had captured prisoners from the German 52nd Division; some of these men stated that fresh troops, the German 5th Guards Division, were due to relieve the 52nd that night. Captain Shipley Thomas, the regimental intelligence officer, advanced with the 2nd Battalion. At 0900 he reported via runner to Col. Erickson, confirming that the 1st Battalion was on their objective and digging in. To the rear, the going was slow.[20]

Many of the scouts who were in connecting files became casualties, and the 3rd Battalion closed too closely upon the 2nd Battalion in support. By 0900 the forward elements of the 3rd Battalion were in the valley east of St. Germain Farm; they were thus probably very close to the forward battalions' positions. The enemy was visible ahead and on the right flank in the outskirts of Bois de Moncy. Major Frasier halted the battalion and sent the battalion scout officer forward to ascertain the situation with the assault and support battalions. Again the 26th's right flank and rear were exposed; in the area of the 3rd Battalion, two machine gun platoons were ordered to be ready to meet any attack from the right flank, while a third platoon and two platoons of riflemen were ordered to the rear to Hill 200, near the jump-off line, to protect the rear from any attack emerging from that area.[21]

Major Frasier, unable to establish telephone communication with the regimental commander, ordered the sergeant from the regimental signal detachment accompanying the 3rd Battalion to find the problem and correct it. Simultaneously, he ordered a detachment of trained telephone and linemen from the battalion headquarters to go forward to repair the lines to the 2nd Battalion, up ahead in support. The platoon commander who had earlier been dispatched to the right flank for protection now reported that they had fought off an attack on their position and that he could observe Germans about 1,000 yards away in Bois de Chene Sec and Bois de la Morine, which "bristled with well placed machine gun nests."[22] He suspected that these forces were preparing for a counterattack down Rau de Mayache, attempting to take the 3rd Battalion, and thereby the entire regiment, from the right rear. This would in turn imperil the entire divisional line.[23]

Presently the scout officer, who had been sent ahead, returned and reported that the 1st and 2nd Battalions had practically merged and that progress was slower than expected. At this time, probably shortly after 0900, or at least two and a half hours after jump-off, it was Maj. Frasier's impression that the other battalions still had not taken Hill 212; parts of the 1st and 2nd Battalions were still fighting their way through the woods ahead. Absorbing all this information, Maj. Frasier ordered the 3rd Battalion to move to the rear to the "high ground northwest of the Tronsol Farm," to protect the right flank and rear of the regiment.[24] The battalions had closed up too much in the advance; there was not enough depth to the regiment to adequately meet an attack from the right flank. The area as far back as the mouth of Rau de Mayache was open to the enemy. Probably the reports reaching Maj. Frasier about the progress of the battalions to his front were confused. According to field messages, the 1st and 2nd Battalions had advanced to and taken Hill 212 by that time but were still engaged with Germans across the ravine in front of Hill 272.

Up ahead, the troops located enemy machine guns in the woods north of Hill 212. Captain Forster's 37mm gun could not, however, acquire any targets, so the enemy machine guns were flanked by infantry patrols.[25] Presently, Maj. Frasier was able to reach Col. Erickson via telephone; the regimental commander temporarily approved Frasier's revised troop disposition, and he came forward to inspect the position. When Col. Erickson arrived at the 3rd Battalion position, he formally approved the disposition and then ordered the 2nd Battalion, now almost merged with the 1st Battalion ahead, to withdraw to Hill 200, just north of Exermont Ravine. This placed the 2nd Battalion in position to protect the regiment's flank and rear, or to advance as the reserve battalion if necessary. Colonel Erickson also ordered artillery fire against Bois de Chene Sec and Bois de la Morine. Two machine gun platoons had been firing on Bois de la Morine, and no threat from that area was observed after this. All during this time all three battalions were under machine gun and artillery fire.[26]

At this critical juncture, some guns of the 7th Field Artillery Regiment, supporting both the 26th and 28th Infantry Regiments, were moving forward to Rau de Mayache. A few guns remained in position near Eclisfontaine, and these were not able to adequately protect the 26th's right flank and at the same time give support to the advance battalion. The idea of attaching a 75mm fieldpiece to each battalion for immediate support had, in the case of the 26th, proved to be a disaster since at least two fieldpieces had been destroyed quickly and several crewmembers killed in these attempts. Instead, the "idea of keeping some guns where the fire could accompany the battalion in every situation was substituted," and this seemed to work better.[27]

By 1000 the 2nd Battalion had taken up position on Hill 200. According to Maj. Frasier, it was noon before the 1st Battalion had driven the enemy from Hill 212.[28] At 1000, as the 1st Battalion paused to reorganize, the 3rd Battalion approached, preparing to pass through and continue the assault. They received heavy fire from the woods south of Hill 272, and they were checked in their advance. At 1040, Col. Erickson, again concerned about progress up ahead, decided to call for a protective barrage before resuming the advance against Hill 272. Accordingly, he ordered the 3rd Battalion, now in the lead, to hold, dig in, and wait for further orders. Colonel Erickson was rather emphatic, his message reading, "Do not advance until you get orders from me. If you have advanced, dig in. Do not advance until your protective barrage begins." To ensure Maj. Frasier would get the point, Erickson repeated his admonition in another message ten minutes later.[29]

Behind the 1st Battalion, the 2nd Battalion continued to protect the right flank and rear. At 1050, Sgt. Roman T. Jones of Company E, the lead right company, reported by message to Capt. Youell that he had achieved liaison with the 2nd Battalion of the 127th Infantry, 32nd Division. Jones reported that the 127th had tried to advance but had been driven back by artillery fire. They were planning to try again. At present, according to Sgt. Jones, the 127th's front line was about "1½ kilometers to the right of our division and about 600 yards in rear."[30] This slower advance was to cause trouble for the 26th for the rest of the campaign. Captain Yuill, commanding Company B, 3rd Machine Gun Battalion, ran into trouble keeping up with the 2nd Battalion. He reported being unable to advance further unless he had infantry and artillery support; his men had been pinned down by machine gun fire in their front and crossfire from the left. He had sent liaison troops forward but had been unable to get in touch with the 2nd Battalion.[31]

In the meantime, Lt. Forster scouted the northern edge of the woods north of Hill 212. The troops were still taking machine gun fire from the woods across the ravine; fog obscured the enemy positions, however. With great difficulty, the men hauled a 37mm gun through "thick underbrush and a mass of wild vines" to get it into place at the edge of the woods. As they waited for visibility to improve to acquire a target, Forster dispatched Sgt. Rimstead to the northeast to reconnoiter.[32] When the sun burned off some of the mist, the 37mm crew fired about fifty rounds at the high ground where the German machine guns were. Since it was impossible to see the machine gun from the 37mm position, Lt. Forster again sent Sgt. Rimstead forward to see if he could determine the effect of the gun's fire. Sergeant Rimstead returned with the information that he could no longer see the German machine gun crew. Lieutenant Forster could not definitely locate other machine guns to fire upon, but he and his crew did fire on positions "along the edge of the Bois De Moncy." Forster recalled that the 37mm gun crew was "constantly in the path of machine gun fire and it is remarkable that more men were not killed." Although they took cover by lying on the ground and in shallow foxholes they'd dug nearby, while they were manning the weapon their only shelter was "the iron shield of the gun."[33]

According to Lt. Forster, this was the extent of the firing for the one-pounders for the day; he further stated that troops later discovered an abandoned German machine gun but no dead bodies.[34] Major Frasier, however, recalled a different scene involving both of the remaining 37mm guns that afternoon. According to his very detailed account, the 37mm guns, one each from the 3rd and 1st Battalions, came forward and directed their fire against four machine guns and a fieldpiece in a small offshoot of Bois de Moncy about 800 yards to the northeast of Hill 212. There then followed a "brilliant duel" at 400 yards range that resulted in the destruction of the enemy fieldpiece and one machine gun. One of the 37mm guns, located in a shell hole for cover, fired only two rounds, the second round entering the firing port of the log emplacement of one of the machine guns. Upon advance later, troops found that the round had killed or wounded every member of the crew. After firing this second round, however, the 37mm gun was itself destroyed by enemy fire; the entire crew, except two ammunition men, was killed.[35]

The second 37mm gun opened fire on the German field piece, firing its first round at the muzzle blast of the piece visible through a cut in the trees at about 300 yards. The German piece responded by a rapid barrage of eleven shells, one of which knocked out the 37mm gun's breechblock lever, killing the gunner and wounding two other men. The officer in charge of the 37mm gun fired the next round himself, and a loud explosion at the German gun heralded its destruction.[36]

While it's difficult to reconcile these two accounts, it is important to note that Lt. Forster, the 37mm platoon leader, was awarded the Distinguished Service Cross for manning and directing the fire of his guns while under artillery, machine gun, and rifle fire throughout the period from October 4 to October 13.[37]

At noon, Col. Erickson sent a message to Maj. Frasier by runner, telling him that a barrage would commence "as soon as possible."[38] The barrage would fall upon le Petit Bois that covered part of Hill 272 ahead, and through which the 3rd Battalion was to pass in its assault. Arietal Farm, "a veritable nest of machine guns," at the right edge of the area through which the battalion was to pass, was also scheduled to receive a barrage. The barrage was to fall for fifteen minutes and then roll forward as the assault waves moved up.[39] The 3rd Battalion was to follow the barrage without further orders.[40] Major Frasier sent a reply to Col. Erickson, telling him that he understood the message and would "go thru if such a thing is possible." He reported heavy casualties, suffered when his battalion attempted to advance beyond the woods north of Hill 212, and decried the absence of the 32nd Division on his right.[41]

It's difficult to ascertain whether this barrage was the one called for in the original attack order, or whether it is the barrage referred to by Capt. Cornish and Maj. Legge in their written reports years later. This latter barrage was ordered by Erickson on specific targets prior to advancing to the second objective. There may have been two barrages, the second of which was called for when Col. Erickson received updated information as to the location of the Germans. In battle, information was key. Regimental officers pressed their battalion commanders for information: Where are your companies? What units are on your right and left? Battalion commanders, in turn, pressed their company commanders who then queried their platoon leaders.

But pressure from division headquarters was constant on the regimental commanders. At one point during the battle, Col. Erickson, while busily directing his regiment, was pressed by division for information. "Yes, yes, everything is fine," he replied distractedly. "Our heavies have just opened up, and it sounds good." One wonders if this answer satisfied division.[42]

In any event, from about 1315 until 1400 the 3rd Battalion, and the others also, waited under artillery and machine gun fire from enemy positions on Hill 272 and in Bois de Moncy off to the right. Machine guns from both the 3rd and 1st Battalions returned the enemy fire, but to what effect is not known.

Around 1345, the promised barrage began to fall in front of the leading wave; due to the aforementioned "thinning" of the supporting artillery pieces, the barrage was not as concentrated as it ought to have been.[43] Fifteen minutes later, the command "'Forward' pierced the uproar … and the front line of the battalion moved down the slopes of Hill 212."[44] As Maj. Frasier wrote eight years later, "There was no use for scouts now. We knew exactly where the enemy was. He knew exactly where we were. Machine guns and artillery which had hitherto awaited our advance opened fire from the woods across the valley and from the Farm d'Arietal." The leading wave, under terrific fire, sprinted across the open ground; "Very few of the men who were in that front line ever will travel again as fast as that." The following wave suffered heavily and merged with the first wave. The American barrage was now past the far side of the valley; officers gave the order to double-time across the open valley to "close with the enemy;" this would give the men the best chance for achieving some cover on the far side, and escaping the enfilading machine gun and artillery fire pouring from Bois de Moncy and Hill 269 off the right flank.[45]

Companies I and K were in the lead, in three lines of skirmishers, the first two lines having blended into one in the initial advance. With ten yards between men, the companies traversed the exposed valley. The men were greeted by artillery fire from le Petit Bois and "veritable sheets of steel" from machine guns in Arietal Farm and the nearby hills. The wicked fire swept the valley knee-high; once men fell, wounded, they were easily finished off. The survivors of Companies I and K engaged the Germans in le Petit Bois and Arietal Farm in hand to hand fighting. So savage was the fighting that enemy cannoneers were bayoneted while they stood at their guns. In only one place did the Germans retreat; they had to be violently driven from the rest. It had taken thirty-five minutes to advance across the valley; in that short space of time "nine officers and approximately one hundred and fifty men had been killed. The number of wounded was never determined."[46]

Major Legge later stated that the 3rd Battalion had reached Arietal Farm and was halted by severe fire from Hill 272 at 1530. He also stated that the 3rd Battalion had made a previous attempt at crossing the valley immediately after passing the 1st Battalion, but that effort was aborted due to heavy casualties, and that Col. Erickson had ordered a two-hour halt for more artillery preparation. This would account for his claim of a 1530 arrival at Arietal Farm, versus the presumed 1435 time suggested by Maj. Frasier.[47] The division history simply states: "Upon reaching the top of the hill [Hill 212] the 3d Battalion was passed through the 2nd and 1st Battalions and fought its way through the woods and occupied the first objective on schedule time."[48]

Once taking Arietal Farm, Companies I and K, the lead companies of the 3rd Battalion, could not stop to rest. In order to provide room for the support companies to move from Hill 212 and cross the valley, they had to push their assault toward the second objective, Hill 272. Accordingly, Company I, commanded by Capt. Paul N. Starlings, pushed forward into le Petit Bois, the woods at the base of Hill 272. At some point, Starlings ordered Lt. Morgan to "take a clump of woods to his front" with his platoon. Morgan had just started forward with his men when he was struck in the forehead by a shell splinter and killed instantly. Company K, commanded by 1st Lt. Dayton Sackett, on the right moved from Arietal Farm into the valley to the north, approaching the slopes of Hill 263 farther to the northeast. The support companies of the 3rd Battalion, Companies L and M, now moved down the north slope of Hill 212 and double-timed the 300 yards across the valley that the leading wave had traversed under terrific fire. Companies L and M, too, were subjected to waves of enemy fire from the right; finally they reached the cover of le Petit Bois.[49]

Machine gun companies supporting the assault and support battalions were very active throughout this time. Company A, 3rd Machine Gun Battalion, in support of the 3rd Battalion, had been delivering "heavy overhead fire" as the rifle companies moved from Hill 212 across the valley and into le Petit Bois; once those companies were in the woods, the machine gunners shifted their fire to Hill 272 proper. Meanwhile, the machine gun company supporting the 1st Battalion had been firing into Bois de la Morine and Bois de Moncy, to the right, prior to the 1st Battalion moving into that area toward Hill 269. A machine gun platoon advanced with Companies L and M and set up position in the fringe of le Petit Bois and covered approaches to Arietal Farm. The machine gun company supporting the 2nd Battalion was located near Exermont Ravine, available for overhead barrage.[50]

Two 75mm guns from the 7th Field Artillery, located in Rau de Mayache, also provided effective support to the 3rd Battalion. These guns "destroyed many machine guns and two pieces of artillery" that had impeded the advance so far. Major Frasier attributed the success of these guns to the battalion's artillery liaison officer, "an exceptionally excellent artillery officer."[51] Some guns of the 7th reportedly fired 1,000 rounds that day.[52] Although artillery fire against the enemy was heavy, one might question its efficacy given the events of the day.

Throughout the day's fighting, liaison with the 28th Infantry on the left was adequately provided by a combat group of two squads from Company I. The 28th advanced in concert with the 26th, and the two regiments kept pace until fire from Hill 272 stopped the 28th about 600 yards north of Hill 240. Liaison on the right was a different story, however. The 32nd Division, meeting difficulties in that zone, had not advanced as far as the 26th; due to enemy fire and due to friendly counter fire in the area around Bois de Moncy, combat liaison patrols were impractical. However, as noted above, the 26th was now arrayed in depth; the 1st Battalion was attacking to the east in that area, and the 2nd Battalion, near Hill 200, was guarding the right flank farther to the rear.

A field artillery liaison officer using a field telephone to communicate with headquarters. (Courtesy Colonel Robert R. McCormick Research Center.)

The advance was now at a standstill due to fire from Hill 272 and from the hills and woods to the east. Company K, on the right, had come up along the eastern slope of Hill 272; they came under fire from Hill 263 to the northeast. Troops could see Germans on the right moving from le Petit Bois across a narrow opening into Bois de Moncy, further threatening the right flank. At this stage, Maj. Frasier contacted Col. Erickson and requested artillery fire upon Hill 272 and Hill 263. Colonel Erickson ordered a half hour barrage on those areas, followed by renewal of the assault at 1600. Unfortunately, some of the American barrage fell on Company K's position east of Hill 272. According to Frasier, "This fire was so deadly and demoralizing that the company commander did not wait for the order of the battalion commander but fell back across the valley." The company lost forty men killed and wounded in this incident. They were now down to about eighty men. Even in the midst of the American bombardment the 3rd Battalion was being hit by "artillery fire from the front and right and by machine gun fire from the right, front and left front."[53]

At 1600, Companies I and K again advanced. As Frasier recalled, "Three waves were mowed down as they emerged from the cover of the woods."[54] Captain Starlings, the commander of Company I, at the vanguard of his men, went down with a bullet wound to the head. Badly wounded, Starlings stayed on the field leading his men until Maj. Frasier ordered him to the rear to seek medical attention. Company K, on the right, managed to re-cross the valley they had fought for, and taken, once already. By now darkness was coming on, and Maj. Frasier ordered a halt. In Company I, with almost all officers and NCOs out of commission, enlisted men began to show leadership initiative. Corporal Charles A. McCoy, although badly wounded, and "in the face of murderous machine gun fire," assumed command of the company and consolidated the position. For his heroism he was awarded the Distinguished Service Cross.[55] Major Frasier later recalled that Company I was down to twenty-eight privates, with no officers and one or two non-commissioned officers; Company K was down to one officer, two non-commissioned officers, and forty-seven privates; however, there was at least one officer, 2nd Lt. William C. Steinmetz, still with Company I. The lead companies dug in. Machine guns moved forward to protect the flanks; the last remaining 37mm gun and two trench mortars took up position on the eastern edge of le Petit Bois to assist in flank defense. When it became dark enough, the support and assault companies of the 3rd Battalion changed positions.[56] The day's fighting had been "vicious in the extreme." For the entire 1st Division, the going had been difficult. First Lieutenant Alban B. Butler, Jr., 1st Division Aide de Camp, remembered that after each advance the infantry "dug in under machine gun and rifle fire from the wooded crests, which seemed always to surround the troops. To reply was almost impossible, for the gun muzzles were hidden and the firing came from everywhere."[57]

At 1620, Col. Erickson sent forward a runner who came from the leading elements of the 127th Infantry on the right. Erickson requested that the man pass on information to both Maj. Legge and Maj. Frasier. Clearly, liaison and flank protection on the right was still a big concern for the officers of the 26th. Accordingly, Col. Erickson sent a message to the commander of the 127th Infantry requesting a sketch of that regiment's position.[58]

While the 3rd Battalion was embroiled in the bloody assault on Arietal Farm, Maj. Legge, 1st Battalion commander, ordered Capt. James R. Manning, commander of Company D, to advance with his company and another company eastward, at right angles to the division's line of advance and assault Bois de Moncy. He also requested food and water and 10,000 rounds of machine gun ammunition, testimonial to the amount of fire the supporting guns laid down during the day.[59]

Sometime before 2000, Capt. Manning moved across the ravine to the east of Arietal Farm and into the northwest part of Bois de Moncy. Once in the woods, Manning deployed his men in a series of outposts forming a rough semi-circle facing north and east. These were placed "to protect the flank in case the enemy attempted either to infiltrate or counter-attack our flank or to our rear, as the 32nd Division had not come up."[60] Indeed, the outposts fought "several sharp engagements" with Germans in the woods that night.[61] In one of these outposts there was a "small hut and short trench" where Manning established his advance PC. The main PC of Company D was located to the west, back across the ravine and on a reverse slope south of Arietal Farm. The 1st Battalion PC was farther still to the west, and runners had to follow a circuitous, lengthy route some several hundred yards to the south and west to avoid the machine gun fire that completely enfiladed the ravine between Arietal Farm and Bois de Moncy. Throughout the time that Company D was in position in Bois de Moncy they were "under severe mortar bombardment" from German mortar emplacements to the north. Manning remembered that the "ravines and hills were steep and narrow, and the Germans had excellent positions for their mortars, which they used frequently and effectively."[62]

Manning sent a patrol directly to Hill 269; that patrol reported the hill unoccupied, and Manning then sent a platoon to occupy the hill. Hill 269 is actually two separate peaks on the same general hill, with a "saddle" between them; this connecting ridge was narrow and "heavily wooded," so that it appeared that the patrol on the western knoll was in possession of the entire summit. The platoon commander, having no map, moved to the southwestern peak of the hill and dug in. However, as was soon discovered, the Germans were still in possession of the taller summit just to the northeast.[63] The 26th reported to V Corps that they had occupied Hill 269; the 32nd Division, in whose sector the hill was, reported, however, that they were still receiving fire from the hill. This was true, since the 26th had only occupied a part of the hill while the Germans remained on the part of the hill to the northeast.[64]

The whole area had been reconnoitered by patrols, under fire from machine guns to the east, and by the officer in command of the troops in the area, in addition to Capt. Manning himself, and by "special Officers [*sic*] sent up by Brigade Headquarters for that purpose."[65] Yet none of these men could determine the exact configuration of the terrain; obviously the woods and ruggedness of the terrain were such that it was very difficult to determine an exact layout of the area in the darkness.

Apparently another patrol from the 26th got as far as Hill 263, well to the north. From there, "they announced that if someone would give them a brigade, they would 'clean out the whole business' that evening." The reinforcements were not forthcoming, and the patrol withdrew.[66] Still, the presence of the platoon on a portion of Hill 269 "several hundred meters" in the enemy's rear caused confusion in the German ranks. Members of this platoon and supporting elements captured Germans moving to and from the front lines through Bois de Moncy. Indeed, Maj. Legge, commander of the 1st Battalion, to which the occupying platoon belonged, wrote that the care and disposition of prisoners was one of his major concerns on October 5.[67] Prisoners were escorted to the rear by one or two riflemen or by some "walking wounded" who were, themselves, on the way to the rear. Once in the regimental PC area, the prisoners were interrogated. Captain Shipley Thomas, 26th Infantry Regiment Intelligence Officer, circulated among these men. Due to his knowledge of the German language, Thomas could sometimes get enough information from prisoners to enable the Americans to identify a target for immediate artillery fire.[68] After initial interrogation, Thomas used military police to escort the prisoners to divisional cages farther to the rear.

A detachment of men was sent to Arietal Farm for further defense against counterattack from that area. At 2010, the 1st Battalion, in support, was in line with two companies just south of Arietal Farm and two companies in Bois de Moncy, facing east, while the left flank bent to the rear to reestablish contact with the 28th Infantry.[69] Major Frasier established listening posts; a combat patrol prowled the ravine east of Hill 272, the area between le Petit Bois and Bois de Moncy. Two patrols were ordered forward. One patrol was to depart at 2200; its mission was to cover the ground in front of Hill 272. The other patrol was to depart at 2330; its mission was to cover the eastern portion of Hill 272.

As the regiment settled into position at the end of the day, the universal question among World War I Doughboys began to be raised: When do we eat? The 3rd

Battalion kitchens were now in Rau de Mayache, probably along with the kitchens from the other battalions. An officer was ordered to ensure food was carried from the kitchens to the men in the line, but this officer failed in his duty. The men in the line went without food. Although the troops carried reserve rations, they were ordered to refrain from eating them unless they had been taken from dead or wounded soldiers. Surely this was an order that was widely ignored. Water was also a problem; "the only water to be had was what was left in the canteens from the morning and from shell holes and from the dead."[70] Although such water in shell holes was muddy and filthy, it posed a temptation to tired, parched soldiers. But drinking this water would at least cause stomach problems such as dysentery and at worst it could be fatal; as stated earlier, such water was often infused with poison gas from the ground. With darkness came the rain, however, and the men were able to catch rainwater in their shelter halves.[71]

This rain, although providing much needed drinking water, added to the misery of the men, especially those who had been wounded and now lay exposed on the battlefield somewhere between the jump-off line and the valley and woods in front of Hill 272. The 3rd Battalion aid station, now consisting of only one Medical Corps first lieutenant, was in the woods just west of Arietal Farm. Normally, men of the regimental band would help act as stretcher-bearers to carry wounded men to the rear; in this case, the bandsmen had been left with the rear echelon of the regiment, along with the regimental clerks. A detachment of men from the pioneer platoon of Headquarters Company had been dispatched to help evacuate the wounded, but they never arrived at the front. Thus the Medical Corps doctor pressed into service some slightly wounded men and prisoners to carry the seriously wounded men back to the regimental aid station and field hospitals. There still remained in the aid station some 120 men too seriously wounded to help themselves out.[72]

The plight of the wounded men of the regiment can best be described in Maj. Frasier's account of the men at this aid station: "Over eighty men died at this aid station, some of them living as long as three days after being brought in. The sight and experience will never be forgotten by those who were present. It shows most convincingly how worthy are the present efforts of the Medical Corps to provide for more effective and certain evacuation of the field."[73] To assist in this evacuation, Col. Erickson granted permission to use unwounded riflemen to carry wounded men to the rear. The men were then ordered to return to the frontline carrying breakfast for the battalion. At 0400 the next morning, only about two-thirds of those who departed returned with marmite cans full of breakfast. Of course some of the others "were killed or wounded by the shell, machine gun and mortar fire which swept the valleys. Some breathed too much gas in the valleys."[74] But some most surely succumbed to the all-too-human temptation of relative safety and comfort in the rear. Some of these men eventually found their way back to the front, but some men were actual stragglers or deserters. Men in combat can take only so much before the overwhelming desire for a break takes hold. Such straggling was common in all armies, however, Maj. Frasier concluded, "It is undoubtedly a dangerous matter to send effectives to the rear unless they are highly trained, disciplined, and experienced."[75]

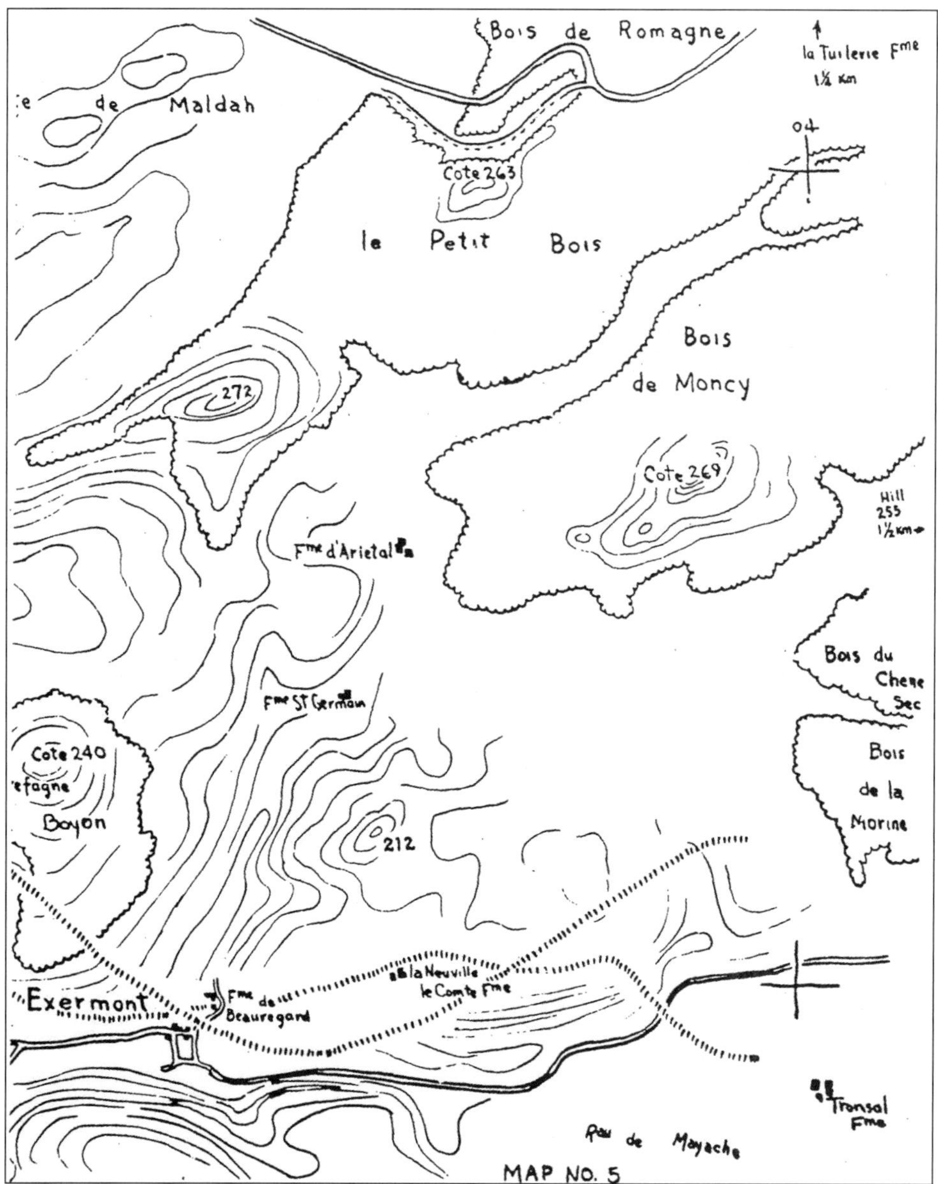

Map showing the 26th Infantry Regiment's area of operations, October 4 through 12, 1918. (Cochran, "The 1st Division Along the Meuse.")

As the wounded were found and cared for, and as men ate what meager food they could find in the rain and mud, commanders began to take stock of their men. The toll on junior officers continued; 2nd Lt. Richard C. Kennedy, a platoon leader in Company K, had been wounded and evacuated to a hospital.[76] As mentioned above, Lt. Morgan Anderson, the twenty-seven-year old Company I platoon leader from Milwaukee, had been killed while leading his men. This steady attrition of officers and NCOs had the effect of greatly impairing the combat leadership of the regiment.[77]

For the 3rd Battalion, the cost was high. They had advanced approximately 1,500 yards at a cost of nine officers and 240 men killed and seven officers and 350 men wounded. At the close of the day, the battalion would count approximately three officers and 370 men. Company I was now commanded by a sergeant (apparently having come forward sometime after the halt).[78] According to Capt. Cornish, the regiment advanced about 2,200 yards on October 5, losing about 310 men of all ranks. The numbers are estimates, but after two days of fighting, it had become apparent that compared to this drive, "St. Mihiel was just a practice game." [79]

Although there was no movement of the lines in the 26th's sector, it would be a gross overstatement to say that quiet prevailed along the line; "spasmodic bursts of [German] machine gun and extremely heavy *minenwerfer* fire swept the area." Likewise, American machine guns kept up intermittent fire on the enemy lines and the ground between the lines.[80] And there were the usual nocturnal prowling and comings and goings: patrols, ammunition carrying parties, litter bearers, liaison groups, etc. The chill night air still smelled of gunpowder, high explosives, and poison gas as shadowy figures moved through the mist like apparitions, on their way to fulfill one duty or another. The patrols dispatched earlier by the 3rd Battalion "accomplished nothing, both having been driven off with losses."[81] Some members of a telephone line guard intercepted a German patrol on the slope of Hill 212, fairly well to the rear, showing just how otherworldly nighttime on a battlefield can be. The Germans were all killed or captured.[82]

The end of the day found the 26th Infantry in line with the 3rd Battalion holding a part of le Petit Bois, the woods in the valley between Hill 212 on the south and Hill 272 on the north, and to the right to Arietal Farm; the 1st Battalion had two companies in line, "entrenched" about 200 yards behind the 3rd Battalion, and two companies "holding the western slopes of Hill 269" to the right. This had the effect of extending the 26th's line over a kilometer.[83] The 2nd Battalion was still in the area of Hill 200 or slightly to the north, toward Hill 212. As of 1900, the 3rd Battalion was still taking rifle, machine gun, and automatic rifle fire from the area to the east of Hill 272. Major Frasier reported, "many signals are going up from woods on top of [Hill 272] tonight."[84]

"On the evening of October 5, Army [the American First Army] ordered all three corps to halt and prepare for a counterattack."[85] So serious was the situation that I Corps, to which the 1st Division belonged, ordered a defensive line to be prepared along the same area from which the division had jumped off on October 4. Accordingly, the 1st Engineer Regiment began preparation of a defensive line along the line Chaudron Farm to Serieux Farm. The 1st Division was to hold its position. The Germans had, indeed, considered a counterattack for October 6, with the goal of pushing the American line back; in the 26th's sector, the German goal was the area near Exermont Ravine. However, this was called off because of an ammunition shortage.[86]

155mm gun and tractor destroyed by German artillery, France, 1918. (Courtesy Colonel Robert R. McCormick Research Center.)

Camouflaged ambulances, October 3, 1918. (Courtesy Colonel Robert R. McCormick Research Center.)

75mm caissons and limbers being unloaded at an artillery park, 1918. (Courtesy Colonel Robert R. McCormick Research Center.)

American soldiers using gas masks, 1918. (Courtesy Colonel Robert R. McCormick Research Center.)

Members of a Field Signal Battalion testing switchboard connections, 1918. (Courtesy Colonel Robert R. McCormick Research Center.)

Ordnance repair truck. Ordnance repair units were attached to each division and operated just behind the lines to keep the division's weaponry in repair. (Courtesy Colonel Robert R. McCormick Research Center.)

Hill 240, in the 18th Infantry Regiment's zone; evidence of their foxholes can be seen in the foreground. From its summit, German observers directed fire against the 26th Infantry. (Courtesy Colonel Robert R. McCormick Research Center.)

Major Thomas R. Gowenlock, 1st Division Intelligence Officer, with an assistant observing German activity during the Meuse-Argonne Offensive. Note close proximity to the front lines. (Courtesy Colonel Robert R. McCormick Research Center.)

Second Lieutenant Samuel C. Gholson, Machine Gun Company, 26th Infantry Regiment, killed in action October 4, 1918. (*Soldiers in the Great War - Mississippi.*)

Second Lieutenant Morgan M. Anderson, Company I, 26th Infantry Regiment, killed in action October 5, 1918. (Girton and Adams, *The History and Achievements of the Fort Sheridan Officers Training Camps.*)

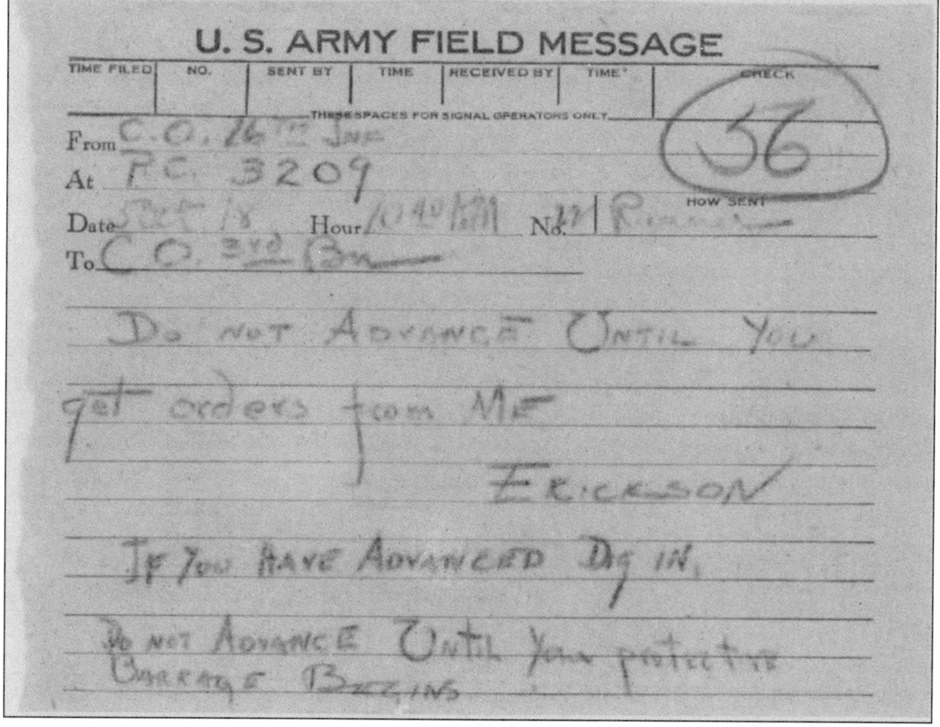

U. S. ARMY FIELD MESSAGE

TIME FILED	NO.	SENT BY	TIME	RECEIVED BY	TIME	CHECK
						56

THESE SPACES FOR SIGNAL OPERATORS ONLY

From C.O. 26th Inf
At P.C. 3209
Date
Hour 1040 AM
No.
HOW SENT
To C.O. 3rd Bn

Do not advance until you get orders from me

Erickson

If you have advanced dig in.

Do not advance until your protective barrage begins

An example of a field message, this one sent by Colonel Erickson to Major Frasier, reminding him to hold his position, 1040 hours, October 5, 1918. (National Archives, Record Group 120, Field Messages.)

Five:

"A RATHER SHARP FIGHT," OCTOBER 6 THROUGH OCTOBER 8

October 6

The morning hours of October 6 found the battalions taking stock of their provisions. At 0640 Maj. Legge sent a message of inquiry to regimental headquarters:

> 10,000 rds M.G. Am, 3 boxes 30 cal., 1 box Chauchat were requisitioned last night and not received. Can you relieve the water situation by having carts come up tonight, or furnish us a Lyster bag. All brought over by this bn. were lost in action. The men are under cover and awaiting order to move. Hospital Corps men are needed, and a direct line to artillery.[1]

Regimental headquarters was also busy processing information gained from prisoners and deserters. At 0730 Capt. Thomas sent two German deserters to division headquarters. The men, one Pole and one Alsatian, had "very valuable information about a relief which will take place tonight."[2]

An American observation post on Hill 212 reported that the Germans on Hill 272 were strengthening their position. Although under orders to hold their position, Maj. Frasier, commanding the 3rd Battalion, decided they could still take Hill 272 if they acted quickly. He had devised a plan to do so on the previous evening, but had run out of time. During the night, the rain gave way to a fog that, in turn, began to dissipate as the sun rose. Major Frasier planned to send his two strongest companies in column across the valley and woods to the east of Hill 272 and strike the Germans on the flank. The 1st Battalion troops in Bois de Moncy and on Hill 269 lent protection from attack from the right flank; the 28th Infantry on the left would lend fire support on Hill 272 until friendly troops appeared atop the hill. Company I, at the left front of the regiment, would extend the line in front of Hill 272 toward the 28th, lending its fire support to the attacking companies. Company L would move to the right to further protect that flank. Company A, 3rd Machine Gun Battalion, still in support of the 3rd Battalion, would fire along the front of Hill 272 and protect the right flank. The 1st Battalion machine guns, from the regimental Machine Gun Company back on Hill 212, would also lend their supporting fire.[3]

The 7th Field Artillery would continue its support, firing on Hill 272 until friendly troops appeared. One suspects that this method of battlefield fire support, basically "fire until you see friendly troops," subjected the attacking troops to a great deal of "friendly fire." In order to secure the element of surprise, there would be no preparatory bombardment.[4]

It was midday before Maj. Frasier received permission to attack, and it wasn't until 1400 that all preparations had been made for the attack. Company K in the lead and Company M in support jumped off. As the assault companies advanced from the southeast, the artillery, machine gun, and rifle fire played savagely upon Hill 272, which became crowned with a "heavy cloud of dust."[5] Second Lieutenant Bayard Brown, second in command of Company K, led the 1st and 2nd platoons to within fifty yards of the Germans when he was wounded in the right hip and left arm. Brown was evacuated to Field Hospital 12 where he died early the next morning; he earned the Distinguished Service Cross for his heroism. Despite losses, the assault made headway early on, but at 1500, artillery and rifle fire was heard to the northeast. It soon became evident that a counterattack was imminent or underway.[6]

Major Frasier, who was in position just south of the leading elements of Company M, the support company of the assault wave, noticed that a German column appeared, "in strength estimated to be a regiment advancing to counter attack our right flank" from the east.[7] Captain Cornish recalled that the Germans seemed to be about battalion strength as they prepared to counterattack from the ravine just north of Hill 269.[8] Soon Frasier saw men from companies M and L streaming past him, reporting that "hundreds of Germans were counter-attacking southwest down the valley east of Hill 272."[9]

Company L, guarding the right flank in the area between le Petit Bois and Bois de Moncy, was subjected to heavy artillery fire, and they fell back. Company M, in support of Company K, also gave way; the company commander, Capt. McClure, managed to rally and hold two squads which returned fire against the on-coming Germans. Company K, concerned because of the attack against their flank and rear, and seeing their supporting company, Company M, give way, began to fall back, giving up ground already won that afternoon. Just then a runner who had been dispatched by Maj. Frasier reached Lt. Dayton Sackett, commander of Company K. Frasier had ordered Company K to hold; Lt. Sackett was able to comply, and the ground lost was minimized. Company I, meanwhile, was too widely deployed in front of Hill 272 to begin an assault against the hill to take pressure off the right flank.[10] In the midst of this confusion and carnage, examples of heroism still shone forth. Corporal Neal D. Fenton, of the regimental medical detachment, advanced through heavy machine gun fire in an attempt to rescue a wounded man. Corporal Fenton was killed in the attempt; he was posthumously awarded the Distinguished Service Cross for his outstanding heroism.[11]

Now Maj. Frasier, on his way to join Company K, tried to rally the men of Company M who were streaming past him. Three veteran non-commissioned officers stopped and managed to gather a group of about forty men. Major Frasier sent two runners, by different routes, back to the officer manning the telephone at the battalion PC. The extension line of the telephone was about 400 yards south of his position; due to casualties among the signal detachment, it was not possible to supply a line and telephone to Maj. Frasier as he moved forward. The runners carried requests that the 1st Battalion, in support near Hill 212, fire their machine guns on the Germans attacking down the valley; also, the message requested that the support battalion commander relay a request to the regimental commander for artillery support. It was normal procedure for the support battalion to relay such requests between the assault battalion and regimental headquarters.[12] Next the runners were directed to find the artillery liaison officer and apprise him of the critical situation on the front line. The artillery officer was in an impromptu observation post in a tree south of Hill 272. The officer left in charge of the telephone at the battalion PC had been killed, but the runners were able to telephone the support battalion themselves.[13]

Two machine guns that had accompanied Company L halted and began to fire upon the Germans from the western edge of Bois de Moncy. Major Frasier, personally taking command of the forty rallied troops, advanced against the Germans in the woods and fell on their left flank. This, coupled with machine gun fire now falling "with uncanny accuracy" from the support battalion, stopped the Germans and thinned their ranks. The forty riflemen had to withdraw slightly since the machine gun fire was falling too close to them. They took up positions upon a hillside and continued firing upon the Germans.[14] Although wounded, 2nd Lt. Ernest H. Pool, an Illinois lawyer in civilian life, led a successful assault against a machine gun nest; he was awarded the Silver Star for his bravery.[15] By this time, the runners reached the artillery liaison officer who, from his position in the trees on the left, could not observe that attack developing on the right. With his own telephone "ladder line" to the 7th Field Artillery, he was able to call down fire upon the Germans on the right flank.[16]

Another group of Germans, approximately company-strength, came through le Petit Bois and attacked the small forty-man group who were on the hillside. Although outnumbered three-to-one, the men had no option but to attack the Germans. The men advanced rapidly, "firing from the shoulder." The rapid advance and a wide interval between men proved deceptive to the Germans, who thought they were being attacked by a much larger force. The enemy retreated into the path of fire from the two machine guns at the edge of Bois de Moncy. The Germans began to flee in disorder; a barrage from the 7th Field Artillery now added to the confusion and casualties among the enemy and broke up the attack. The attempt had cost the Germans approximately 800 casualties.[17]

A soldier using a field telephone. (Courtesy Colonel Robert R. McCormick Research Center.)

Salvage dump near a field hospital, Meuse-Argonne front. Clothes, weapons, and equipment were examined for possible repair and reissue. (Courtesy Colonel Robert R. McCormick Research Center.)

Typical dressing station behind the lines, Meuse-Argonne front. (Courtesy Colonel Robert R. McCormick Research Center.)

Traffic congestion around a supply dump behind the lines, Meuse-Argonne front. (Courtesy Colonel Robert R. McCormick Research Center.)

An American officer examining a German machine gun ammunition belt. Note the concrete gun emplacement, typical of those against which the troops of the 26th Infantry Regiment advanced. (Courtesy Colonel Robert R. McCormick Research Center.)

Exermont, October 7, 1918. Note smoke from areas of the town which were burning even after 1st Division troops had passed through. (Courtesy Colonel Robert R. McCormick Research Center.)

By 1600 the American advance and the German counterattack were over. Major Frasier summed up the situation: "We had gained a foothold on the slopes of Hill 272. We had practically destroyed an enemy regiment. On the other hand we had failed to accomplish our full mission and had suffered heavy casualties. The strength of the [3rd] battalion that night was three officers and one hundred and eighty-two men." Frasier now set about reorganizing his battalion. Companies L and M were badly scattered and "confused." Company L was assembled and sent forward to relieve Company K, the original assault company, which had suffered heavy casualties. Company K took up position in support of Company L. Only three platoons from Company M could be gathered, and they were placed in support of Company I, the left front company. The fourth platoon of Company M was found four days later "in an old quarry in a high state of demoralization."[18]

Supporting machine guns continued to fire upon the enemy; this fire, along with the weakened condition of the Germans, stopped any further attack from developing that night. The six machine guns left in support of the 3rd Battalion were now repositioned. Two were situated to support Company L on the right front, while the other four were placed near Arietal Farm to cover the whole right flank, a source of worry ever since jump-off on October 4. Also, a 75mm field gun from the 7th Field Artillery was sent forward to the area near St. Germain Farm later that night.[19] One battalion of the 7th Field Artillery also moved north, from Rau de Mayache up to the ridge north of Exermont Ravine, near la Neuville le Comte Farm, some 1,700 yards south of the front lines. From this position they hoped to better support the infantry during the next advance.[20]

For his actions on this day, Maj. Frasier was awarded the Distinguished Service Cross for extraordinary heroism in action, his citation reading in part:

> While conducting a flanking movement to reduce the enemy defenses on Hill 272, at the head of his two assaulting companies, Maj. Frasier met a battalion of enemy, formed for counterattack against our advanced positions, in Bois de Moncy. Disposing of his force with excellent judgment, Maj. Frasier himself conducted an assault that routed the enemy, driving him from the field in complete disorganization. Later in the action, when wounded, he refused to relinquish command, and continued to direct the operations of his battalion until he had placed his troops on their final objective.[21]

During the 3rd Battalion's efforts to seize Hill 272, the 1st Battalion had not been inactive. Sergeant Robert Blalock from Company D led a patrol of ten men against a machine gun position in Bois de Moncy on Hill 269. Blalock used the accepted strategy against machine gun nests by maneuvering and flanking the position, and attacking from the rear. In the process, Blalock expended all his ammunition; he then utilized two captured German Luger pistols that he had brought along. Blalock himself, although wounded, killed eight Germans. Nine machine gun nests were put out of action as a result of this patrol; the guns were then organized for defense against their former owners. Sergeant Blalock was awarded a Distinguished Service Cross for his actions on this patrol.[22] The patrol, however, was not strong enough to occupy the entire hill; the woods were "very dense," and infiltration by Germans throughout the area was "a serious menace."[23] Later in the day, the patrol turned their portion of the hill over to a group from the neighboring 32nd Division. All three battalions of the 26th had been subjected to German artillery fire throughout the day, and the 1st Battalion had to contend with "some short shooting by [American] 155s."[24]

As the fighting died down, the wounded were collected, treated, and evacuated if possible. The tired, cold men improved their positions as best as they could. Outguards and patrols were sent out and liaison established. And hungry men sought out rations. Most of the men in the regiment had not eaten a hot meal since the start of the attack; the officer responsible for delivering the meals had failed in his duty on October 5. Colonel Erickson "personally assured" Maj. Frasier by telephone that "a hot supper was on the way forward" on the evening of October 6.[25] However, once again the officer responsible for this delivery failed, and neither the 3rd nor 1st Battalions received hot rations; probably the 2nd Battalion went hungry also.

Providing for the care and safety of the men is of vital importance to military officers; of prime concern is the provision of adequate rations. Failure to feed the troops is a major problem. Major Frasier described what happened next:

> "After considerable heated telephone conversation the three battalion commanders and the officer detailed to see that food reached the forward troops were assembled in conference with the regimental commander. A dramatic and tense moment took place. The regimental commander spoke somewhat broken English. He said, in effect, 'Dere is von officer here vot is a -----. He vill at vonce get himself out of my P.C.' Needless to say the officer concerned with rations left and did not stop going until he was safe within the continental limits of the United States."[26]

Eventually, the company kitchens, by this time probably located in Exermont Ravine or Rau de Mayache, used machine gun carts to haul rations to the men. These carts also took forward rifle and machine gun ammunition. The same mules that pulled the carts on this evening also had spent the day bringing forward rifle and machine gun ammunition using improvised carriers made from shelter halves. By using cover and being clever, the mule drivers managed to make it through the day without losing a single mule in this service, despite the fact that they had, at times, come within 300 yards of the firing line.[27]

It is interesting to note that Maj. Frasier calculated that his men on this day fired approximately 200 rounds each while each machine gun fired approximately 4,800 rounds. This high rate of fire he attributed to the emphasis by officers and non-commissioned officers upon the use of fire against the enemy. They "tried to make the men understand that they could only save their lives by killing the enemy and the best means at their disposal with which to kill the enemy was fire."[28]

October 7

German guns off the left flank of the 1st Division, in addition to German positions on Hill 272, barred further advance. "To the 1st Division, its troops exhausted and with thinning ranks, it seemed that the fate of battle rested on the capture of the guns at Cornay, across the Aire, and the capture of Hill 272."[29] To this end, the 82nd Division moved into position on the 1st Division's left on October 6. That night they attacked and drove the enemy back along the Aire River and into the Argonne Forest. This relieved the pressure on the 1st Brigade, the 1st Division's left brigade; this in turn helped relieve the 2nd Brigade, on the right. The 26th Infantry, on the far right, still had to contend with pressure on their right, outside of the division's allotted zone. Thus, on October 7, the division's right boundary was shifted farther to the right, to the line Hill 269-Tuillerie Farm. The 26th would have to shift their forces accordingly. Also on the 7th, the division was placed under V Corps control.[30] The 181st Infantry Brigade, part of the 91st Division, was also placed under 1st Division command and became the right flank element of the division, supporting the 26th Infantry.[31]

During the morning, the 37mm gun with the 3rd Battalion was called upon by Maj. Frasier to fire on targets to their front. Although Lt. Forster could not positively identify targets, he did fire at supposed enemy positions; invariably, the Germans replied with fire from their "high angle firing weapons from Hill 272 and Hill 263." Once again the gunners and nearby riflemen were on the receiving end of this retaliatory fire. Officers decided to suspend firing until targets could be definitely identified.[32] The other one-pounder in position, "covering the two companies of the 1st Battalion in the Bois de Moncy," fired upon a German horse-drawn machine gun. The Germans soon disappeared from view, and return fire against the one-pounder killed several riflemen and three of the gun crew. By nightfall, neither of the two 37mm guns had more than five men left to man them.[33]

In the meantime, the men of the 26th spent the day improving their positions, digging foxholes and wiring the area with captured German wire. Work was suspended from about 1400 until 1600 as the 3rd Battalion was subjected to a heavy gas attack.[34] Despite the "drenching" to which the 3rd Battalion was subjected during that afternoon, Maj. Frasier recalled only two casualties. He stated that, in his battalion, the men in general showed no fear or worry during gas attacks. Frasier attributed this "to the confidence in the gas mask and the discipline in the use of that piece of equipment that our non-commissioned officers had acquired from long experience."[35] The NCOs spread this confidence to the men. The 26th, at this time, contained a large number of replacements. Many of these replacements had seen action at St. Mihiel in mid-September, but others had only recently arrived. If this positive state of affairs regarding gas mask discipline existed in the 3rd Battalion, it is a marked tribute to the NCOs and the men alike.

The shelling and gas affected the other battalions, too. The constant attrition due to enemy fire impacted the platoon leaders and the men alike. In Company E, Lt. Gordon B. Knowles was severely gassed and evacuated; there were now no officer platoon leaders in Company E. Knowles, a twenty-six-year-old Florida lawyer, was later cited for gallantry in action in 1st Division general orders.[36] Also in the 2nd Battalion, Company F, between October 4 and 9, lost thirty men "from old mustard gas seeping about the position we occupied." The company was now down to sixty men.[37]

At 1735, the patrol from Company D that had been relieved by elements of the 32nd Division on Hill 269 were ordered to move to the northeast slope of the hill and dig in to protect the division's right flank. Still unknown at this time was the fact that Germans held the northeast slope and summit. Still later, at 2150, a battalion from the 1st Engineer Regiment and "one company of machine guns, 1st Division," were ordered to relieve the troops from the 32nd Division on Hill 269.[38] According to Capt. Manning, the machine guns "never arrived, for what particular reason, I never knew." The other elements of the group, however, moved into action. The engineers moved "along the southern edge of Hill 269, and along the narrow ridge connecting the two summits"; simultaneously, a squad from Company D moved out through the thick woods to the northwest before swinging around to the east. The infantry squad joined up with the engineers on the northeastern slope of the hill.[39]

At this point a "rather sharp fight ensued" as the Doughboys came upon Germans who still occupied that part of the hill. The Americans prevailed and in the process captured a large dugout, along with two or three machine guns. The precise number of men captured is uncertain; the unit history states that the number was sixty, all of them machine gunners; Capt. Manning, writing some eight years later, thought it was "in the neighborhood of some twenty."[40] In any event, this maneuver "relieved the source of annoyance of machine guns which the 32nd Division had complained of during the days of October 6-7."[41]

In the evening of October 7, Col. Erickson sent a message to the 2nd Brigade Headquarters giving his regiment's strength:[42]

1st Battalion: 8 officers, 200 men
2nd Battalion: 10 officers, 419 men
3rd Battalion: 7 officers, 260 men

These numbers are Col. Erickson's best figures based upon reports received from the battalion commanders; those reports, in turn, were based upon the efforts of company commanders to make counts among their platoons. Men were lost, wounded, straggling, or mixed in with other units; final accounting would come much later.

By now the battlefield in the 26th's zone presented a gruesome picture. The dead of the 35th Division extended back to the original jump-off line; since that point, the 26th had added to the grim toll all the way to the slopes of Hill 272. Men had gone down, killed and wounded, in woods and among thick bushes; they had fallen in ravines, shell holes, and small crevices, some never to be found. Burial details did their best to find and bury the dead as close behind the active front as possible. Usually, these details consisted of men from Headquarters Company, led by a regimental chaplain, who scoured the ground looking for the dead. Out of necessity because of the active fighting still on-going, the burial party gathered the dead together close to where they fell; the chaplain would remove one of the dog tags from each man, while leaving the second dog tag with the body. He would record the man's name, serial number, and regiment, along with a rough description of his burial place. Finally, the removed dog tag would be affixed to a wooden cross or other burial marker. The list would then make its way through channels. At a later date, graves registration units would move through the area, disinterring the men as they were found, cross-checking identification, and transporting them to American cemeteries.

From October 6 through 8, however, enemy shelling as far back as Montrebeau Woods disrupted the burial details and halted their work. Typical of the brave men who undertook this hazardous task was regimental chaplain 1st Lt. Howard R. Sisson. All during this time he not only conducted burial parties, but he also attended to many wounded men while under shell and machine gun fire. For his heroism in action, Lt. Sisson was awarded the Distinguished Service Cross. Also participating in this work were chaplains 1st Lt. W.T. Jones and 1st Lt. Roberts Williams, among others.[43]

The shellfire in the rear areas brought danger and some excitement to the regimental headquarters. A 77mm shell landed four feet from Lt. Charles Fullerton, who was seeking shelter in a hole. Fullerton reported, "my sheepskin coat was literally blown from my back, my field glass case ruined, and gas mask too. Had I not had on all my impedimenta, I should have been wounded in no less than twenty places. I am lucky." Fullerton reported that two pieces of shell passed through his glass case only slightly scratching the field glasses, his canteen was punctured, and his musette bag was blown into a bush a few yards away. The only thing untouched was his raincoat that was "flat on the ground." Fullerton escaped with "a scratch on the wrist and cheek." He lamented that his sheepskin, a treasured garment for some officers, was "no longer cozy."[44]

Despite the terrible shellfire throughout the entire rear area of the 26th Infantry, hot meals did get through on October 7. Following the dismissal of the officer who had been appointed to arrange for delivery of rations to the front lines, a veteran mess sergeant had been appointed to the task. This man was extraordinarily capable; according to Maj. Frasier, "it would have taken a large contingent of the German Army to have prevented the delivery of food on this night."[45] As darkness fell, Capt. Thomas, the regimental intelligence officer, moved to the front lines and crawled forward, alone, through the brush and woods to reconnoiter the enemy line. He brought back important information about the location and strength of the enemy lines.[46] Once again the men faced a cold, rainy night.[47]

Privates Sampsell and Steel, left to right, Headquarters Company, 26th Infantry Regiment. (Courtesy Colonel Robert R. McCormick Research Center.)

Private Aubrey Harris, Headquarters Company, 26th Infantry Regiment. (Courtesy Colonel Robert R. McCormick Research Center.)

Private Benjamin F. Allgood, Headquarters Company, 26th Infantry Regiment. (Courtesy Colonel Robert R. McCormick Research Center.)

Privates Steel and Nicoles, left to right, Headquarters Company, 26th Infantry Regiment. (Courtesy Colonel Robert R. McCormick Research Center.)

Private Carmine Ferritto, Company C, 26th Infantry Regiment. (Carmine Ferritto Collection, Veterans History Project, Library of Congress.)

Captain Charles Bushnell Fullerton, regimental adjutant, 26th Infantry Regiment. The two chevrons on the left sleeve of Fullerton's uniform indicate between 12 and 18 months of overseas service; the single chevron on his right sleeve indicates that he had been wounded in action. Fullerton wrote the official history of the 26th Infantry Regiment (Courtesy Patricia Fullerton Hamman.)

Private Cohan, Headquarters Company, 26th Infantry Regiment. (Courtesy Colonel Robert R. McCormick Research Center.)

Second Lieutenant Bayard Brown, Company K, 26th Infantry Regiment, killed in action October 7, 1918. (Girton and Adams, *The History and Achievements of the Fort Sheridan Officers Training Camps.*)

Captain Raymond D. Wortley, commander, 2nd Battalion, 26th Infantry Regiment, killed in action, October 4, 1918. (Courtesy Janice Buchanan.)

Captain Shipley Thomas, Intelligence Officer, 26th Infantry Regiment. Drawing by Captain Joseph C. Chase, AEF. (SC-111, WWI Signal Corps Photo #59473, National Archives.)

October 8

Whatever repose the men of the 26th enjoyed was interrupted at 0300 on October 8; the Germans began a "violent fire" all along the lines of the 3rd Battalion, crouching in their foxholes near the dominating prominence of Hill 272. American machine guns and artillery returned the nocturnal "compliment." Shortly after this display, Col. Erickson again ordered the 3rd Battalion to attack Hill 272, leaving the particulars up to Maj. Frasier, the battalion commander.[48]

Frasier decided to send all four companies against the eastern slope of Hill 272, the enemy's left flank. He planned to put two companies in assault and two in support; all four companies were under-strength by this time. This would open a gap between the 3rd Battalion's left flank and the right flank of the 28th Infantry. Frasier considered that the 28th would be able to cover this gap. Once atop the hill, one company was to turn and face the rear, thus providing protection from attack from the right-rear. The 3rd Battalion had only four machine guns left, and these were to be left in le Petit Bois since they would be able to support the attack as well as lend cover to the left flank from that position. Although Maj. Frasier wanted to attack at once, the 0300 flare-up had ruined any chance at catching the enemy troops asleep in their foxholes. Furthermore, it was 0400 before the few officers and NCOs could get everything ready.[49]

Now, as the men readied for the attack, the Germans began a heavy shelling of the 3rd Battalion's positions. The men immediately dove for cover. Their handiwork in improving their foxholes the previous day paid off as very few men were killed during this half-hour barrage. By 0500 daylight was beginning, and the battalion jumped off. Part way up the slope the lead companies came upon machine gun outposts, each one protected by about fifteen riflemen. Once again the men used the tactics they had developed out of necessity; they methodically infiltrated forward and flanked each position. By this method, they put the outposts out of commission. It had, however, cost the battalion precious time and even more precious manpower.[50] In the meantime, the 155mm howitzers of the 5th Field Artillery Regiment of the 1st Division bombarded Hill 272 with high explosives, shrapnel, and gas.[51]

At this point, an officer of the 3rd Battalion left the line. As Maj. Frasier recalled:

> One of the three remaining officers [in the battalion] became confused now and left the field. He was not found until after the battalion had been relieved from the sector [October 12]. This officer is not to be censured, however, because he had received a wound in the side on October 6th and a wound in the leg on October 7th, and had gallantly refused to be evacuated. It was fever and not lack of the offensive spirit that had carried him beyond helping us.[52]

In combat officers bore the heavy responsibility of caring for their men in addition to ensuring the orders of higher echelons were unhesitatingly carried out. Junior officers in the Argonne were pressured to advance at all costs, without regard to their flanks. Officers, like the men, were subject to the hostile elements, the enemy, and discomforts such as lack of food and water. It is not surprising that, as with enlisted men, there should have been some officers who gave way to the pressure. By now three of Maj. Frasier's companies were commanded by sergeants.[53]

Following the reduction of the machine gun nests on the slope, the attack resumed and had neared the eastern summit of Hill 272 when scouts reported that enemy columns were approaching from Hill 263 and from the northwest, over the summit they were then attacking. Major Frasier ordered the two support companies forward, and the battalion formed a single line, the left half facing northwest and the right half facing northeast. The Germans approached in column of twos with about seventy-five yard intervals; the 3rd Battalion was able to open fire upon the enemy columns before they could fully deploy into attack formation. At the same time, observation posts on Hill 212 to the rear saw the approaching enemy and relayed the information to artillery and machine guns units; these guns opened fire shortly thereafter.[54]

The combined rifle, machine gun, and artillery fire stopped the German attacks, but the 3rd Battalion was also stopped. Further advance was "impossible because no man succeeded in advancing more than fifty yards."[55] The 3rd Battalion simply did not have enough surviving manpower to continue the advance. The German column that had been approaching from Hill 263 had been a strong one; the survivors of that column posed a serious threat to the right flank of the 3rd Battalion that lay exposed upon the slope of Hill 272. Should the battalion be hit in the flank, it would have been an easy thing for the Germans to roll up the 26th and continue on to the 28th, thereby jeopardizing the entire division. Major Frasier therefore ordered his men to withdraw to their positions of the night before. The men accomplished this difficult task by withdrawing a few men at a time down the hill and back to their foxholes, the NCOs calling each man's name to begin the withdrawal.[56]

As an illustration of human nature and the strength of morale, Maj. Frasier noted that the men who had fled two days earlier now "fought as well as could be asked of any troops." This display erased any doubt in Maj. Frasier's mind regarding the ability of his battalion to hold until the end. The Germans, for their part, seemed content to let the Americans withdraw to their previous positions. A few enemy patrols ventured through the woods to reconnoiter; these the men of the 3rd Battalion dispatched with ease. Soon no more patrols came, the Germans apparently satisfied that the Americans were where they thought and were holding.[57]

From 1100 to 1330, the Germans shelled the American lines with *minenwerfers* and heavy 210mm high explosive shells. The men were rocked by the "terrific concussions of the exploding shells." Afterwards relative quiet reigned, punctuated occasionally by ripping bursts of German or American machine gun fire. Snipers were still a concern, but by now the men had learned not to expose themselves unless absolutely necessary.[58] Lieutenant Mansfield, the platoon leader in Company E who had been wounded and evacuated on October 4, later gave an explanation of one way to protect oneself from enemy snipers during an advance. It was, he said, "accomplished by lying flat on one's back, digging with a side arm movement, pretending the last sniper's shot was good, then suddenly digging like hell until another zing which signaled you were being observed through a telescopic sight."[59]

In any event, after 1330, the casualties in the 3rd Battalion were few. The 3rd Battalion was now down to two officers, one of whom was suffering from a painful wound, and about 118 enlisted men, about twenty of whom had been slightly wounded.[60]

In the midst of the carnage, while men fought and died, the river of administrative paperwork still flowed. At 1100, Col. Erickson sent a message by mounted courier to Gen. Summerall requesting the immediate promotion of Capt. Rice Youell, commander of the 2nd Battalion, to the rank of major, noting that he'd been recommended three times previously and commenting upon the "exceptionally able manner" in which he was leading his battalion in combat. He desired that the promotion would reach Youell in the field.[61] As stated earlier, Lt. Mansfield, an officer in Company E, and Capt. Cornish, commander of Headquarters Company, believed that Youell had already received and turned down a promotion to major.

Throughout the remainder of the day, the Americans continued their bombardment of Hill 272 while the Germans sent over shells and gas, all three battalions being subjected to this fire. A new plan was developed that called for the 3rd Battalion to shift to the right while the 28th Infantry moved into the 26th's positions. A fresh battalion from the 16th Infantry Regiment would then fill in on the 28th's left, with the task of finally capturing Hill 272, the thorn in the side of the 1st Division. All this was to accommodate not only the 26th's new territory to the right, but also to prepare for the 1st Division's proposed assault to begin the next day. The 2nd Battalion was to move forward into the assault position with the 3rd Battalion in support, while the 1st Battalion was ordered to Hill 212 as division reserve with the additional assignment to protect the regiment's right rear.[62] "The night was cold and disagreeable," and rain fell as the men prepared to move.[63]

Since the zone of the regiment, and indeed the division, was to extend to the east to include the eastern summit of Hill 269, senior officers acted to bolster that area. According to a 1900 field message, orders from the 2nd Brigade sent an officer and men from the 1st Machine Gun Battalion to Hill 269, "to consolidate the position ... particularly paying attention to trenches along the northern and eastern slopes." The men were to help the engineers "hold the hill at all costs," and they were, upon arrival, to relieve all elements of the 26th Infantry.[64]

At about 2000, Maj. Legge ordered 1st Lt. Calvin D. Richards, commander of the regimental Machine Gun Company to take two of his guns "and go to Hill 269 as reinforcement to the Engineers who were at that time holding same."[65] Richards, who had "lost all but five of my guns out [of] the twelve that I had started over with," arrived at the PC of the major commanding the engineers at 2200. The major sent a runner to guide Lt. Richards and his machine gunners "to his advance troops on top of the hill a considerable distance" from the PC. Upon arriving atop the hill, an engineer lieutenant told Richards that there was an infantry outpost "a short distance further on the nose of this hill directly opposite the enemy." Richards left one gun with the engineer outpost and took the other gun forward to the infantry outpost that he discovered was from Company D, 26th Infantry Regiment.

Leaving both guns in charge of a sergeant, Richards retraced his arduous route back to the 1st Battalion PC; upon arrival he reported to Maj. Legge, who ordered

Richards to take his remaining three guns "to this position from which [he] had just come." Richards did so, arriving just before dawn.[66]

Sometime around 2300 Col. Erickson made his way forward to see his battalion commanders and deliver orders in person. At 2310 he met with Maj. Frasier and directed him to send runners to elements of the 28th Infantry that were to relieve the 3rd Battalion. Erickson told Frasier that the 3rd Battalion would support the 2nd Battalion at a distance of 440 yards. "You will conform to the movements of the assault Bn and be prepared to assist its advance, by fire and movement. ... Caution your men to use their rifle fire to the utmost."[67] Next Col. Erickson relayed his orders to Maj. Legge, commander of the 1st Battalion. The 1st Battalion was ordered to the edge of the woods in the draw between Hills 212 and 272, about 200 yards southwest of Arietal Farm. In an effort to redistribute the auxiliary weapons to the attacking battalions, the 1st Battalion was to turn over two trench mortars and one 37mm gun to the 2nd Battalion and the remaining trench mortar and 37mm gun to the 3rd Battalion. Once in position, Legge was to "be prepared to defend the valley on [his] front."[68]

Finally, at 2340, Col. Erickson met with Capt. Youell, commander of the 2nd Battalion. Erickson ordered the 2nd Battalion to move to Bois de Moncy and to jump off at H+22, or 0852. The 2nd Battalion would attack toward the northeast in normal formation with liaison with the 28th Infantry on their left, and the 1st Engineers on their right. Advancing to the northeast up the east side of the hill, the battalion's left flank was to circle to the east of the peak of Hill 263. On the far side of the peak, the left flank would join with the 28th Infantry while the support wave of the battalion helped to mop up the hill. Captain Youell was also requested to make frequent progress reports to regimental headquarters. Although the meeting ended at 0200, the officers' work for the day was only just beginning.[69]

Also that night, regimental headquarters dispatched some enemy prisoners, under military police (MP) escort, to division headquarters.[70] The prisoners had already been interrogated by the 26th Infantry's intelligence section, and now they would be subjected to further interrogation and processing at the division level. The next day, Col. Erickson would request the return of the MP escort; no doubt he was anticipating the accumulation of still more enemy prisoners.[71]

During October 6-8, the 26th Infantry lost about 800 men. The division history stated that "there was never a more trying period for the First Division than October 6th, 7th, and 8th."[72] The men of the 26th lay in their muddy, cold foxholes under artillery, machine gun, and rifle fire; all areas, especially the valleys, were drenched with gas. Many of the dead lay on the battlefield adding to the horror of the scene. The 3rd Battalion also suffered during at least two attacks; streams of wounded flowed back through aid stations to field hospitals and eventually to evacuation hospitals.

And the weather continued to be dismal. Lieutenant Fullerton, writing in the early morning hours of October 9, said: "It has rained nearly every day and the nights are damp and cold beyond description."[73] Fullerton's struggle during the previous week illustrates the sickness and fatigue that gripped the regiment:

For a week I just followed along, laid in my hole all day and all night, too weak to do more than advance when the P.C. was moved forward and give such orders as necessary. I did not retain a morsel of food for four days and I certainly look it. Have lost pounds and my whiskers, they say, are white. If they don't relieve us soon, I will be a Rip Van Winkle.[74]

Six:

"MACHINE GUNNERS ... FOUGHT LIKE WILD MEN," OCTOBER 9 AND OCTOBER 10

October 9

The 1st Division's mission was to continue to drive ahead taking Hill 272 and the woods and heights beyond. H-hour was set for 0830; at that time, a barrage would fall 200 yards in front of the attacking troops, and the 1st Brigade, on the division's left, would advance against the high ground in their sector and Hill 272, the latter of which was newly allocated to that brigade. Then, at H+22 minutes, the 2nd Brigade was to jump off toward Hill 263 and the woods beyond. Orders from the division headquarters required regimental commanders to use all available men in their Headquarters Company and similar support units. Consequently, numerous clerks and cooks made their way to the front line, rifle in hand.[1]

In many ways, the Meuse-Argonne Offensive for the 26th Infantry consisted of a battle for high ground. From the areas north of Exermont Ravine to Hill 212, Hill 269, and Hill 272, the 26th had plodded on, attacking hills that were studded with machine guns and artillery pieces, while under perfect observation from the same high ground they were attacking. Regimental adjutant 2nd Lt. Charles Fullerton recalled that the 26th "pushed through the very worst part of France, where there are no roads, no towns, and just hills and woods – and machine guns." The 26th was now tasked to drive northeast farther into le Petit Bois and capture Hill 263; after that, they were to continue to and through Bois de Romagne.[2] To the right of the

26th were now the 1st Engineer Regiment of the 1st Division and the 361st Infantry Regiment, on loan from the 91st Division. These two regiments were to protect the right flank and right rear of the 1st Division in the upcoming assault.

Indeed, it was an odd situation on the precarious right flank. To the immediate right of the 26th was the 1st Engineer Regiment. To their right was the 181st Infantry Brigade of the 91st Division (361st and 362nd Infantry Regiments), temporarily assigned to the 1st Division; they were to attack north from a line running between Hill 269 and Hill 255, further to the east. Their advance was to take them into Bois de Moncy in a narrowing triangular zone that culminated in Tuillerie Farm at the north apex. At that point the 181st Infantry Brigade would become part of the 32nd Division.[3]

Before the assault could be renewed, the 28th and 26th regiments had to complete their shift to the right. Thus, yet another night passed in which the 26th got no rest. Sometime during late night of the 8th and early morning of the 9th, the 2nd Battalion moved forward through the gloomy, still-hazardous Bois de Moncy, then across a small clearing, and into the south edge of le Petit Bois, in front of Hill 263. Relief elements of the 28th arrived at the 3rd Battalion positions at 0330 on October 9. The 3rd Battalion then moved off to the right in four columns. As the battalion traversed a ravine near Arietal Farm they encountered a "strong German patrol," and the Germans were all soon killed or captured. The battalion then moved into position at the north edge of Bois de Moncy; just across a small valley to the north waited the 2nd Battalion.[4]

It is of some interest to note how a battalion under combat conditions moves laterally, from one area to another, while virtually in touch with the enemy. The 3rd Battalion formed in two main columns, one about 100 yards behind the other. Each main column consisted of two companies, one following the other by about twenty-five yards. Each company formed in two columns of two, "a formation resembling closely the right and left formation utilized when a column of squads is passing through a town when there is a possibility of being fired on."[5] In this case the battalion moved through wooded and open areas. Such a move, even in more favorable conditions, was fraught with problems. In the pitch black of night, the usual method was for each man to grasp the pack or shoulder of the man ahead in order to keep the line intact. Even so, sections of men were lost during the march, and it was with great difficulty that everyone arrived at the correct place at the correct time. By 0550, Capt. Youell's 2nd Battalion was in place and receiving sniper fire on the right flank of Company E.[6]

Thus, we have the final disposition of the 26th Infantry Regiment just prior to the start of the assault on October 9: The 2nd Battalion, leading the assault, was formed up in the southern edge of le Petit Bois, approximately 800 yards south of Hill 263, the eastern slope of which was their objective, with two companies in the assault wave and two companies in support, and what remained of Company B, 3rd Machine Gun Battalion near the support wave. The left half of the 2nd Battalion faced a climb of about 240 feet up the steep, thickly wooded slopes of Hill 263; the right half of the battalion's line would advance along the east slope of the hill.

1st Division troops near Exermont, possibly a dressing station, October 9, 1918. (Courtesy Colonel Robert R. McCormick Research Center.)

The 3rd Battalion, in support, was located about 300 yards behind the 2nd, across the narrow valley from le Petit Bois in the northern edge of Bois de Moncy, with Company L in the left front, Company M in the right front, Company I in the left rear, and Company K in the right rear, and Company A, 3rd Machine Gun Battalion, with only four guns remaining, immediately to the rear. One 37mm gun was to accompany the 2nd Battalion in the lead and one was to accompany the 3rd Battalion in support. The 1st Battalion, in division reserve, was on Hill 212; the 26th's Machine Gun Company, supporting the 1st Battalion, was for the moment still on Hill 269 in support of the 1st Engineer Regiment.[7] Throughout the night, the American artillery continued their bombardment of the German lines, to include firing approximately 3,000 gas shells into German positions.[8]

Before the regiment's main action got underway that morning, off to the south and east another drama was playing out in the woods and knolls around Hill 269. In the early morning hours, Lt. Richards, commander of the regimental Machine Gun Company, had taken his five remaining machine guns out to bolster the defenses that the battalion from the 1st Engineers had erected on and around Hill 269. He had placed three of his guns with the engineer outpost near the summit, and, just before dawn, took one gun forward to join another gun he had emplaced hours before with an infantry outpost of Company D from the 26th Infantry. As he ordered this second gun crew to dig in, Richards moved over to where he had emplaced the first gun and "found that all the infantry had been withdrawn and that the Engineers had made no attempt to relieve or replace the infantry leaving my gun way out on the nose of this hill holding by itself."[9] Just after dawn, Richards was making his way back to his second gun when Germans attacked the entire position.

According to Richards, "there were about seven of us and we killed and wounded about fifteen or twenty of the enemy in a hand to hand encounter. Only one other man and myself escaped, the other five having been killed." In the wild melee, a German struck Richards in the nose, breaking it, before a "sergeant killed him in his tracks." Years later, Richards recalled "those five machine gunners who fought like wild men, kicking, biting, shooting and cussing and who gave their lives in helping hold off this attack and rioting a much greater number than that which opposed them." The attackers were, indeed, "rioted," as they retreated around the nose of the hill and prepared to stage another attempt.

Richards and his surviving gunner withdrew to the engineer outpost where they secured the assistance of an engineer sergeant. Together, the men deployed what engineer and machine gun troops were available over the slopes of the hill. Richards, the only man who knew the location of the engineers' PC, moved off to request reinforcements. The attack was imminent, and Richards "had not been back to the troops on the hill more than two minutes before here they came." The weary men fought with machine guns, rifles, pistols, and grenades; they "let them have all we had and held this position until about noon when reserve troop arrived after which we advanced and took a number of prisoners."[10]

For his actions, Lt. Richards was awarded the Distinguished Service Cross; Sgt. Andrew Charles, Cpl. Casper L. Johnson, Privates First Class David O. Jones and Walter Waldroop, Privates Oliver H. Downs, Frank P. Lozupone, and Ralph B. Manwaring were awarded the Silver Star for their part in this action that was "of the utmost tactical importance." Sergeant Edward J. Lynch of the Machine Gun Company was also award the Silver Star for his actions in defending this position; Pvt. Ennie Townsend, although badly gassed, remained on duty throughout this period, and he, too was awarded a Silver Star.[11] Sometime after this action, the 1st Battalion was ordered forward from Hill 212 to a position about 500 yards behind the 2nd and 3rd Battalions.[12]

While all this was going on, the main regimental attack continued in preparation. Just after 0800, Col. Erickson contacted his battalion commanders and requested that they send runners back to regimental headquarters. Further, Col. Erickson told them to establish blinker communication using "Hill 240 [as] a central sending and receiving station."[13]

At H hour, 0830, the 1st Brigade, to the west, jumped off and began their assault. Soon the barrage began in front of the 26th's positions in the woods; at 0852 the 2nd Battalion began their advance in a dense fog, hoping to keep pace with the barrage that was advancing at the rate of 100 yards in six minutes. Captain Youell used a prismatic compass, one of his prized possessions, to determine the direction of his advance. Once satisfied with his readings, he placed the impossible-to-replace compass on the ground, ordered the advance, and stepped off. When he next thought of his valued compass, it was long gone.[14] Over the din of the outgoing rolling barrage the advancing soldiers of the 2nd Battalion soon could discern the moan of incoming rounds. This would be followed by the ear-splitting crash of the exploding shells. The air was filled with thousands of metal shards of various sizes, each of which, propelled with deadly speed, turned into a lethal projectile. In wooded areas, the explosions would cause what in World War II were known as tree bursts; this added wood splinters into the mix of airborne death. If enemy shellfire wasn't bad enough, Capt. Edgarton, commander of Company F, stated that, "our own barrage, that is, some shells of it, detonated in the trees over our heads but did no damage."[15]

Despite the confusion of friendly fire, the barrage in front of Company F seemed to have worked as ordered; Capt. Edgarton reported that, "The south edge of the Petit Bois, bristling with machine guns the night before, must have been evacuated when our barrage struck it." Edgarton, who spoke German, talked with a prisoner who claimed that, "they had retreated ten kilometers." It might have been true that some Germans retreated, but there were still plenty of Germans in the woods and hills prepared and willing to give battle to the 26th, as shall be seen.[16]

About this time, as the 3rd Battalion moved forward in support, Lt. Dayton S. Sackett, commanding Company K, came upon a small clearing. Sackett decided to walk across the clearing himself to check whether it was under enemy observation. Lieutenant Sackett was severely wounded in this attempt, and he was later awarded the Distinguished Service Cross for his actions during this day.[17]

Up ahead, the 2nd Battalion ran into stiff resistance in the thick woods. Before advancing 200 yards they were stopped by heavy machine gun fire from the right flank. Company E continued to lose officers as Lt. Levis Bune, who had assumed command on October 4, went down with a wound.[18] Major Frasier ordered Company M forward to provide support to the right flank; the supporting machine guns moved forward to take Company M's place. In about thirty minutes, the resistance on the flank was reduced; at the same time, a terrible barrage of German 210mm heavy artillery descended upon Company M, causing great destruction.[19] As usual, the medics proved their bravery. Sergeant Thaddeus Wilkinson of the Medical Detachment, was severely wounded as he ran through heavy fire trying to reach a wounded man. For his heroism, he was awarded the Distinguished Service Cross.[20]

The 37mm guns, owing to the difficulty in their maneuvering, did not reach the 2nd and 3rd Battalion PCs until after they had moved out. Lieutenant Forster, accompanying the one-pounder gun that was assigned to the 2nd Battalion, followed the 2nd Battalion telephone wire, being laid by linesmen ahead, in order to find his assigned position. Forster recalled that "the going was slow, with three men pulling the gun and two carrying ammunition." The men struggled with their guns; the "path was overgrown with brush and the telephone line followed a winding route often fifty yards off the path and then back on it." Little wonder that Lt. Forster later recommended that, "husky men should be considered … in the make-up of the personnel for gun crews." So slow was the going that the leading elements of the 3rd Battalion, in support, began to catch up with Lt. Forster's gun and crew. German artillery fire was severe even in the rear of the 2nd Battalion; the gun crew lost an ammunition carrier as they moved up the slope of Hill 263.[21]

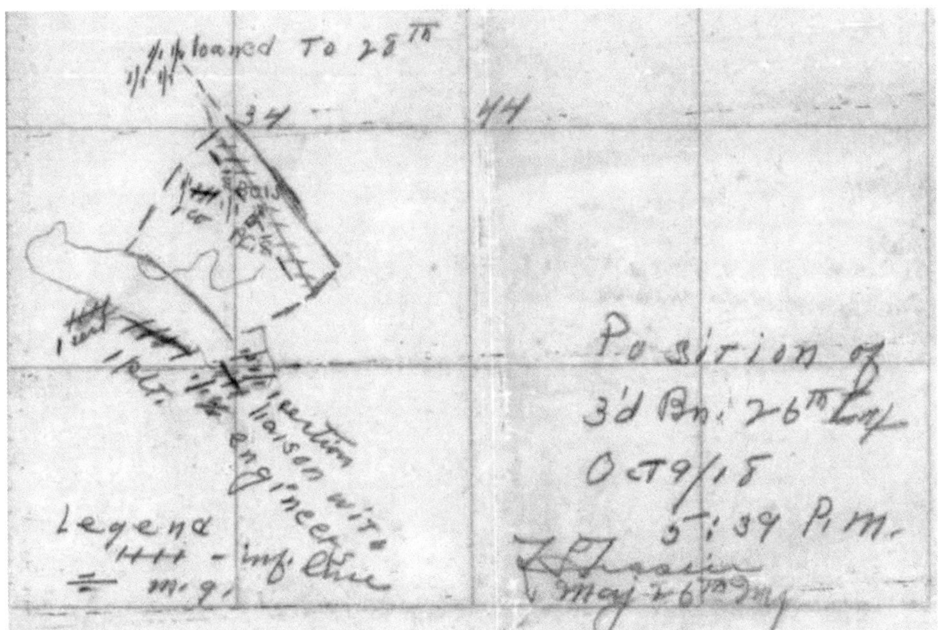

Major Lyman S. Frasier's sketch of 3rd Battalion positions in support of the 2nd Battalion, Hill 263, October 9, 1918, at 1739 hours. (National Archives, Record Group 120, Field Messages.)

The 2nd Battalion once again moved forward in the woods with the 3rd Battalion following. The Germans now blasted the entire area of the advance with 210mm shells. The result was horrific; the tremendous blasts felled trees and vaporized men; survivors were often knocked senseless from the concussions. As Maj. Frasier recalled: "An entire squad would from time to time be blown from the face of the earth."[22] Still the line moved forward, albeit very slowly. The 2nd Battalion began the hazardous ascent of Hill 263 under severe fire; at some points the men had to grab hold of saplings and roots in order to pull themselves up the steep, wooded slopes.[23] The 3rd Battalion in support continued to suffer casualties. Second Lieutenant Phillip C. Sheridan, a recent replacement officer leading a platoon in Company L, was killed by machine gun fire. Sergeant Waclaw Darkoski, a platoon leader in Company K, engaged in a hand-to-hand fight with some Germans defending a machine gun position. Sergeant Darkoski prevailed in this desperate struggle and succeeded in capturing two guns, for which action he was awarded the Distinguished Service Cross.[24]

Despite Col. Erickson's earlier pleas to use runners and blinkers for communications, the paucity of information flowing back to him was evident. At 1000 he sent a message to the 1st Battalion, asking for information on the progress of the battle ahead: "Have you any information at all of the situation forward? Is the shelling heavy? Is there much machine gun fire to be heard? Can you hear rifle fire?"[25]

An analysis of "sent" and "received" times of the field messages shows an approximate transit time averaging over one hour and sometimes up to three hours. The toll

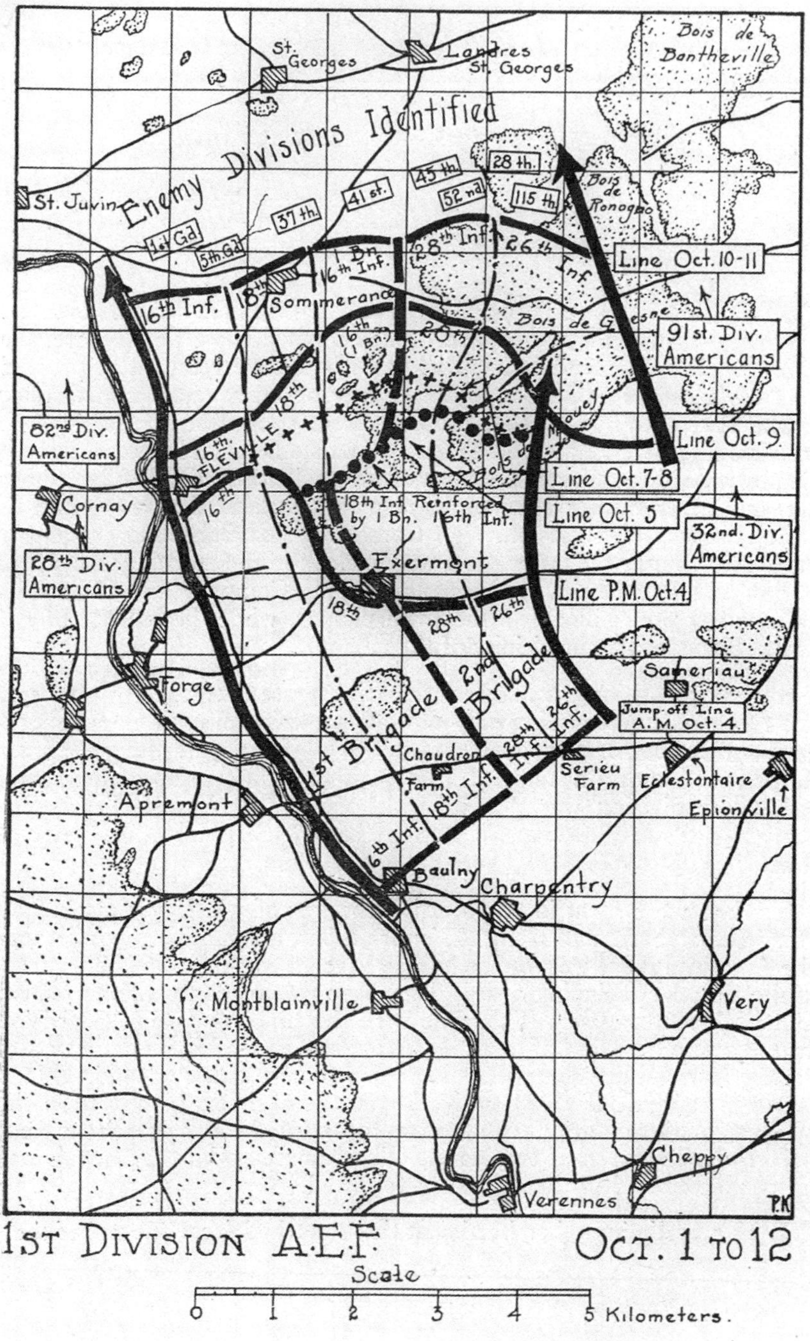

Map showing the 1st Division area of operations, October 4-12, 1918. (Captain Ben Chastaine, *History of the 18th U.S. Infantry*.)

among the runners was tragic; many men were gunned down or blasted with artillery before they had made two strides from their shelter. In rapidly changing circumstances, these inherent delays could be catastrophic. The concern for timely information led Col. Erickson to send various officers from headquarters to the front line battalions for liaison. Captain Cornish, commander of Headquarters Company, and Lt. Ridgely went forward into the woods seeking the precise location of the lines. Lieutenant Ernest Pool, the regimental operations officer who had already led an assault against an enemy machine gun nest, also acted as runner in bringing messages forward. Ridgely had trouble finding Capt. Youell and would not be in position until October 10.[26]

Shortly before noon, Capt. Cornish started forward. Upon reaching the southeast corner of les Petit Bois, he reported back that he could find no sign of enemy infiltration thus far, although he noted heavy artillery fire in the valley between les Petit Bois and Bois de Moncy and in the area to his left and left front. This was probably the artillery barrage that wrought such havoc mentioned by Maj. Frasier.[27] Troops had captured fourteen prisoners, including one officer, from the German 170th Regiment and had identified enemy soldiers from the 211th Regiment in les Petit Bois. Later that afternoon Capt. Thomas would send back at least sixty-seven prisoners to division headquarters.[28]

The figurative and literal fog of war affected communication with regimental headquarters as well as communication with lower levels of command. As Capt. Youell advanced through the thick woods of les Petit Bois he lost contact with Company F and his supporting machine guns. Noticing machine gun positions of Company A, 3rd Machine Gun Battalion, in the northern edge of Bois de Moncy, across the valley from les Petit Bois, Capt. Youell sent a message via runner: "I have crossed the Valley with sixty men and will continue the attack. Please send up the rest of my Battalion and Machine Gun Company. Who are you?"[29]

Shortly after noon the 2nd Battalion reached their objective, having gained the hillside east of the peak. Captain Youell formed a strong outpost at the right flank of the line where it abutted the valley between the two wooded areas; German troops still infested the area to the east and northeast. Communications with the rear, including the support battalion, were extremely difficult. So severe and thick was the artillery fire that telephone lines were cut "as fast as they could be laid."[30] Captain Youell reported that his phone wasn't working and that while he had "most of E, G, and H Co's, F and M.G. Co have not arrived yet." As an example of the time lag for runner-borne messages, this message was sent at 1208 and received at headquarters at 1506, almost three hours later.[31] In reply, Col. Erickson ordered the 2nd Battalion to "mop up Hill 263. Plant machine guns and hold." He also requested that both the 2nd and 3rd Battalions send sketches of their positions using two runners departing at ten-minute intervals.[32]

At 1500, when all communications between the assault and support battalions were cut off, Maj. Frasier took three runners and went forward to meet with Capt. Youell commanding the 2nd Battalion. To the front, Frasier could observe, in the clearing between Hill 263 and Landres-et-St. Georges to the north, three batteries of German artillery "in full flight," along with what he estimated to be two machine gun companies and three battalions of infantry. The two battalion commanders could only watch the distant flight helplessly. They had, at their immediate disposal, no machine guns, telephones, or artillery; they even longed for a squadron of cavalry that could ride amongst the fleeing enemy to cut them down.[33]

Captain Youell, by actual count, had only forty-three men and no officers with him on that portion of the crest of Hill 263.[34] He reported that "several of our men have straggled to the rear. Not enough of officers & NCO to watch them." It must not be assumed, of course, that all of the rest of the men had become casualties or had straggled. As men struggled forward through thick brush and rough terrain under such tremendous fire, some became lost; others drifted away and joined neighboring or following units. Still others dropped, exhausted, into a convenient shell hole to catch their breath. Such men would eventually make their way back to their proper unit as the day wore on. And as of 1513, Company F still had not joined up with the rest of the 2nd Battalion. Captain Youell had located Capt. Yuill, commander of the machine gun company that was in support of the 2nd Battalion, and had asked him to send the machine guns forward. Upon arrival of these guns, Capt. Youell sent four of them to support the weakened 3rd Battalion, 28th Infantry, to his left. There was no one to the left of the 28th; this small force seemed to be alone on Hill 263.[35]

But now, on the crest of the hill, Capt. Youell and Maj. Frasier decided to combine their depleted battalions for the time being. One company and the machine guns stayed behind with the support battalion to provide protection for the rear and right flank.[36] Both battalions had formed liaison with the 28th Infantry on the left, but neither battalion had established contact with friendly troops on the right.[37] German machine guns continued to fire on the 2nd Battalion from the left-rear and from the draw in front of and extending northeast from Hill 263, causing them to have trouble digging in. Some of the resulting casualties could not be evacuated. At 1700 Capt. Youell requested litter bearers to evacuate his wounded; he also requested signal rockets. Concerned about the enemy to his front, Capt. Youell also asked, "Can the artillery fire on the line where barrage stopped to-day? If so have them fire some there during the night."[38]

The one-pounder assigned to the 2nd Battalion remained on Hill 263 since it was the only area from which it could fire. Still, the gun crew failed to acquire any targets, and Lt. Forster functioned as "scout officer for the 2nd Battalion." Indeed, the one-pounders did no more firing after October 9.[39]

At 1739 the 2nd and 3rd Battalions formed a line just to the east and slightly north of the peak of Hill 263. One depleted company from the 3rd Battalion was pulled back to the left rear of the front line. Other detachments were to the rear, on the far side of the draw between les Petit Bois and Bois de Moncy. To the right of these men were four machine guns and a section of infantry in liaison with the 1st Engineers.[40] Sometime during the day, Lt. Cornell and 100 men from Company A of the 1st Battalion in reserve were dispatched to help the 2nd Battalion. This much needed boost in manpower was helpful for the small band of men clinging to the eastern and northern slopes of Hill 263, and Capt. Youell requested that the detachment be allowed to remain with his battalion.[41]

The area was still very hazardous; sniping continued to take a toll on the men on the hill. Several men were selected "to crawl out and locate the snipers and kill them." In time, all but one of the sniper-hunters returned; the mission was a success. The men encountered enemy patrols and carrying parties during the night, and many Germans were captured. Indeed, as late as October 10, 1st Lt. Harry Spring, 37th Engineer Regiment, reported that, "machine guns were sweeping Exermont yet."[42] That night word was received from division, through regiment, to exploit the day's gains, with the 2nd Battalion again in the lead, on the following day.[43] The entire 1st Division was to consolidate its gains and push patrols forward on the morrow.

Once again night fell on the battlefield, and the weary men improved their precarious positions as best they could. There was no food or water to be had, unless one still had one's emergency rations, or could find rations on the dead. On their way to the rear for rations, men creeping through the dank, dark woods became disoriented and lost, further depleting the available forces, at least temporarily. Captain Youell and Maj. Frasier sent some of the men to the forward slopes to dig in. The Germans shelled the area, and "that night the hill top became a seething inferno."[44] The division on the regiment's right had not yet advanced past Hill 269, and the enemy was still present in that area. The 26th's men were subjected to fire that seemed to come from the rear.[45] The Division Operations Report stated that it had been the "bitterest day of fighting yet."[46] To the 26th's commanders, it seemed that the Germans were "fighting a strong rear guard action, principally with [machine guns] and artillery," and that they were "fighting desperately."[47] On the hilltop, 1st Lt. Daniel E. Stedem, battalion surgeon for the 2nd Battalion, had his hands full treating the wounded. Stedem, who had lost all his aid men as casualties on October 4, had been treating the battalion's wounded under shell and machine gun fire by himself since that day. The twenty-six-year old native Philadelphian would be cited for bravery while saving many lives during this campaign.[48]

"Troops from a regiment of pioneer infantry were sent forward during the night" to evacuate the many wounded men. Pioneer infantry regiments during World War I were similar to the combat engineers of later wars. Most often, however, these men were used to build and maintain roads, dugouts, and trenches, and they had only basic infantry training. In this case, the lieutenant commanding the pioneer troops balked at sending his men to the front lines. Some of the pioneers, however, did come forward and began to carry back some of the wounded men. But most of the pioneers appear to have not performed their duty conscientiously, as Maj. Frasier reported that most of the wounded thus evacuated "were left in the way to be killed by shell fire or die on their stretchers from want of proper attention."[49]

October 10

Throughout the night, the men who had straggled or become lost during the advance filtered forward to join their units. The 2nd Battalion was finally able to dig in, and they passed a quiet night on the slopes of the hill. Around 0600 Company F finally reported to Capt. Youell, greatly boosting his manpower.[50] According to Capt.

Edgarton, Company F "landed in the middle of a battalion of the 28th Inf. on the pinnacle of Hill 263." Edgarton immediately set off to report to Youell, whom he found about 200 yards to the right. Edgarton's Company F, which had started the climb up Hill 263 with sixty men, could muster only forty-one survivors to join the rest of the battalion. The front line, consisting of the 2nd and 3rd Battalions, remained substantially the same as the night before.[51]

By early morning October 10, the depleted condition of the regiment was evident. In the 1st Battalion, still in reserve to the rear of the other two battalions, there were only 192 men and twenty-three machine gunners left. A company-by-company itemization showed: A Co.: sixty-one men; B Co.: thirty-eight men (with three NCOs); C Co.: thirty-seven men (with three NCOs); D Co.: fifty-six men (with nine NCOs); MG Co.: twenty-three men.[52]

The 2nd Battalion, still in the assault position, could field only 200 riflemen, five officers, and seventy machine gunners; the battalion had no food and water, and they needed telephone wire. The 3rd Battalion, in close support of the 2nd, had seven officers, 245 men, and fifty-five machine gunners present. The 2nd and 3rd Battalions, comprising the front line, were badly intermingled and in need of reorganization.[53] When one considers that at the start of the campaign on October 4 each of these battalions fielded almost 1,000 men, one can see just how terrible the toll had been. One may also compare these numbers to those given by Col. Erickson in his message on the night of October 7; the fighting on October 9 had been severe indeed, especially for the leading 2nd Battalion. The wounded suffered on the hillside since both the 2nd and 3rd Battalions reported they were in need of stretcher bearers.[54]

The north slope of Hill 263 was wooded; the path of advance for the regiment crossed these woods, Bois de Romagne, and then a road that traversed the sector, east to west. North of the road the woods remained thick, but the terrain descended more gradually. It was about 1,400 yards from jump off to the northern edge of Bois de Romagne. North of the woods the ground rose slightly and the woods diminished to almost a meadow. Further north and to the right were la Musarde Farm and the wooded Côte de Châtillon. Some 2,200 yards north of the northern edge of Bois de Romagne lay the town of Landres-et-St. Georges.

At 0700, the 2nd Battalion jumped off for the day's attack, moving through woods so dense that liaison and contact even between platoons was difficult.[55] Captain Youell's method to advance through Bois de Romagne was to send a combat group forward to a designated line first. The group would clear whatever resistance it encountered, if possible, and then dig in on the line. Once again, as the men encountered machine guns they would work their way around the flanks and rear of the guns. Once in position the men would attack the guns using rifles and grenades; this method was very effective. If more serious resistance was encountered, the patrol would send back information regarding the location and type of resistance, and calling for artillery on the target. Once established on the new line, the combat patrol would summon the rest of the battalion to move up; these companies would eliminate any resistance as they moved forward.[56] As Capt. Edgarton euphemistically put it, "in the morning we took a little promenade to the top edge of the Bois de Romagne." Even the 3rd Battalion, following in support, found the hills and woods filled with machine guns.[57]

As the 2nd Battalion advanced to the second exploitation line, Capt. Youell requested that the supporting 7th Field Artillery Regiment withhold fire south of that line.[58] At one point, as Company G worked its way forward, the air was rent by the sputter of German Maxims, and many men went down. The advance was held up as the machine gun inflicted severe losses; Capt. William C. Acklin, commander of Company G, went down with a serious wound. Eschewing for the moment the usual methodical flanking attack, Pvt. Eddie J. Parent advanced alone, crawling forward under heavy fire. Private Parent succeeded in silencing the enemy gun, allowing his company to resume the advance. For his heroism, Pvt. Parent was awarded the Distinguished Service Cross.[59]

Lieutenant Ridgely finally arrived at Maj. Frasier's PC, on his way forward to Capt. Youell, and at 1215, submitted the following report:

> Guide got lost. Have just reached P.C. Frazier. [*sic*] ... Am on my way to Youell now. His patrols are advancing again. No sound of small arms ahead. Third Bn. goes forward now. Everything seems to be going nicely. Artillery not heavy. Youell understands that he is to dig in at northern edge of B. de Romagne.[60]

An hour later, Company F was in place along the northern edge of Bois de Romagne with Companies E, G, and H directly behind and moving forward in the thick woods. The 2nd Battalion had continued liaison with the 28th Infantry along the same line to their left. To the right, the battalion still had not established liaison with the 362nd Infantry at the farthest point of advance. The battalion slightly refused the right of the line for protection; machine gun fire still came from that flank.[61]

The 3rd Battalion was in position just behind the 2nd Battalion, about where they were the night before. The support line was manned by two companies with the other companies and machine guns just behind, forming in columns of twos, preparing to advance. A corporal and three men had been dispatched to the right flank to establish liaison with the support troops of the 362nd Infantry. As of 1215, the 3rd Battalion was preparing to advance to support the 2nd more closely. Their reported strength was now 174 riflemen with seven officers, and seventy machine gunners with four officers.[62]

By 1230, Capt. Youell could report "no resistance from enemy." He had sent two eight-man patrols to the second exploitation line and had finally established liaison with the 362nd Infantry on his right, while maintaining liaison with the 28th Infantry on his left. He reported his battalion's strength as 179 riflemen, seven officers, eight NCOs, and seventy machine gunners. The men were without reserve rations and still in need of food and water. Patrols pushed forward and reported German soldiers to the north, near La Musard and Tuillerie farms. The main line was now just south of a road traversing the front from west to east in the center of the Bois de Romagne. An outpost was in position just north of the road.[63] Shortly after this Company F reached the north edge of the woods.

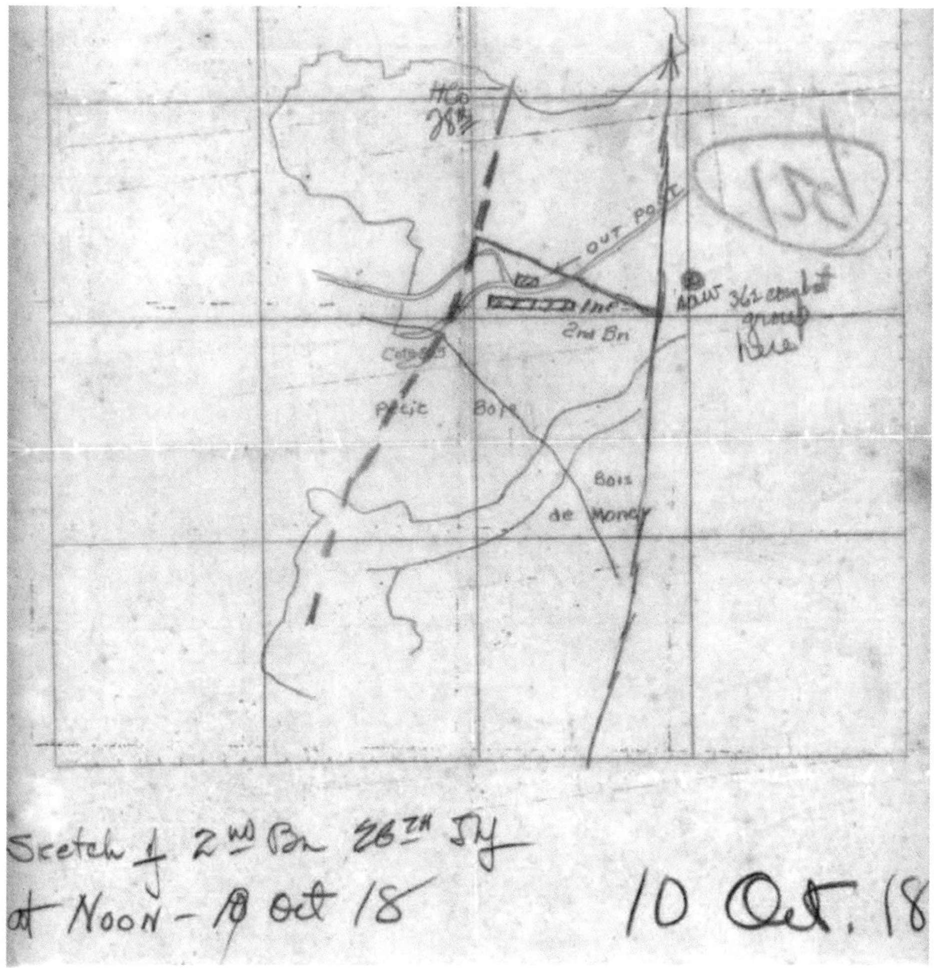

Sketch showing the position of the 2nd Battalion on Hill 263, noon, October 10, 1918. Note position of the 362nd Infantry Regiment combat group to the right. (National Archives, Record Group 120, Field Messages.)

To the northeast of the 2nd Battalion was the high ground of Côte de Châtillon, still in German hands. At 1500 Col. Erickson directed Youell to send two patrols forward into woods on Côte de Châtillon in order to contact the enemy. He also wanted Youell to reconnoiter the "top of hill and trench system to the west. Do not bring on an engagement but see what is between you and 3rd Exploitation line. If your patrols succeed in gaining the line without being perceived, they should dig in and you should hold the position." Colonel Erickson concluded this message to Youell with some good news: "I congratulate you on your promotion to Major which dates from today."[64] It's not known if Maj. Youell had any major's insignia to affix to his uniform, but he did, in ensuing messages, continue to refer to himself as "Captain Youell" out of force of habit.

The patrols sent out by Maj. Youell did, indeed, meet resistance. This information was relayed up through the chain of command, and by 1655 Col. Erickson sent word

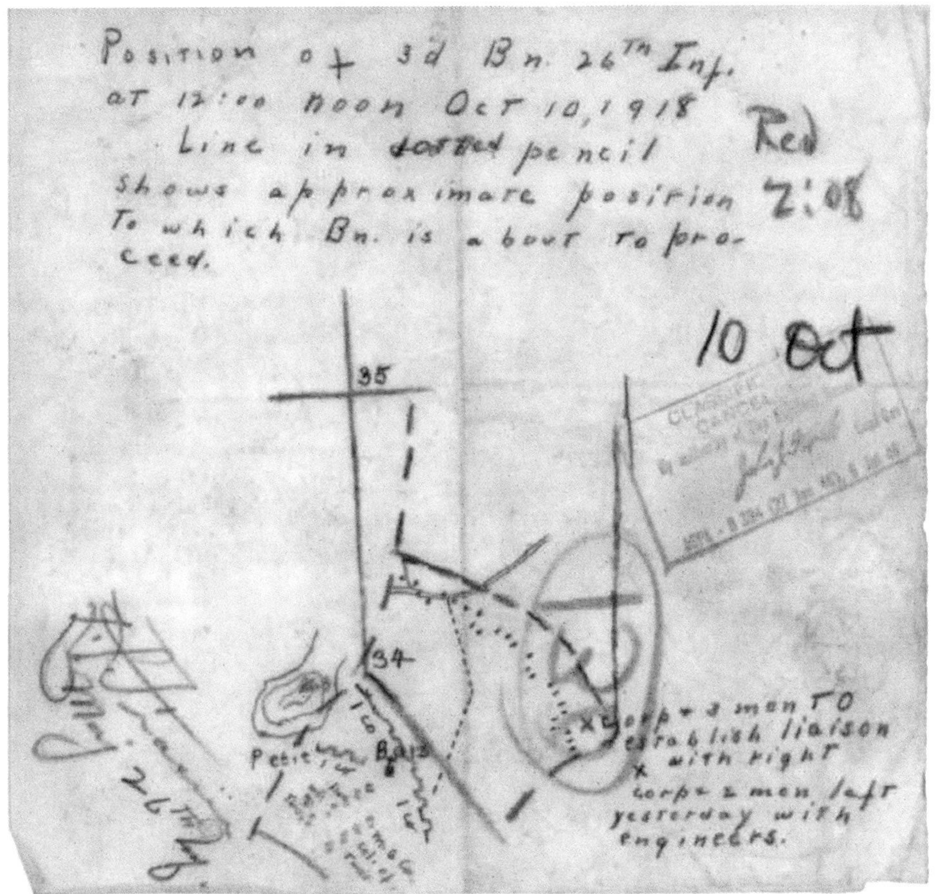

Major Frasier's sketch showing the position of the 3rd Battalion in support of the 2nd Battalion on Hill 263, noon, October 10, 1918. The 3rd Battalion was planning to move forward to the area then occupied by the 2nd Battalion as that battalion advanced. (National Archives, Record Group 120, Field Messages.)

that the division commander directed that the patrols withdraw to Bois de Romagne and there consolidate a position. Just after 1700, Maj. Legge sent word forward to 1st Lt. Cornell and 2nd Lt. John C. Coughlin, commanding Companies A and B, which had been sent forward to support the 2nd Battalion, that they should withdraw their men to their previous positions. Major Legge told the officers to "send them back in small detachments if necessary to conceal the movement."[65]

To the right, the Germans poured heavy fire upon the 2nd Battalion. Major Youell reported enemy troops digging in in front of Company F and to the right, rear. This area was too close to request an artillery bombardment. So great was the pressure that Maj. Frasier, commanding the 3rd Battalion in support, sent Companies K and I forward to bolster the right flank of the 2nd Battalion. The companies soon faced severe fire, and Company K, under the command of a sergeant, fell back. Major Frasier stopped and rallied part of the retreating company, but a large number of

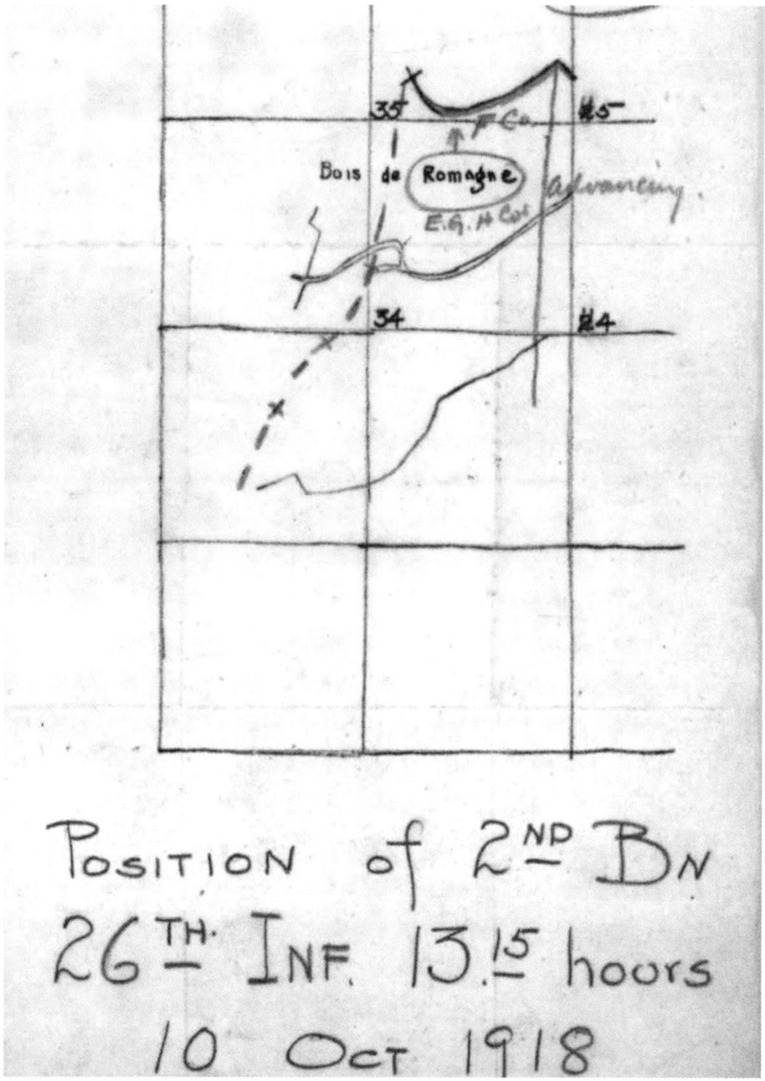

Sketch showing the position of the 2nd Battalion on Hill 263, 1315 hours, October 10, 1918. Company F is along the northern edge of Bois de Romagne with the other companies of the battalion coming forward. (National Archives, Record Group 120, Field Messages.)

them continued to fall back and were "not put under control again until after the battle was over."[66]

To replace Company K near the right flank of the 2nd Battalion, Maj. Frasier ordered Company M forward. Captain Walter R. McClure, commander of Company M and one of the few officers left in the battalion, moved his men forward; machine gun and artillery fire sifted the ranks of the men as they struggled forward through the thick woods. One-third of the men in the company became casualties just getting into position, but the company held and relieved the pressure on the 2nd Battalion in line at the north edge of the woods.[67] For his heroism during the campaign, Capt.

McClure, a native Oregonian who had been a member of the 1912 US Olympics track team, was awarded the Distinguished Service Cross.[68]

At 1835, Maj. Frasier sent a message to Col. Erickson detailing his battalion's position. Major Youell was in liaison with the forward battalion of the 28th Infantry on the left; Frasier, likewise, was in liaison with the support battalion of the 28th and, on the right, with the 361st Infantry. According to Frasier, "our left is all right." The right, however, continued to be "very dangerous." The road leading to the east in the southern part of Bois de Romagne was subjected to enemy fire; machine guns still infested the hills to the right. Despite the presence of some American troops from the 91st Division in areas to the right, the eastern part of the draw south of Bois de Romagne was still in control of the Germans. The 361st Infantry had tried but failed to drive the enemy from this draw, and their presence was a serious threat to the 26th's right flank. Occasional salvos of 77mm fire struck the area.[69]

At the end of the day, the 2nd Battalion stood at the northern edge of Bois de Romagne, with two companies of the 3rd Battalion in line next to it. The rest of the 3rd Battalion was behind the 2nd, with the 1st Battalion, in brigade reserve, further still to the rear. In front of the regiment to the northeast was Côte de Châtillon and La Musarde farm. To the north was the high ground leading to Landres-et-St. Georges. Thus ended October 10; that night, the 1st Division was ordered to continue the attacks in the same manner on the following morning. Also that night, chow had once again failed to arrive at the front lines for the weary, hungry men.[70]

1st Division observation post on Hill 240, October 11, 1918. (Courtesy Colonel Robert R. McCormick Research Center.)

Another view of the 1st Division observation post on Hill 240, showing the panoramic vista that presented itself to observers. (Courtesy Colonel Robert R. McCormick Research Center.)

German prisoners arriving in Exermont under shell fire, October 10, 1918. (Courtesy Colonel Robert R. McCormick Research Center.)

1st Division troops in a ruined church in Exermont, October 11, 1918. (Courtesy Colonel Robert R. McCormick Research Center.)

Seven:

"IT WAS WICKED TO ORDER OUR MEN TO ATTACK AGAIN," OCTOBER 11 AND OCTOBER 12

October 11

In the early morning hours of October 11, Col. Erickson sent orders forward stating that the 3rd Battalion was to lead the attack with the 2nd in support. The 1st Battalion was to remain in Brigade reserve. Elements of the 181st Infantry Brigade, 91st Division, were slated to relieve the 2nd Battalion, which would then move to the left rear to form up behind the 3rd Battalion in the woods.[1]

The orders dictated that the 3rd Battalion attack at daybreak, however the attack was contingent upon the 28th Infantry, to the left, attacking and making progress half way up the slope leading to Landres-et-St. Georges. If the 28th Infantry failed to advance, the 3rd Battalion was not to advance beyond Bois de Romagne. These orders did not reach Maj. Frasier until 0635. At daybreak, Maj. Youell sent out two fourteen-man patrols to establish the location and strength of the enemy to the front.[2]

The 3rd Battalion had only two officers and eighty-five enlisted men in the line; the assault battalion of the 28th was not much stronger. The 28th tried several times to move up the hill toward Landres-et-St. Georges but without success. The "heroic efforts" of the 28th only resulted in more casualties as the assault waves were mowed down before they advanced fifty yards beyond the edge of the woods.[3] Patrols from the 3rd Battalion moved forward but soon came into contact with wired positions. The Germans were in a fortified, wired trench line to the north; this was the vaunted Kriemhilde-Stellung, part of the line of fortifications and trenches the German forces had building up since 1914.

The depleted condition of the attacking troops is reflected in a message that Maj. Frasier sent to Col. Erickson at 0815: "Most of the men have had nothing to eat in forty-eight hours and no water. Some of my officers and many of my men are sick and cannot go much farther. I do not want to complain but I would like the CO to know the situation we are in. … Will move forward as soon as possible."[4] The front line troops were also lacking in basic tools: "My phone will not work. Have no more wire. The 2d Bn has no more wire. I can get no wire cutters." Still, Frasier, under "fairly heavy artillery fire," began to move his battalion into position for the advance.[5]

The stress of being under fire for eleven straight days, coupled with the strain of almost constant combat in deplorable weather and rugged terrain, with minimal food, water, and sleep, began to show on officers and men alike. Frasier had some difficulty in getting his men up through the woods to the jump-off line. Some of his companies were failing to establish the line; he was also having trouble with liaison with the 28th Infantry on his left and the 361st Infantry somewhere to his right. The dense woods made it difficult for him, personally, to find officers and men with whom he needed to consult.

His frustration is quite evident in a message he sent to Col. Erickson some time during the morning:

> I had K & I Co's up here on proper line, explained in detail to officers where they were to go, pointed out direction of line to NCO. The shelling was heavy. I do not understand why the Co's went back. I then had my hands full with the situation as regards the 28th and 361st, trying to find Youell, trying to find Lt. Crossland [3rd Battalion adjutant], the officer I sent to 28th as liaison. I gave him a map & full details of where I would be. He has never yet reported. Had to do all running myself. Gave my Telephone Corp. full details of my new position. Have seen nothing of him since. I am not yet in touch with Youell. Lt. Sackett [commander of Company K] is sick and not responsible but there is no excuse for Lt. Steinmetz, comdg Co. "I." I showed each his position and then when I looked for them, they were not here. Did not let me know of leaving. Explained to them that P.C. would be to left rear of Co "M" and close to it.[6]

The entire 1st Division was depleted and in a weakened condition. Lieutenant Butler, 1st Division aide de camp, wrote in his journal that he thought it, "was wicked to order our men to attack again this morning. … Since we have entered this sector … we have lost between nine and ten thousand men."[7] At about 0930, the regimental PC advanced to a cottage 300 yards east of Arietal Farm.[8]

The 2nd Battalion was relieved by a battalion of the 362nd Infantry of the 181st Infantry Brigade, 91st Division. During the relief, the 2nd Battalion received artillery and machine gun fire from Germans in trenches to the right rear, resulting in the loss of six men, and the relieving battalion lost more.[9] Major Youell moved the 2nd Battalion back into the woods 1,200 yards behind the 1st Battalion in a position of support.[10] The 1st Battalion moved forward and by 1000 were in position "on military crest on Hill 263, three companies holding and 1 company in reserve."[11]

Colonel Erickson was anxious to use Maj. Legge as a conduit for information about the front lines, asking him to contact the 2nd and 3rd Battalions to his front and request that they send runners to the regimental PC; he also asked that Legge forward any messages through to the regimental PC, something that was standard operating procedure anyway. In order to find out more information on the activity to his front, Legge sent Lt. Forster, commander of the 37mm platoon, forward to report on the situation ahead. Forster established his observation post on the left of the front line, at the edge of Bois de Romagne.[12]

Up ahead, Maj. Frasier and the 28th's battalion commander conferred and decided to deploy their men in a manner best calculated to allow them to hold their ground. This they had to do with only about 200 men and nine machine guns to cover a front of about 1,800 yards. Among the eighty-five men now present in the 3rd Battalion there were but sixty-three automatic rifles. The auto riflemen also carried Springfield rifles, and Chauchats were also placed with some of the machine guns.

Lieutenant Ridgely finally was able to contact Maj. Youell; he found that the battalion of the 362nd Infantry that had relieved Youell had only 200 men with no machine guns and only eight Chauchat automatic rifles. Youell's PC, by 1100, was along the north fork of a crossroads in the southern part of Bois de Romagne, in support of the 3rd Battalion, which was just to the left of the position just vacated by the 2nd Battalion. Ridgely also relayed to Erickson his opinion that the situation on the right flank was serious. An officer in the battalion that had relieved the 2nd Battalion reported severe fighting on a hill to their right rear. He concluded, "In my opinion it is dangerous to press out with right in present shape."[13]

Lieutenant Forster, from his observation post on the left of the line at the edge of the woods, reported at 1102 that Company H of the 28th was awaiting elements of the 3rd Battalion of the 26th to relieve them. No doubt all this delay was a result of the trouble reported by Maj. Frasier in an earlier message. He also reported that Companies H and I of the 26th (probably he meant Companies K and I, both in the 3rd Battalion) were forming to the rear, and that Lt. Crossland was awaiting Maj. Frasier with Companies L and M. Forster reported seeing men walking in front of the woods without drawing fire. Forster, having spoken with Maj. Youell, who told him the details of the relief of the 2nd Battalion, also repeated the concern over the presence of Germans "in the trenches to his right rear." While there appeared to be no enemy activity directly to his front, Forster reported that patrols from the 28th to the left had advanced and met with machine gun fire about 875 yards out.[14]

The precarious nature of communications between battalions and regimental headquarters in the rugged woods with heavy artillery fire is evident in Forster's request that Maj. Legge "send me two or three runners and I will keep you informed what is going on but I must have runners." Likewise, Lt. Crossland, 3rd Battalion adjutant, reported that Maj. Frasier had "no telephone at all."[15] The value of runners was obvious under these circumstances.

Colonel Erickson was still very concerned about the possibility of enemy resistance in front of the 26th. At 1155 he once again cautioned Frasier that he was not to advance beyond the edge of the woods if his patrols encountered resistance; he said that the "situation will be handled from the right by 181st Brigade." Showing his thirst for information, Erickson concluded his message: "Send your runners to my P.C. thru Youell's P.C. in your rear. Send me a statement & for God's sake send me more frequent reports."[16]

At noon, Maj. Legge, still in position on the reverse slope of Hill 263 with the 1st Battalion, reported that Maj. Youell's 2nd Battalion was in position in support of the 3rd. Youell had earlier sent forward an officer and two men to find Frasier. Legge reported that, "Germans reported dug in and strong in Cote de Châtillion. Machine gun and rifle fire from this direction [to the right front]."[17]

Lieutenant Ridgely also dispatched a message at noon, showing that the confusion at the front continued. Ridgely reported that the 2nd Battalion of the 28th Infantry had, earlier in the day, moved to the left and then advanced. The battalion had encountered heavy machine gun fire from both flanks and from the road between Sommerance and St. Georges. When heavy artillery fire hit the battalion, they had withdrawn and were now, at noon, back in their original position awaiting the arrival of Maj. Frasier's battalion. Ridgely had not yet located Frasier, but he had found Lt. Crossland who apprised him of the above facts. Ridgely also reported that Youell's battalion (the 2nd) would hold their position until they found Frasier. Major Legge's message, mentioned above, arrived at the regimental PC at 1230; ten minutes later, Lt. Ridgely's message arrived. No doubt the arrival of these two messages added to the haziness of the picture of the battle in the mind of the regimental commander and his staff.[18]

An hour later, at 1300, Ridgely reported he had, "located [Lt.] Sackett with 'K' and 'I' Cos. 3d Bn. in trenches in last night's position. He [Sackett] has lost Frasier. I have Frasier's adjutant [Lt. Crossland] and three patrols looking for Frasier and the other two Cos. [L and M] … Shelling us heavily here." Taking these messages as a whole, it would seem that Maj. Frasier had ordered Companies I and K into position at the north edge of thc Bois de Romagne, to the left, but for some reason, the companies didn't arrive at the point where Frasier had expected them to take up position. With his other companies, L and M, Frasier was probably farther to the right. But at 1300 Frasier himself sent Col. Erickson a sketch purporting to show his battalion's position. The sketch shows Companies K and M in the front line, left to right, further to the left (west) of their previous position. In support were Companies I and L, left to right. Farther to the left is the 28th Infantry and to the right is the 362nd Infantry. It is difficult to exactly reconcile all these messages and sketches; obviously there was great confusion in the woods as to the location of individuals and units.[19] Persistent enemy machine gun and shell fire didn't help the situation.

At 1400, Col. Erickson began to send out messages to his battalions and other regimental elements directing them to prepare for relief by the 168th Infantry Regiment, 42nd Division. These messages no doubt took at least an hour to arrive at the elements furthest north, the 2nd and 3rd Battalions. The messages were all the same, directing each unit, upon relief, to "proceed to Vauquois, five kilometers south of Cheppy. Your kitchens are there at the old Regtl. P.C. east of La Neuville le Comte Fme where a hot meal will be found. Send one guide per Co. and one per Bn Hqrs to this P.C. at once."[20]

Meanwhile, the enemy artillery and machine gun fire in the woods became very heavy. The shot and shell destroyed the woods, and all the troops in Bois de Romagne suffered badly. The telephone line guards patrolling the area between the 3rd Battalion and the 2nd Battalion, looking to repair broken lines, reported coming upon strong German patrols to the rear. Consequently, Maj. Frasier sent sixteen men and a machine gun to an area about 400 yards south of the northern edge of Bois de Romagne to protect the battalion's rear against attack. At 1500, the battalion of the 362nd Infantry, to the right, suffering heavy casualties from the artillery and machine gun fire pounding the woods, withdrew. Once again the 3rd Battalion was left to occupy the entire northern edge of the woods on the right flank.[21] The men had had no food the previous night, and no food for breakfast and lunch this day, other than the meager reserve rations which could be found on the dead. Consequently, when they spied a German aircraft drop what they supposed to be food on German positions on Côte de Châtillon, many men wanted to move forward to retrieve the package. Prudence triumphed over gnawing hunger, however; "nothing so foolhardy could be permitted."[22]

With about seventy men left, Maj. Frasier decided that the 3rd Battalion had to shift position to protect the right flank. Two squads were ordered from the front line to move to the right and take position along an unimproved road, facing to the right, to guard against a flank attack. The squads spread out, twenty yards between men, each man armed with a rifle and an automatic rifle. Two machine guns were also sent to this road. These guns moved up and down in a ditch behind the road, keeping up an incessant fire, hoping to deceive the Germans as to the strength of the troops in that area. The battalion now had two squads deployed to the rear and two squads deployed to the right.[23]

As these men took up positions along the road, they spied German scouts approaching through the trees in their front. In a "vicious fighting mood," the men opened fire; when the smoke cleared, few of the German scouts were left standing. Throughout the afternoon and evening small enemy patrols attempted to infiltrate the position, but these were driven back; apparently the Germans were convinced that the position was held in force.[24]

It was now evident that a strong, organized attack by fresh troops would be necessary to attain the high ground beyond Bois de Romagne. The formal news finally arrived that the 1st Division was to be relieved. At 1700 the regimental operations officer arrived at the 3rd Battalion with the welcome news that a battalion of the 42nd Division was to move into position at 2200 that night. The 3rd Battalion had to dispatch guides to escort the relieving battalion forward, as had the other two battalions. According to Frasier, "Six dependable men were sent to regimental headquarters to act as guides." This, of course, further reduced the strength of the front line. Danger lurked in the dark woods; the small detachment ran into a German patrol, and in the ensuing firefight two of the men were killed. Still, "never was the news of relief more welcome."[25]

Thus during the night the 26th was relieved by the 168th Infantry Regiment, 42nd Division. The exhausted, hungry Doughboys filed through the darkness over ground for which they had fought during the previous week. "They were tired, weary but never disheartened."[26] The men had been under fire continuously for eleven days; they had advanced steadily over wooded and broken ground; they had assaulted hills and ravines and had advanced against farms and open areas swept by enemy fire. As they passed through those same areas one wonders what thoughts occupied their minds. The men were described as "hollow-cheeked, pale and silent ... dazed and bewildered"[27] They were a "forlorn procession" moving through to the rear.[28]

October 12

The 3rd Battalion, now consisting of two officers and sixty-eight men, moved back to Rau de Mayache where they found the company kitchens. The men devoured hot stew and sipped hot coffee, letting the warmth from each soak into their bodies. The food tasted better "than the finest of food in ordinary times," but the men could not eat much of it; their stomachs had become shrunken due to the dearth of food during the previous few days.[29] The rest of the regiment experienced similar episodes as they moved farther to the rear on the way to Cheppy. They arrived at that "battered village" on the morning of October 12. They spent the night about one mile south of Cheppy, prior to finally receiving rest, replacements, equipment, food, supplies, and a bath.[30] The companies began to take stock of who was left; Lt. Glen M. Brody of Company C wrote, "Of the two hundred and twenty men in the company that started the attack, sixty were left when we came out." Private Carmine Ferritto, with a different perspective, recalled that Company C "came out with a total of thirty-five men."[31] Captain Edgarton of Company F left Bois de Romagne with forty-one men; by the time he reached the woods of Vaux after the relief, "I had forty-six, having accumulated somebody." The men who had rejoined Company F were not shirkers, however. According to Edgarton, there "was no skulking whatever. The number of small wounds [on the returning men] was very large," indicating that the men had been wounded and lost or at least seeking medical aid.[32]

The other companies were equally shocked at the thin lines of men marching to the rear. Years later, groping for the right words to express his impressions of those days, Lt. Calvin Richards, Machine Gun Company commander, recalled the battle as "ten or eleven days of pluperfect H____ ... I shall never forget it."[33] For some men, the memories were just too painful. In 1928, responding to a question about his experiences as commander of Company L during part of the battle, 1st Lt. John H. Ducket stated that "I doubt if I could have helped much, as this phase of the war all seems like a night-mare to me now."[34]

During this phase of the Meuse-Argonne Offensive, the 1st Division "suffered the heaviest casualties of its history likewise the losses of the 26th were the heaviest. The regiment entered the attack with 3,300 men and eighty-four officers. It came out with 1,600 men and forty-one officers."[35] The numbers given above show that the 26th lost forty-three officers and 1,700 men killed, died of wounds, wounded, and missing. The other infantry regiments of the 1st Division suffered equally badly. The 16th Infantry Regiment lost thirty-five officers and 1,600 men, the 18th Infantry Regiment lost thirty-eight officers and 1,384 men, and the 28th Infantry Regiment lost a total of 1,677 officers and men.[36] The 1st Division as a whole lost 196 officers and 7,324 men.[37]

A graphic description of the battlefield provided by Lt. Col. William Donovan, commander of the 165th Infantry Regiment, 42nd Division, which moved into the area just west of the 26th on October 11, reveals the horrors of the fighting. Donovan wrote that his men moved "past freshly killed and yet unburied Germans, through unmistakable smell of dead horses to a farm in a valley." The farmhouse had been used as a dressing station, probably for the 28th Infantry. The sight that greeted the new occupants must have been unsettling: "Outside was a huge collection of torn and bloody litters, broken salvaged equipment, reddened underclothing and discarded uniforms, all of our own men – the cast off of the dead and wounded." Donovan wrote that the 1st Division "had a terrific fight just three days before and the ground was a stew of dead Boche and Americans." Donovan found the remnants of an American attack: dead bodies "laid out in rows. It was easy to determine the formation." He also found wounded Germans and Americans.[38]

Another member of the 165th Infantry, in passing over the ground taken by the 26th and 28th Infantry Regiments, noted the German defenses: "Machine gun bunkers made of concrete, and their dugouts were also framed in concrete, with electric lights and telephones ... some even had running water installed. Their defenses were superb." Remembering this, Pvt. Albert M. Ettinger reflected, "It was amazing that human flesh could endure what had been inflicted on the [1st Division] in capturing these positions."[39] On his way north to Hill 272, Ettinger, too, was horrified at what he saw: "I had never before seen so many bodies. There must have been a thousand American and German dead in that valley between the two ridges. They were an awful sight, in all the grotesque positions of men killed by violence."[40] Still other members of the 42nd Division recounted what they experienced on Hill 263 and the area to its north on October 12: "Everything bore signs of the previous week's battle by the 1st Division. Mud-covered bodies of German and American soldiers were strewn about, and the large proportion of American bodies was unnerving. The green residue of mustard gas marked everything."[41]

The regiment had advanced almost five miles and fought against elements of four enemy divisions while capturing 400 prisoners, a battery of four 77mm cannons, and a large number of machine guns, not to mention other weapons, ammunition, and stores.[42] Considering the severity of the fighting and the heavy losses suffered by the regiment, it seems that the Germans showed an inclination to fight and a reluctance to cede ground. But one company commander, however, felt that on

October 4, at least, the Germans fought a rearguard action while withdrawing.[43] While this may be a matter of perspective, there is no denying that the regiment faced a well-organized, tough resistance.

The importance of the 26th's costly advance to the overall First Army effort is best seen in the effectiveness of the 1st Division as a whole. The division succeeded in clearing the fortified woods and hills before the Heights of Romagne. Their advance, coming at a time when the American effort had, for the most part, bogged down, permitted the insertion of the 82nd Division to their left. The combined advance of the 82nd and 1st Divisions resulted in outflanking the Germans in the Argonne Forest and caused their withdrawal to the north. In particular, the 26th's struggles in Bois de Romagne set the stage for the eventual successful assault against Côte de Châtillon by the 42nd Division. Côte de Châtillon was a heavily fortified, partially wooded hill that was the gateway to the more open area to the north. All this paved the way for the advance to the Meuse River and the eventual fall of Sedan and the German railroad hub there, one of the main objectives of First Army to begin with.

Eight:

"ANXIOUS TO SHOW THEIR METTLE," RELIEF AND REPLACEMENTS, OCTOBER 13 THROUGH NOVEMBER 5

October 13 to October 16

It took days for officers and clerks to sort out who had survived and who had not. Indeed, even as the regiment withdrew, their ranks increased as men who had been separated from their units now rejoined them. These men were either shirkers or men who had legitimately become separated from their company. As an example, the 3rd Battalion, while withdrawing, grew from sixty-eight men to about 140. By October 13, they had 240 men present for duty. According to Maj. Frasier:

> Our increase was due to the men who had miraculously and suddenly discovered which way was north and had, therefore, found their proper organization. Some of them had, undoubtedly, been lost but most of them could well be characterized, as they were by the soldiers who had fought through the battle … [as] "Shell-hole Rats." It may well be taken into the consideration of all officers who may be called upon to lead troops in battle that there will always be a certain number of these men who become conveniently lost and as conveniently find themselves when the show is over.[1]

Although such straggling would be disheartening to a commander and the men, and detrimental to unit effectiveness, a commander might find "great moral value" if he considers "that there are in every fighting unit a certain number of men who can be depended upon, as a general thing, to begin and end all military operations."[2] Such has always been the case in every army, everywhere.

The company morning reports reflected the confusion in accounting for everyone. For example, Company E's morning report for October 18 lists Lieutenants Levis Bune, William Mansfield, and Gordon Knowles as missing in action since October 11; in fact, all three men had been wounded and evacuated. Also listed as missing in action on that day were 145 men (six sergeants, twenty-four corporals, and 115 privates). It wasn't until October 24 that Lieutenants Bune and Mansfield were correctly listed as wounded in action, and it wasn't until late October 27 that Lt. Knowles was listed as "gassed, Oct 5-18."[3] And at least fifteen men from Company I who, as late as November 1918, were listed as missing in action between October 4 and 10 were later found to be on duty.[4]

As the days wore on, something like a final reckoning was made. The numbers listed here do not include those captured or missing in action, nor do they include men of Companies A and B, 3rd Machine Gun Battalion, who supported the 3rd and 2nd Battalions, respectively, throughout the campaign. Likewise, the numbers do not reflect the hundreds of men who were wounded or became sick. Included

Brigadier General Frank Parker, commander of the 1st Division as of October 11, 1918. Parker had been commander of the 1st Brigade. (Courtesy Colonel Robert R. McCormick Research Center.)

here are twelve men who died in the time frame from October 13 through October 29, after the active fighting. Certainly some of these men died of wounds, but others died of disease, and those are included in the numbers because it is likely that their illness was caused or exacerbated by the strenuous ordeal of the battle.[5]

The following table gives the numbers of men, by company, killed and died of wounds or disease, October 1 through October 29, 1918:

COMPANY	OFFICERS	ENLISTED MEN	TOTAL
A	1	49	50
B	0	31	31
C	2	24	26
D	1	35	36
E	0	31	31
F	0	26	26
G	0	9	9
H	1	20	21
I	1	15	16
K	1	10	11
L	1	20	21
M	0	10	10
MG	2	20	22
HQ	0	5	5
HQ, 2nd Batt.	1	0	1
Med. Det.	0	4	4
Sup.	0	1	1
Totals	11	310	321

It is important to note the number of leaders, that is, officers and NCOs, that were killed or wounded during this phase. Eleven officers and 51 NCOs were killed or died of wounds, and a much greater number were wounded and evacuated; this represents a huge loss of the regiment's junior leaders. Since each one of these men had to be replaced, on the spot, by a man of lower rank – a sergeant, corporal, or private – one can readily sense the loss of unit cohesion and effectiveness that must have resulted. Many of the men were fairly new replacements, having joined the regiment only about a month previously; unit cohesion, even in early October, was still undergoing a solidifying process. It speaks much about the enlisted men in the regiment when we consider the fact that they persevered, despite breath-taking losses, and achieved their strategic goal.

Although the 26th Infantry and the rest of the 1st Division had suffered great losses, they had achieved their objectives. Colonel Hjalmar Erickson was later awarded the Distinguished Service Medal for the period 1-11 October, for "displaying marked tactical ability, courage, and resourcefulness in the handling of numerous critical

Charles P. Summerall as a Brigadier General. Summerall was named commander of V Corps on October 11, 1918; at his request, Brigadier General Frank Parker was named commander of the 1st Division to replace him. (Courtesy Colonel Robert R. McCormick Research Center.)

situations, thus enabling his regiment to advance steadily to all its objectives."[6] Colonel Erickson was promoted to brigadier general and sent to the 1st Brigade in mid-October; Lt.Col. Theodore Roosevelt, Jr., replaced him in command of the 26th. Roosevelt, son of the former president, had been a battalion commander in the 26th before being wounded in July.

Upon his recovery, Roosevelt had been detailed to be an instructor at the AEF school of the line at Langres, France. Sometime in mid-October, Brig.Gen. Erickson stopped by to visit Roosevelt, bringing him tidings and news from his old regiment. This meeting prompted Roosevelt to seek a return to the 26th. First, he had to be medically certified as being able to return to combat. Deciding to "take the bull by the horns," Roosevelt left the school before receiving formal approval; "I was technically A.W.O.L. [Absent Without Leave] for a couple of weeks, but they don't court-martial you for A.W.O.L. if you go in the right direction, and my orders came through all right," reasoned Roosevelt later. He showed up at 26th headquarters with "a cane and a limp." Lt. Fullerton was able to remain as regimental adjutant, and this pleased him; Fullerton said of Roosevelt, "he is a wonder."[7] Roosevelt was, of course, delighted to return to his former regiment as commander.

On October 11, Gen. Summerall left to assume command of the V Corps, and, at his request, Brig. Gen. Frank Parker, who Summerall called "the ablest combat leader of the war," was appointed to command the 1st Division. The 26th had suffered so many losses that each company had to be rebuilt around a core of surviving veterans. Leaves and passes were cancelled in order to have all available men ready to train replacements and to prepare for further operations; both Summerall, and Parker told the troops to be ready for further combat operations.[8]

October 16 to October 31

The 1st Division arrived at Vavincourt on October 16. Private Carmine Ferritto of Company C recalled staying in "billets that had electric lights and good bunks," and the men "got new clothing and equipment and got cleaned up." In the next few days, about 8,000 replacements from depot divisions or replacement divisions reached the 1st Division. According to Maj. Frasier, about 2,000 of these were assigned to the 26th Infantry Regiment.[9] For a typical example, Company E received forty-six men on October 16 (one sergeant, one corporal, two cooks, and forty-two privates); on October 21, twenty more men went to Company E. Private Ferritto reported that Company C received 130 new men.[10] Many of these men had been drafted in July and had had minimal training before heading overseas; it now fell to the veterans of the infantry regiments to train these new men.[11]

The state of training in the National Army is evident when one examines the fitness and training of the newly arrived replacements. Some of the men had never fired a rifle, and none of them had fired a pistol. They had no idea of attack formations or the use of hand- and rifle-grenades. A look at how the 3rd Battalion approached the training of these new men will give us insight into how the rest of the regiment approached this difficult problem.[12]

The 3rd Battalion, along with, assuredly, the rest of the 1st Division began to inculcate the esprit of the division into the new arrivals. As Maj. Frasier wrote, "We believed in that esprit as we believe in our own religion. It was a sacred thing."[13] The veterans then trained the men to shoot. The American army placed great emphasis on a rifleman's use of his primary weapon, the rifle. Under the instruction of the veterans, including officers who declared that only by accurate, deadly fire would they live to return home, the newcomers fired their rifles at tin cans.

On a borrowed blackboard, the veterans diagramed an attack formation. The nucleus of veterans remaining in the depleted companies then formed up to show the men what a small unit deployed in attack formation looked like. The recruits then formed up in similar fashion. Captain Cornish recalled that training the new men in attack formation "was a case of, 'Here Green, you follow Smith, and keep abreast of Jones over there.'" Within four days the 3rd Battalion was making progress; soon the new men were able to assume an attack formation, and some of them could at least shoot accurately.[14] In the end, the replacements were "anxious to show their

1st Division G-2 (Intelligence) Section, October 29, 1918. (Courtesy Colonel Robert R. McCormick Research Center.)

mettle." For their part, the veterans "were more than eager to make good their prodigious boasts" regarding their past exploits and combat prowess.[15]

In addition to the new replacements bolstering their ranks, the regiment also benefited by the return of some veteran officers. On October 12, as the regiment withdrew from the front lines, 1st Lt. George W. Andrews returned to Company L after spending time recuperating from wounds he had received at St. Mihiel. First Lieutenant Eugene A. Dye, also released from a hospital, returned to Company D to resume command of a platoon. Before the end of October, Dye would be promoted to captain and would take command of Company D.[16]

Although this was technically a rest period, it was anything but truly restful. Lieutenant Fullerton, suffering from dysentery and gas exposure, wrote: "We are very, very busy in 'rest' again, preparing for another crack at the Hun. ... If I were not a mule and could only get good and sick, sick enough to be carried off on a litter, the only honorable way to be sick, I might enjoy some good sleep and rest."[17]

In rainy, miserable weather the regiment participated in maneuvers over rough ground, in anticipation of the battle to come. In these maneuvers an American observation plane took aerial photographs showing the efficacy of using ground panels to mark the various PCs and the front line; this impressed upon the infantrymen the value of these marking panels in establishing the correct location of ground troops in battle and thereby enhancing artillery effectiveness.[18]

On October 29, the regiment boarded French trucks and moved to the woods north of Parois, on their way to what everyone hoped would be their last battle. For the next two days, as the regiment awaited further orders, they continued to receive replacements. These men must have been rather awed at having to join a regiment on the eve of a battle; the older men did their best to give the newcomers the benefit of their experience, hoping that would at least improve their chances of survival.

Despite the infusion of replacements and the return of veteran officers, the regiment suffered from a serious lack of experienced leaders. The table below shows how many officers, and the highest rank, that each rifle company of the 26th had at the start of the next phase of operations:[19]

COMPANY	NUMBER OF OFFICERS	HIGHEST RANK
A	2	Captain
B	2	Captain
C	4	First Lieutenant
D	3	Captain
E	3	Second Lieutenant
F	4	Captain
G	4	First Lieutenant
H	4	First Lieutenant
I	3	Captain
K	3	First Lieutenant
L	3	First Lieutenant
M	3	Captain

On the last day of October, Gen. Summerall addressed each regiment in the 1st Division, priming them for the battle to come. "Men, you belong to a fighting division. You have pushed the enemy back on three fronts. You have gone far. You will go farther. You have suffered much. You will suffer more. You have gone long without food. You will go longer. You have faced death. You will face it again." At the conclusion of these remarks, a muleskinner in the regiment stood atop his water cart at the edge of the assembly and said, "Who in the hell is that guy, anyway?" The men wanted to laugh; surely the muleskinner spoke what many men felt. "He, too, was sincere; and he, too, spoke from the heart."[20]

November 1 to November 5

The men moved north; they were assigned to support the veteran 2nd Division during the upcoming assault. The 26th marched past familiar, bloody ground. On

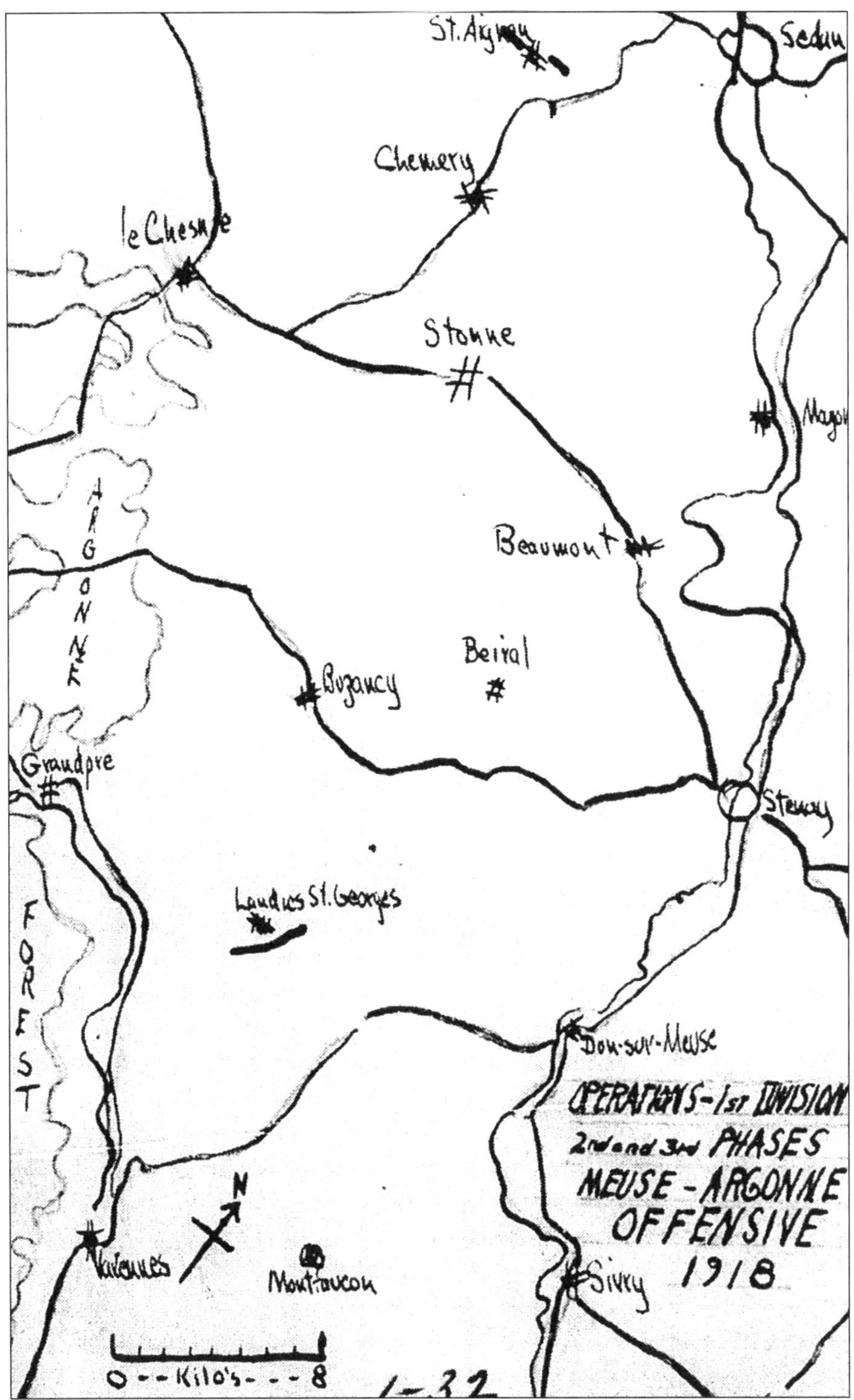

Then-Captain Frasier's post-war sketch showing the area of operations of the 26th Infantry Regiment, November 1 through 8, 1918. (Captain Lyman S. Frasier, "Operations of the Third Battalion.")

the morning of November 1 a terrific artillery and machine gun barrage erupted from the American lines. A total of 608 guns of all calibers were amassed for the barrage, dwarfing anything that the 26th Infantry had seen in the earlier phase of the fighting in October. The two-hour "fire for destruction" covered the enemy ground to a depth of 1,300 yards with a blanket of steel death. Every known German artillery piece and machine gun nest was targeted. The "fierce, savage" barrage impressed even the veteran Doughboys of the 26th; one can only imagine its effect on the replacements fresh from the United States. Probably it had the same effect on them that the barrage prior to the St. Mihiel Offensive, in the early morning hours of September 12, had on the then-newly arrived rookies. At 0530, the 2nd Division jumped off with the 1st Division, including the 26th Infantry, following in support. The attacking Doughboys followed closely behind the thick curtain of artillery and machine gun fire as it swept over the German defenders. The 26th did not come under a great deal of fire during the next couple of days; their harassment was limited to aerial bombardment and strafing.[21]

On November 2, they entered Bois de Romagne where the 2nd Battalion had led the assault on October 9 and 10. The 42nd Division, which had relieved the 1st Division on October 11-12, still crouched in foxholes that the men of the 26th had dug three weeks earlier. In the rain and mist, the trails through the woods quickly became a quagmire. All through November 2-3 the 26th moved forward, passing through Landres-et-St. Georges, Landreville, and Bois de Folie, as the 2nd Division drove the Germans back.[22] Under these conditions, with the regiment moving forward at a relatively quick rate, over rough, broken ground, under aerial attack, the feeding and supply of the men was difficult. Often the drivers had to unhitch the mules from the carts while men lifted, pulled, and pushed the carts and wagons across trenches and through swampy fields. A platoon of riflemen was detailed to the Machine Gun Company for this purpose.[23]

Despite the muddy morass and the traffic jams, the supply train, under battalion supply officers Capt. Robert Scott, 1st Lt. Charles M. Cook, and 2nd Lt. Joseph B. Card, actually managed to beat the infantry to one rest area. When the infantry column arrived, they found the kitchens by the roadside, fires going, "and the food spreading a comforting aroma through the rain-rotted woods."[24] Such an occurrence warmed the hearts and stomachs of cold, tired infantrymen and endeared the supply and kitchen staffs to the men.

On the afternoon of November 4, as the 26th advanced northward in support of the 9th Infantry Regiment of the 2nd Division, Baron Richthofen's Flying Circus attacked and strafed the men. This famed German Air Force unit, with their distinctive red-nosed aircraft, often attacked the 1st Division, and this would be their final appearance to the soldiers of the 26th Infantry. There were no Allied aircraft in the area at the time, and the Flying Circus "performed many antics, among others the shooting up of one of our columns, happily with trifling damage."[25] One man in the 3rd Battalion was shot through the ear while, ironically, he was taking a rifle shot at the passing aircraft against standing orders to do so.[26] According to Capt. Cornish, "a few moments before the [German] planes appeared, the sky seemed full of Allied planes, but when the attack on the column was made, all of our planes evidently found business elsewhere."[27] The regiment halted at dusk south of Bois de Belval.[28]

The word was received that the regiment was to go into line to protect an exposed left flank of the 9th Infantry; the men continued the advance through Bois de Dieulet, and there a line was established at 0500, November 5. Up to this point, since the beginning of this phase of the offensive on November 1, the regiment had been almost continually on the march "over roads in the worst possible condition."[29] The traffic jams behind the lines were monumental; huge tractor-drawn artillery pieces churned the roads into impassible muddy sloughs. These behemoths had trouble negotiating narrow village streets, further halting traffic. The Doughboys of the 26th, on foot, had to detour around these impasses, hiking across mired fields pocked with shell holes. Trudging through the mud in the rain with full packs soon exhausted the men. One man in the 3rd Battalion was found, complete with his rifle and pack, dead of exhaustion by the roadside.[30]

Lieutenant Colonel Roosevelt called his three battalion commanders, Majors Legge, Youell, and Frasier, into his PC to issue attack orders for the next day. While doing so, Lt.Col. Roosevelt discovered that he had to slightly amend some portion of the order. He turned away for not more than five minutes; when he returned, he found all three battalion commanders, each young and vigorous, asleep on the wooden benches upon which they were sitting. Such was the mental and physical fatigue present even in the battalion leaders.[31] At 1800 on November 5, the 1st Division was ordered to go into line on the left of the 2nd Division.

Nine:

"A NIGHTMARE OF MARCHING," NOVEMBER 6 THROUGH NOVEMBER 11; POST-WAR DUTIES

November 6

To get to the jump-off line, the 26th would have had to pass through Beaumont; that town, however, was at the time, undergoing heavy shelling. The regiment therefore marched cross-country to reach the line of departure, the Beaumont-Stonne road. Members of the regimental intelligence section moved ahead and guided the men, in the dark, toward their destination. In this manner, the 26th "avoided many losses" and "saved considerable time in reaching the line of departure." Elements of the regiment were in place by midnight; the remainder were in place by 0400.[1] The jump-off area was "subjected to un-aimed and intermittent shelling," and occasional bursts of machine gun fire ripped through the cold night.[2] As the 26th moved into position, they relieved a "scattered detachment of the 80th Division."[3] The officers of the 26th had had no time to conduct a reconnaissance of their front; the regiment would have to attack without it.

The 26th Infantry went in on the 1st Division's right; to its right was the 9th Infantry Regiment of the 2nd Division. To the 26th's left was the 18th Infantry; to the 18th's left was the 16th Infantry. The 28th Infantry and parts of the 18th were

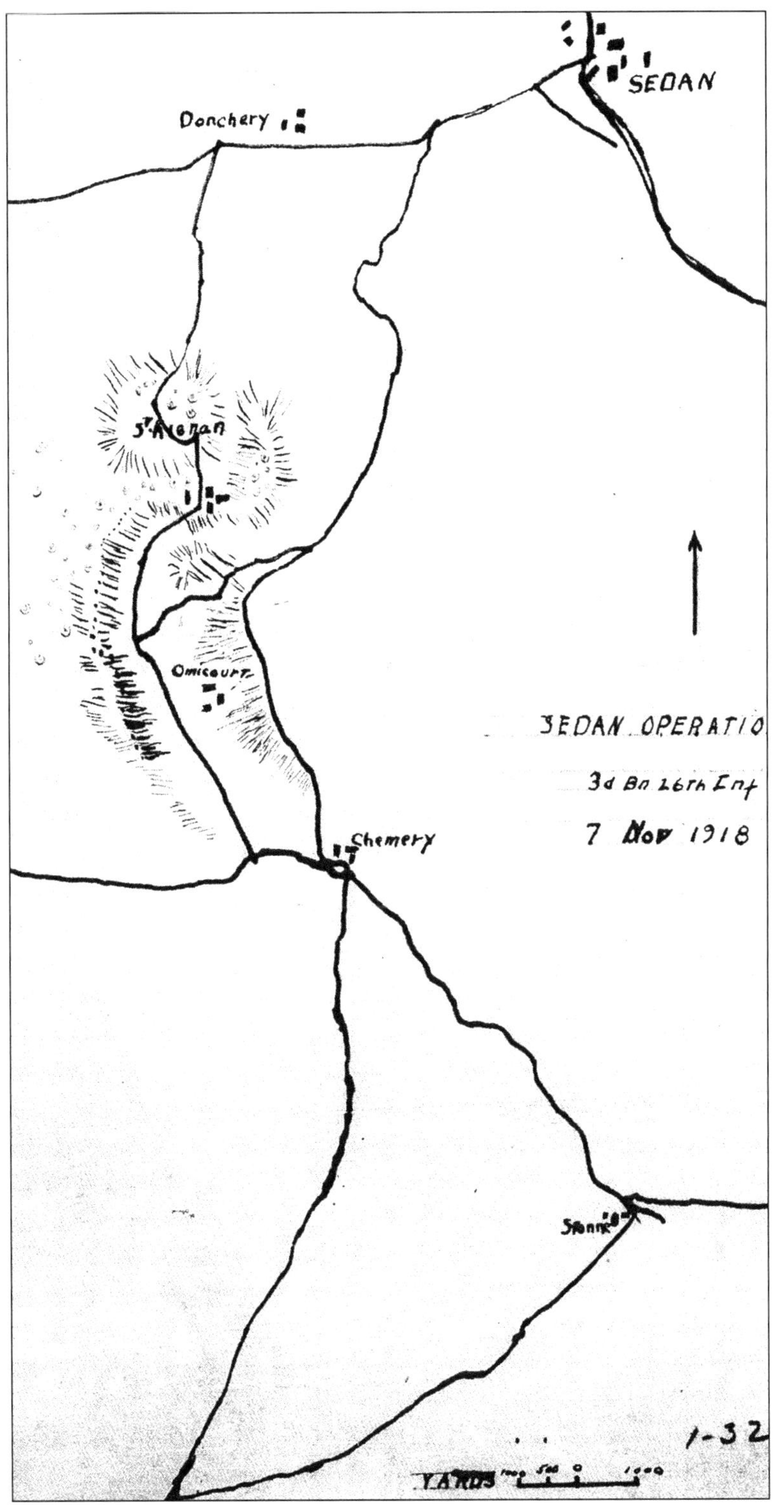

Then-Captain Frasier's post-war sketch showing the area of operations of the 26th Infantry Regiment for the march on Sedan. (Captain Lyman S. Frasier, "Operations of the Third Battalion.")

division reserve. The 26th went into line with the 2nd Battalion on the right and the 1st Battalion on the left; the 3rd Battalion was in reserve 1,000 yards south of la Thibaudine Farm, on a ridge due west of Beaumont.[4] The 7th Field Artillery Regiment moved into position near Beaumont to support the 26th Infantry during the attack.[5] Both the 1st and 2nd Divisions were to jump off at 0530; the 26th's objective was the town of Mouzon and the west bank of the Meuse River.[6] The direction of advance was to be northeast. The 26th had three intermediate objectives before reaching Mouzon.[7]

The 1st Battalion, the 26th's left assault battalion, formed with Companies D and C, left to right, in the front line on the Beaumont-Stonne road. Company D's left rested on the intersection of the Beaumont-Stonne road and the road leading north to Yoncq. In the second line, just south of the road, were Companies A and B, left to right. Each of the 1st Battalion companies was allocated a 600-yard front. The 2nd Battalion, to the right, formed up along the road, nearer Beaumont, with Companies H and E, left to right, in the front line and Companies F and G in the second line. The battalions were on the reverse slope of a large hill; directly ahead was rolling ground with patches of wooded areas. La Harnoterie Farm was about 1,100 yards away in front of Company C and Company H. About 1,000 yards beyond that the attacking battalions would come upon the Yoncq-Beaumont road that ran down a defile coming off a plateau in the 2nd Battalion's zone. The first objective was a northwest-southeast running line just south of the Yoncq-Beaumont road.[8] Upon reaching this first objective, the 1st Battalion was to shift the direction of their attack about thirty-five degrees to the east to allow the 18th Infantry to take Yoncq.

North of the Yoncq-Beaumont road the ground rose to form two large plateaus, one in front of Company D and one in front of the 2nd Battalion. The area between the two plateaus was a woods, Bois du Fond Limon. The second objective, about 1,750 yards northeast of the first objective, was a line running across the tops of both plateaus. The eastern part of the 26th's zone, over which Company E advanced, was a steep slope down to the Meuse River on the right. Beyond this objective, the regiment had to advance from the ridge-like plateaus, and the steep, wooded valley between them, until they came to their third objective, a line running through the northern "nose" of the plateau in front of Company D on the left and through the outskirts of the village of Villemontry, along the Meuse River, on the right. There the regiment would pause before attacking Mouzon, almost 3,000 yards to the northeast of the third objective.

Per the attack order, the 26th jumped off at 0530. Captain Dye, commander of Company D on the left, recalled that, "we went over in a fog that was so thick we could see only a few yards for the first half hour." The left flank of Company D advanced immediately into a dense woods; Dye sent a platoon into the woods while the rest of the company flanked it, ready to "cut in if they raised any M.G. nests." The company met little or no resistance and made the first objective "without incident."[9] To the right, Companies C, H, and E moved up the slope of the high ground to their front, then through la Harnoterie Farm and on to the objective line. The support companies followed.

The situation in Company B, the 1st Battalion's left support company, was probably typical of the rest of the regiment. Due to losses suffered in the savage fighting in early October, officer manning in the company was critical. Second Lieutenant James A. Clarkson Jr., recalled:

> I entered the battle when I should have been in the hospital. I was suffering with a severe cold and fever but, as we were overburdened with men and had such a scarcity of officers and especially since most of our men were replacements, green from the U.S.A., I didn't see how I could very well be evacuated and so I decided that I had better stick as long as I could.[10]

Company B's commander, Capt. Ethelbert Van Ness Burrell, was in the hospital, Lt. David Meeker had sprained his ankle on the night march to reach the area, and "Lieutenant Lewis [*sic*, Capt. Brown Lewis] broke his arm before we went up."[11] Thus Company B, with "300 men or over," went into action led by only two lieutenants, Clarkson and 1st Lt. L. L. Smith.[12]

South of la Thibaudine Farm, the 3rd Battalion, in reserve, moved forward starting at 0545; they had waited a few minutes to allow the 1st and 2nd Battalions, ahead, to gain some ground. Major Frasier was comfortable with the situation on his left flank; the Germans in that area were in retreat before the rest of the 1st Division. Still, the 3rd Battalion had a difficult time with the advance; they "encountered gas and wire. The roads were muddy and rough. The fields and woods ... were little better than water soaked swamps."[13] The battalion received little enemy shellfire. Frasier reflected on the mental stress these conditions imposed on the men, in addition to the obvious physical stress: "It is disconcerting to march along silently through the rain and blackness of night, stumbling over wire and slipping in the mud and wondering when the next messenger of death is going to strike from the black wall ahead into which one is advancing."[14]

Up ahead, at the first objective, Capt. Dye found "about a half dozen machine gun emplacements with plenty of ammunition and part of one gun which the Germans had abandoned, apparently very shortly before." These were the guns that had been firing upon the front line the night before. The lead battalions then shifted direction slightly to the northeast and continued their advance. Company D took some prisoners, "two young Germans. They said they were tired and had declined to go back with their outfit which had retired, they said, an hour before. They said there were few if any troops this side of the Meuse."[15] But there was still plenty of fight left, even among those Germans retreating across the Meuse River. Crossing the Yoncq-Beaumont road, the Doughboys continued up the slope of the plateau; at about 0650, the 2nd Battalion, to the right, entered Bois du Fond Limon and Bois de l'Hospice.[16]

The third objective "was a line of German practice trenches in a thick woods on the forward slope of a rather steep hill," the "nose" of the plateau in front of the 1st Battalion. To the left front of Company D arose Mt. de Brune, a 215-foot prominence that dominated the area. To the right front, in the distance, was Mouzon itself. The

26th had orders to halt at the third objective and send patrols forward to the Meuse River. By this time the fog had given way to a cold, persistent drizzle. The visibility was still poor, but the soldiers in the line could see that, "parts of Mouzon were burning." Company D sent a patrol of nine men to get as close to the bridge over the Meuse River as they could.[17]

At 0700, Company C came up abreast of Company D to its left, with Companies A and B in support at the top of the hill just behind. Up to this point, Pvt. Ferritto in Company C remembered advancing "without having to fire a shot and without even hearing or seeing anything of the enemy." The 18th infantry, to the left of Company D, began to advance; Capt. Dye, hoping to help protect the right flank of the 18th, brought Company D forward and to the left, about 650 feet, partway up Mt. de Brune. Meanwhile, the patrol from Company D had advanced about 2,600 yards; they reported that they could not get any closer to the Meuse than about 200 yards due to heavy machine gun fire. Dye ordered them to remain near le Faubourg, just southwest of Mouzon. The 18th Infantry, dug in on the reverse slope of Mt. de Brune to the left of Company D, also sent patrols forward, and they, too, drew heavy machine gun fire.[18] At 0740, Lt.Col. Roosevelt moved the regimental PC forward to la Harnoterie Farm.[19]

Other patrols from the 1st and 2nd Battalions moved down toward Mouzon, Villemontry, and Givodeau Farm. These areas were lightly held, but Germans on the high ground across the river showered the Doughboys with heavy artillery and machine gun fire. Second Lieutenant Charles D. Mulvey of Company H recalled sending a detachment to Mouzon, or possibly le Faubourg at Mouzon's southwestern outskirts. One of the men of this detachment, Pvt. Fred W. Smith, was the last man killed in Company H.[20] In Mouzon, the Doughboys of the various patrols, their uniforms and equipment soaked with cold rain, engaged in street fighting with the Germans in strong positions. They finally succeeded in driving the enemy out of the area of Mouzon on the west bank of the river and forcing them to the east bank. The Germans detonated delayed action mines in Mouzon, setting fire to some structures. In the face of heavy German fire, patrols crossed the Meuse River and found the enemy in great numbers on the heights east of the river.[21]

Now a thirty-seven-man patrol from Company E, led by 2nd Lt. William F. Leck, company commander, advanced upon Villemontry. As the patrol neared the village from the southwest, they encountered intense fire. Lieutenant Leck left most of his men under cover and entered the village with three men to reconnoiter the enemy's position. The men soon came upon a company of Germans in the process of destroying a footbridge across the river. Leck sent one man back to his patrol to bring it forward, while he and the two other men opened rifle fire on the Germans. Their initial fire killed about twelve Germans as the balance of Leck's patrol came forward. The patrol opened fire and drove the surviving Germans into the water, where many of them "were shot while attempting to swim to the east bank." Lieutenant Leck and his patrol secured the village while under tremendous *minenwerfer* and machine gun fire from across the river. They found many civilians hiding in cellars, some of whom, young girls, had been about to be forcibly taken across the river by the Germans.[22] To this point, the 1st Division had lost seven officers and 347 men killed, died of wounds, wounded, and prisoners.[23]

At about 0900 the fog and drizzle lifted, allowing good visibility for the Germans across the Meuse. Accordingly, they opened up, "with 77s and some larger stuff. Most of it was high explosive, but some other stuff." The German artillery zeroed in on the third objective, shelling the troops still on that line. Company D, which had moved forward and to the left to the reverse slope of Mt. de Brune, escaped serious harm, but "the [other] companies suffered as high as thirty casualties." Dye recalled that from their position on Mt. de Brune they "could see our outfit [i.e., the rest of the 1st Battalion] getting plenty of hell, but nothing we could do as we only had one battery of 75s, called a sacrifice battery."[24]

At this point, two guns from the sacrifice battery, from either the 6th or 7th Field Artillery, came down the Yoncq-Mouzon road. Stopping about 1,500 yards from Mouzon in plain view of the Germans, the horse-drawn guns unlimbered and went into action. The guns, on the level ground between Givodeau Farm and Mt. de Brune, "opened point blank fire on a church in which German machine guns had been located and were making toothpicks out of the bridge which [the Germans] had blown up but failed to completely destroy."[25] The gun was immediately targeted by the Germans, and it looked, "as though all hell was dropping around it, so thick were enemy shells." After finishing their task, the gunners limbered up their guns and then "leisurely trotted back to cover." This made a great impression on all who saw it; Cornish said that this "feat must have been witnessed by at least a thousand infantrymen and must have strengthened their conviction that the First Artillery Brigade was their truest ally."[26] Clarkson declared that this "impression stuck because it was the first time I had ever seen artillery fire point blank at a target."[27]

The outstanding, gallant performance of the artillery was, however, not without its downside. Lieutenant Clarkson, in support in the woods atop the plateau, remembered that the Germans "began to burst a few shrapnel and H.E.s in the woods where we were." Captain Dye recalled that the result of the guns' firing was to draw "fire on the infantry because they insisted on helping us." Company B also "stayed in the woods all day under desultory shell fire."[28] Behind, the 3rd Battalion's platoons were positioned on the slopes southwest of Yoncq, near la Harnoterie Farm.[29]

The 1st Battalion's surgeon, twenty-four-year old 1st Lt. John G. Skilling, was a 1917 graduate of the University of Maryland School of Medicine and College of Physicians and Surgeons, who had just started his civilian medical career. Now he was responsible for the health of a battalion of young men engaged in violent, mortal combat. Throughout the battle, Skilling had bravely tended the wounds of the men while under heavy shell and machine gun fire.

During this action, Skilling saw some wounded men from Company C ahead. Although warned to wait for stretcherbearers, Skilling, "with absolute disregard for his personal safety," began to cross an area under German artillery fire to reach the men. The shellfire was so intense that Skilling was forced to take shelter in a shell hole. According to Pvt. Willard Hollat, an enlisted medic:

> I was about twenty yards from [Lt. Skilling] when he was killed. … I saw him hit, he was killed instantly. We were like a pair of brothers. I had to take care of a wounded Sergeant. I saw that Lt. Skilling was dead, saw his legs blown in the air. We were in the first wave going over when he was killed. He was identified by his shoes.[30]

Lieutenant Skilling's death was a serious loss for the men of the 1st Battalion.

Although the resistance encountered by the 26th was comparatively less than that they had experienced in early October, it, coupled with the grueling march in bad weather, was enough to wear men down. It was probably fear and exhaustion that drove a recent replacement in Company D to shoot himself in the leg to avoid further combat. Captain Dye had to, "raise hell with a non com to keep him from shooting the recruit in a more effective place."[31]

The regiment was ordered to withdraw in preparation for another march. Company D, having lost only two men wounded during the operation, was ordered to withdraw about 4,400 yards to la Harnoterie Farm, just south of the day's first objective. The 3rd Battalion was in this area, and one of their platoons had entered Yoncq and joined up with other troops in that village.[32] The other companies pulled back to the same area during the evening.

What happened next was a source of extreme controversy then and for a long time afterward. One of the objectives of the renewed offensive was the city of Sedan on the Meuse River. This strategically important city was a transportation hub for the German armies fighting the British and French to the west, as well as for the Germans currently engaged against the Americans and French in the Argonne area. Lieutenant General Hunter Liggett, commander of the American First Army, issued a memorandum stating that Gen. Pershing desired "that the honor of entering Sedan should fall to the First American Army." Liggett's memorandum further stated that his 1st and V Corps should begin an advance on Sedan that night and that unit "boundaries will not be considered binding."[33] The order filtered down to V Corps and finally to the 1st Division.

General Summerall, commander of V Corps, and former commander of the 1st Division during the earlier fighting in the Meuse-Argonne Offensive, ordered the 1st Division to proceed to Sedan to assist in taking the city. In moving to Sedan at night, the division had to march on the muddy, rutted roads in horrible condition. There were two options for the march. First, the division could march northwest along roads in the Meuse River valley until they reached the high ground southwest of Sedan. This would expose both flanks of the regiment to hostile fire, and, with such a narrow front, deploying to confront the enemy would be troublesome. The second option, to have the regiment march on a wide front in five columns further south, was the one chosen by the division commander, Gen. Frank Parker. The 26th was assigned to the fifth column, the one farthest to the southwest on the Stonne-Chemery-Omicourt-Hannagne-St. Martin road, with the 3rd Battalion leading the march. The 3rd Battalion was also to lead the actual attack on Sedan, with the 1st Battalion in support and the 2nd Battalion in reserve. The desired rapidity of the

General Charles P. Summerall as he appeared at his retirement as Chief of Staff, US Army, 1930. (Courtesy Colonel Robert R. McCormick Research Center.)

Aerial view of Sedan, objective of the 1st Division's ill-conceived march. (Courtesy Colonel Robert R. McCormick Research Center.)

move necessitated that the men would leave behind their packs and travel as lightly as possible; further, the wounded men would be left behind and cared for as best as possible.[34]

News reached the 3rd Battalion as they were digging in for the night. Their wounded were gathered together and left under guard of two riflemen at the intersection of the Beaumont-Yoncq and Beaumont-Mouzon roads. As speed was a necessity, the battalion discarded their packs prior to departure.[35] Captain Manning, now commander of Company I, recalled that the men "left the lower half of the pack containing their blankets piled for the trains to collect the next day. So far as I know these blankets were never recovered."[36] Captain Dye, commanding Company D in the 1st Battalion, remembered that by 2100 the men had assembled and, after "cutting equipment to the bone," departed for Chemery. Lieutenant Clarkson also recalled digging in before receiving the order to commence the march on Sedan.[37]

A regimental runner sent to the patrol from Company E in Villemontry was killed before he could deliver his message. Still, unofficial word reached Lt. Leck, the patrol leader, that he should pull his patrol out and join his regiment for the march. Leck, thinking that the order was a mistake, refused to withdraw saying, "The First Division never gives up any ground it has taken."[38] Thus, Company E marched away minus its commander, Lt. Leck, and one platoon, still in Villemontry. (Throughout the following two days, Lt. Leck and his men held their ground in the village despite

Another aerial view of Sedan. (Courtesy Colonel Robert R. McCormick Research Center.)

desperate measures by the Germans to kill them or force them out. On November 7 and 8, Leck, with sixteen men, took and held le Faubourg. When, on November 8, a messenger with official orders finally reached him, Lt. Leck was proceeding with his command northwest along the Meuse, hoping to join up with the rest of the regiment near Sedan.[39]) Lt. Leck was not alone in his insistence upon proof of the authenticity of the order to withdraw; one of the 26th's battalion commanders, upon receiving the order over the telephone, "made the Colonel positively identify himself before he would agree to withdraw."[40]

After dark, the regiment set off in the cold rain, the 3rd Battalion, with Company I leading, in front. Behind them came the 1st Battalion, marching with Companies A, B, C, D, and Machine Gun Company in column, and finally the 2nd Battalion, minus one platoon of Company E. Leading the whole column was a point guard; patrols also protected the flanks during the first part of the march. The Doughboys of the 26th were none too happy to engage in this forced march. Although "insufficiently fed and with practically no sleep," the Doughboys set off. As Maj. Frasier recalled: "The sufferings of that night march will remain one of the most memorable of the war's horrors."[41] Frasier, who led the march, best describes it:

> The men had had no supper. It was raining a cold, desolate penetrating rain. The roads over which we marched were what the soldiers called,

> "Shot to pieces." The men were so tired and worn out that it was necessary for the officers to shake them after the expiration of the hourly ten-minute halts. The officers did not dare sit down because of the utter sleepiness which fell upon them whenever they relaxed. We found that by standing against a tree we would be awakened by violent contact therewith if we should go to sleep and fall.[42]

The road from the regiment's position to Stonne was a straight shot of about four miles along hilly, slightly wooded terrain. From Stonne, the road turned northwest and proceeded along steep ridges, some of which were wooded, more than four miles to Chemery. It also passed through some small villages. For tired men, hiking in the cold, wet darkness along muddy roads, carrying, even with having shed some of their equipment, perhaps forty pounds, the march was a grueling ordeal. As the men plodded along in their dreary, cold misery, the slings of their rifles cut into their shoulders. With each step, the web belts around their waist supporting ammunition, canteen, and first aid kit, dug into their hips. Throughout the wet night, more and more mud clung to their boots adding weight with each bone-wearying step. Still the 26th marched on.

November 7

All through the cold, wet night and into the morning the men plodded on. Approaching Chemery in the early morning hours of November 7, the leading officers captured two German horses. Major Frasier mounted one of these but had to give it up since he fell asleep and rolled off the horse. Captain Dye, Company D commander and "a corking good officer," fainted from exhaustion while on the march. He lay in the mud for an hour before coming to and rejoining the march.[43] He later recalled: "We moved pretty fast in this show and as a company commander I was so busy looking after my own duties that I had little time to look over the adjoining units other than to be sure we were not getting out on a limb."[44] Lieutenant Fullerton remembered the difficulty of the march:

> We hadn't seen our kitchens for twenty-four hours, all mounts with us had been wounded, motorcycles and cars hopelessly mired … bridges blown up and detours over hastily constructed ones, gaps blown in the road, an occasional long range shell bursting along the column, horses down, men down, wagons and huge trucks overturned and pushed to one side, orders and curses, but, overall, a morale the Hun could not beat.[45]

This march took the division across the path of the advancing I Corps consisting of the 77th Division and the 42nd Division. Although Gen. Parker had sent a messenger to I Corps headquarters to warn them, no one had contacted the divisions through whose zones the 1st Division would advance. All five columns encountered hostile and friendly troops. These confrontations were dangerous; none of the troops were aware of the presence of the others. The commanders of the 77th and 42nd Divisions, and the commander of I Corps to which they belonged, were irate over what they considered to be tactical shenanigans and glory hunting on the part of the 1st Division. As they made their displeasure known to Gen. Liggett, the 26th marched on.

The advance guard, basically the 3rd Battalion, had been ordered to march in squad columns "until resistance should be developed." Frasier had taken the precaution to march with columns of twos on either side of the road. Near Chemery the main body of the 26th took enemy shellfire and suffered casualties. However, due to the march formation, the losses were kept to a minimum. The men had to now leave the road and deploy as they approached Chemery. Machine gun fire rained down upon the men from the hills to the west and added to the casualties. Company I alone lost, "five or seven Non-Commissioned Officers hit by the same salvo."[46] The 2nd Battalion passed through Chemery and deployed, but they did not contact any Germans.[47]

At Chemery, located on the slope and at the base of the "nose" of a ridge, the route entered a wide valley that it traversed, mostly east to west, before crossing the Bar River and a canal and then entering Malmy. There, the road turned north and ran along a shallow slope for about two and a quarter miles, to Omnicourt.

As the column moved through the black morning, some men joked, but others were quiet, dead tired. Lt.Col. Roosevelt rode up and down the column checking on the men and sometimes joking with them. Just prior to entering Malmy the entire column had to cross a small footbridge single-file. At places the road was mined and the men had to take detours across mysterious, sodden fields in the pitch-black.[48] As the column turned north out of Malmy and marched along the valley, they were vulnerable to attack from the heights on both sides of the valley. Captain Manning recalled that, "the whole regiment could have been very readily shot up, if not practically wiped out, there being no protection along the route of march."[49] Luckily, the Germans had vacated that area prior to the arrival of the column. Just north of Malmy, the advance guard surprised and captured a German machine gun crew of four men and a gun.[50]

As one of the Doughboys in the advance guard approached Omicourt before dawn, he came upon three German soldiers. These he bayoneted before they could open fire. As the main column passed the area later, they came upon the dead bodies as evidence of the anonymous Doughboy's morning efforts. The regiment had planned, once Omnicourt was taken, to drive northeast along the plain of the Bar River for about 1,600 yards before turning north and pushing up the steep, thickly wooded ridge that separated the two legs of the Bar River as it meandered to the east and back to the west. Atop this ridge, the regiment would be looking down, due north, upon St. Aignan, in the Bar River valley, in position to attack.

For the entry into and passage through Omnicourt, we have four almost irreconcilable accounts, two from Maj. Frasier, commander of the 3rd Battalion, one from Capt. Manning, commander of Company I leading the column, and one from Capt. Cornish, commander of Company C in the 1st Battalion. According to Maj. Frasier, the column came under German artillery fire about 1,300 yards south of

Omnicourt. As the column neared Omnicourt it was subjected to both artillery and small arms fire. Frasier deployed Company M to take the village, which it did at 0800. In Omnicourt, a very old French woman crept out of her cellar to greet the Americans. Apparently the only civilian left in the village, she was so overcome by her rescue that she fainted. The men did not have time to care for her, so they gently carried her back to her cellar and moved on.[51]

Next, Frasier sent Company M farther north out of Omnicourt, in the direction of St. Aignan. To the right of Company M was Company K; one platoon of Company I acted as a guard for the left flank, driving out several German machine guns as it advanced "along the heights in the Bois d'Omnicourt." One platoon of Company L maintained liaison with the 28th Infantry to the right. As the battalion pushed north into the wooded high ground they were peppered with German machine gun fire. Although the area to the right was free of German artillery, enemy guns north of St. Aignan began to hit the battalion as it moved north. After "a short, sharp fight," the Germans withdrew to St. Aignan, and the 3rd Battalion took up a line on the top of the ridge south of St. Aignan. By 1115, the battalion was in a long line on the northern fringe of the woods on the slope overlooking St. Aignan to the north.[52]

In his version of the events, Capt. Manning stated that, as Company I approached Omnicourt, leading the regimental column, the village was being shelled. Accordingly, Manning halted his company just south of the village, off the road, which "brought the whole regiment to a halt."[53] Manning eventually entered Omnicourt between 0700 and 0900. Once in the village, Manning found the headquarters of a French battalion that was conducting operations in the area. The French colonel in charge, he was informed, was in the hills north of Omnicourt directing his soldiers. Manning sent one platoon, later augmented by a second platoon, north of Omnicourt to establish contact with the French commander. The French commander refused permission for the Americans to pass through and assault St. Aignan; indeed, the French were preparing to do just that, and a French one-pounder was firing upon German positions to the east, on an extension of the ridge that the Americans and French were then occupying.[54]

Manning, unable to convince the French commander to allow him to follow orders and move upon St. Aignan, prepared to send his two platoons north against the village anyway. Manning remembered that, in the midst of these complicated negotiations, Lt.Col. Roosevelt, regimental commander, and Maj. Frasier arrived in Omnicourt; "very soon [we] had a full-fledged French-American argument in regard to what action should be taken." At this point, according to Manning, advice was sought from brigade and division commanders; this eventually resulted in the order for the Americans to withdraw. While Company I was in Omnicourt, the Germans shelled the town frequently, damaging houses "and wounding some few men."[55]

According to the versions of Maj. Frasier and Capt. Cornish, as the men moved north of Omicourt they came upon troops from the 40th French Division. This was a surprise to both Americans and Frenchmen. The Frenchmen "presented a wonderful sight" as they moved through the 26th and took up positions to its right. According to Capt. Cornish, the French "officers and men were spick and span, dressed as for a gala occasion and presented a great contrast to the sleepy, hollow-eyed, mud-spattered but grim and determined 26th Infantry."[56] The French kitchens then came up through the 26th; "the smell of hot food, although garlicky, presented a tremendous temptation to the men of the First Battalion of the 26th" who were nearby when the kitchens rolled along the road. Captain Cornish reported that, "very few of the men moved on the kitchens, which spoke a great deal for the discipline in the 26th."[57]

The French battalion commander thought he was supposed to relieve the Americans; Maj. Frasier sent word back to Lt.Col. Roosevelt at regimental headquarters requesting clarification. Meanwhile, in the face of increasing German resistance, the attack continued. Considering the terrain over which his battalion was advancing, Frasier had chosen to attack initially with only one company, Company K, deployed in line. This deployment, however, was insufficient to overcome German fire, so Frasier ordered Company M to come up and deploy on Company K's right. Major Frasier had requested to use a 75mm gun that the French troops had with them; this gun now sprang into action. The two battalion commanders, one American and one French, conversed and decided to commence a joint attack with the 26th Infantry, 3rd Battalion leading, advancing north upon St. Aignan, and the French troops advancing up a valley southeast of the town, attacking the German left flank. Thus far, at the point of the advance, collaboration between the Americans and French had gone as well as could have been expected.[58]

Trouble now developed as Company M was slow in coming forward. Major Frasier sent runners to find out what was happening with Company M; these men returned with the bland news that the Company M commander had "nothing to report." Major Frasier then checked into the situation and found that the commander of Company M, sensing that the end of the war was near, was loath to order his men into danger and had therefore kept them under cover in the woods. Frasier, irate at the disobedience of his company commander, stated later that, "the officer in question paid rather dearly for his action."[59] While acknowledging the failure of his company commander, Frasier also blamed himself for not advancing with two companies in line and for "not pushing the advance more aggressively throughout."[60]

At this time, according to Frasier, regimental orders came halting the 3rd Battalion. Frasier organized his men to meet any possible counterattack. Patrols advanced to within 100 yards of St. Aignan and brought back word that German machine gun nests were arranged in a checkerboard pattern throughout the woods in front of the town. The 1st Battalion leapfrogged the 3rd to continue the attack. With Companies C and D in the front line, left to right, and Companies A and B in the support line, left to right, the 1st Battalion moved up the hill in front of town.[61] The 3rd Battalion, in support of the 1st, pulled back about 500 yards into the woods.[62] The 2nd Battalion was still in reserve behind the 3rd.

The French moved against the town from the southeast, as planned. The Germans began an evacuation of St. Aignan depositing, as they left, a heavy artillery barrage on the leading wave of the 1st Battalion. On the right, Capt. Dye took a platoon from Company D and passed through the French lines; arriving at the edge of the woods overlooking St. Aignan, the platoon immediately drew fire from farm buildings in the plain below. Dye called for his automatic rifles and waited in the woods.[63] Patrols from the 1st Battalion infiltrated around St. Aignan; some of them ranged as far as the wooded knoll just north of the village. These patrols confirmed news of the German withdrawal north toward Donchery.[64]

These patrols represent the farthest-north advance of the 26th Infantry Regiment during the offensive. The regiment was now spread from these elements of the 1st Battalion north of St. Aignan, south to the main body of the 1st Battalion on the ridge south of St. Aignan, then to the 3rd Battalion in support in the woods on the reverse slope of the ridge south of St. Aignan, and finally to the 2nd Battalion, probably in Omnicourt or even as far back as Chemery.

While all this was going on, the commander of the French 40th Division visited Lt.Col. Roosevelt in his PC. The irate general demanded that the 26th withdraw. He stated that they were advancing in an area his division was preparing to bombard prior to an attack. Lieutenant Colonel Roosevelt replied that he had his orders, and he intended to follow them regardless of the presence of the French troops. According to Roosevelt, the general "protested a little further and I am afraid I lost my temper. That is about the long and short of it."[65] At this time, orders came to the regimental PC from 1st Division headquarters ordering the 26th to turn over the sector to the French.

Another account comes from 2nd Lt. Charles B. Fullerton, regimental adjutant, who was an eyewitness to the discussion:

> Just as we were preparing to attack the French General came to our P.C. and very politely wanted to know what in hell we were doing in his sector, that his division had been ordered to take Sedan, that his division *would* take Sedan, and that furthermore if the American officer did not pull his troops out at once, his gunners with guns already laid would come down on us with "*le grande precisione*." You see it was a matter purely sentimental with him, while to us Sedan was just a place to "shoot up."[66]

The French general "worked himself into a fever heat" as the debate progressed. The arrival of the 1st Division French liaison officer meant that the whole argument had to be rehashed; in due course, the French general caught the name of the 26th's commander, Theodore Roosevelt Jr. This bit of news made an impression on the general, as Fullerton recalled:

> Not the son of that great American, that noble friend of France! No, it could not be! Well, it was. The General saluted us all about forty or fifty times and then the old 26th could have taken Sedan with the "frogs" backing us up."[67]

Earlier, at 1400, Gen. Summerall had shown up at 1st Division headquarters in Chemery; he had learned of the havoc caused by the 1st Division cutting through the support train of the US 42nd Division as that division moved north; likely, he had also heard of troubles with the French and other American divisions. Consequently, he issued the order for the 1st Division to pull back to the east, the order that was just now, at about 1700, reaching the advanced elements of the 26th Infantry.

Immediately the men stopped digging in; the patrols were recalled, and the weary Doughboys began to retrace their steps along the route over which they had just come. Not everyone was convinced, however. Captain Dye, manning the ridge just south of St. Aignan, waiting in the woods to begin an attack, wanted some confirmation before he began a withdrawal. He recalled, "I refused to leave until we had a note from the C.O. and so we remained until about 8 p.m. when we got the order and retired back through the French."[68] So, during the night of November 7, the "regiment withdrew from the battle line for the last time in the World War." The entire "race to Sedan" episode was a sore spot for many of the senior officers involved.

The troops had not eaten during the day; as they passed through Chemery, they were treated to hot soup and coffee from the kitchens. Everyone was dead-tired. Lieutenant Colonel Roosevelt followed the men to Chemery, and he found the three battalion commanders fast asleep in the stalls of a stable. One of them, upon awakening to find Roosevelt in the stable, said, "Sir, I never knew until this minute what a lucky animal a horse is." As Lt. Fullerton remembered: "We pulled out and went to sleep along the road, and slept as only a tired doughboy can sleep."[69] Captain Dye remembered that it was "a hell of a march and I do not yet see how the division stood up."[70] Second Lieutenant Clarkson's list of things he had to contend with could have been repeated by almost all the men: "Sickness, night marching, scarcity of provisions, etc." He recalled the episode as "a nightmare of marching at night, going hungry, advancing by day and being too tired to care what happened." Lieutenant Fullerton concurred, saying, "I never spent such a night, and hope never to spend another like it."[71] Finally, the regiment arrived at their designated bivouac site in the woods south of Yoncq.

Major Frasier summed up the end of the final day of combat for the regiment:

> Neither the muddy ground nor the cold nor the noise of the guns could disturb the dead slumber of these men who had marched and fought almost continuously for five days and nights with little food and little rest. Between [1630] November 5th, and midnight November 7th, the 26th Infantry had marched seventy-one kilometers [about 45 miles] – the record of the A.E.F.[72]

The other infantry regiments in the 1st Division marched as follows: 16th, fifty-four kilometers (thirty-four miles); 18th, fifty-three kilometers (thirty-three miles); 28th, fifty-two kilometers (thirty-two miles).[73]

It is worth examining the different versions of the reactions of the various American and French units with which the regiment came into contact during the march toward Sedan. Captain Manning, commander of Company I, stated that he never got cooperation from the French commander with whom he spoke north of Omnicourt. The Frenchman refused permission for the Americans to pass through his lines or to advance upon St. Aignan. Indeed, the French commander "inferred that if we insisted upon moving ahead that he would not be responsible for any of his guns that might fire into us."[74] As stated above, Manning, under orders to attack, intended to proceed with or without French cooperation.

Major Frasier, however, recalled that he had secured the assurance of cooperation from a French major, whose battalion was to participate in a joint attack upon St. Aignan. The French commander also assisted the 3rd Battalion in evacuating some wounded men using "a squad of litter bearers equipped with rubber tired wheeled stretchers."[75]

Both Manning and Frasier had mixed feelings about the forced march on Sedan. Manning remembered that "we met with considerable criticism from American troops whose lines we crossed and the movement of the division for a time was looked upon as unwarranted."[76] In a postwar paper, Maj. Frasier opined that:

> The reasons for the forced march on Sedan are not entirely clear. There were divisions nearer Sedan than the First. However, no participant in that memorable forced march ever regretted that he was present and the writer prefers to ascribe the reasons to the desire to grant the glory of taking Sedan to a deserving division. ... The First Division was the freshest and strongest division present.[77]

The feelings of the junior officers and men can be summed up by Frasier's comment: "Suffice it to say that we are satisfied to have let the French have the glory of taking historic Sedan. It meant far more to them than to us."[78]

Even while the dust of the Sedan controversy was still swirling, Brig. Gen. Frank Parker, commander of the 1st Division, wrote glowingly of the division's interaction with other units during the march. In an operations report Parker stated that his division encountered "elements of the 77th Division, the 42nd Division and the 40th French Infantry Division." He insisted that, "nothing but the warmest and most cordial relations existed at all times between the First Division and these troops and there was not a single instance of any unpleasantness reported to me." Parker stated that, as far as he knew, all the divisions felt that they were to cooperate in a joint attack on Sedan, and that, therefore, they presumably didn't begrudge the 1st Division's presence in the area.[79]

Parker claimed that, "nothing but the best feeling existed at all times in all echelons." Further, he claimed that the 26th Infantry "reported the most friendly relations existing between that regiment and the 40th French Division troops."[80] But Parker perhaps came closer to the truth when, after he visited the commanders of the 42nd and 77th Divisions, he stated, with a healthy dose of understatement, that those commanders were "a bit annoyed at the First Division's appearance on what they considered their sector."[81]

For this phase of the battle, 160 men of the 26th were killed, wounded, died of wounds, or missing. Using the division and regiment histories, a breakdown of the men killed and died of wounds or disease follows:[82]

COMPANY	OFFICERS	ENLISTED MEN	TOTAL
A	0	2	2
B	0	1	1
C	0	0	0
D	0	1	1
E	0	2	2
F	0	1	1
G	0	0	0
H	0	2	2
I	0	3	3
K	0	0	0
L	0	0	0
M	0	1	1
Machine gun	0	5	5
Headquarters	0	4	4
Medical Det.	1	0	1
Supply	0	0	0
Totals	1	22	23

Thus a total of 344 men of the regiment were killed, died of wounds or disease, or missing in action for the entire Meuse-Argonne Offensive; this represents more than 10% of the total number of men present at the start of the battle.

November 8 to November 11 and Postwar Duties

In the early morning of November 8 the 26th arrived near the Chateau de Belval. There, "on the cold, bleak, battle-scarred hill-side," and in a chilly, soaking rain, the men bivouacked until November 11. At daybreak on the 11th the men assembled on the "cold and muddy hills" for a rumored march to Metz to the southwest. Sometime after 1000, a mounted courier delivered the incredible news that an armistice had been signed to take effect at 1100 and that hostilities would cease at that time. The men were directed to go into bivouac in Bois Folie. This was sudden; Maj. Frasier states that, "some of our dead still lay unburied in the woods." Initially, as the men looked at their watches, they could still hear the rumble of the guns up front, and some wondered about the veracity of the message. Soon, however, the men noticed that the gun and artillery fire that had been their constant noisy companion for months was beginning to die out. At 1100, the war was over; still, the final shot heard by the 26th didn't come until 1120.[83]

Lieutenant Fullerton recalled the night of November 11:

> That night in our camp looked like Lake Shore Drive [a busy thoroughfare in Chicago, where Fullerton practiced law] or Coney Island on the Fourth of July. Everybody had his own campfire and everyone who had a Very pistol shot rockets, red, white, green, and blue. It was a wonderful sight, but it was a frightful night. I spent it trying to keep warm and dry near a fire which threatened to go out every minute.[84]

The regiment next marched across the entire Meuse-Argonne battlefield, toward Verdun. On November 15, they crossed the Meuse River north of Verdun, "headed unmistakably for Germany."

Lieutenant Fullerton described the state of the French refugees the regiment encountered on their way to Germany:

> The poor wretches have suffered untold hardships. They have no food, except that provided by the American Relief and no clothing except that discarded by the Hun. Their horses, cows, chickens, everything has been taken from them.[85]

Fullerton, writing from a room that had been occupied by a German general, mentioned a blackboard in the room that showed "the work table for 220 civilians. … It is the baldest truth of the Hun's flagrant disobedience of the laws of nations and humanity. For example, children under eight years worked four hours daily, Sunday included."[86]

The 1st Division had been assigned to the newly formed 3rd Army as part of the Army of Occupation, bound for duties in Germany. After receiving an issue of warm weather winter clothing, the regiment next marched to Luxemburg, which they reached on November 20. The men thoroughly enjoyed themselves there before finally crossing the Moselle River into Germany at Wormeldingen on December 1, 1918. The entire 1st Division assembled at Coblenz on December 12 and, the next day, crossed the Rhine River "with the Band playing and the Colors flying."

In Germany, when not patrolling their assigned area, the troops occupied themselves with "maneuvers and problems"; later, in the spring, they enjoyed target practice, "combat firing, welfare work, athletics, and amusements."[87] Soldiers were offered the opportunity to take leave in France, Belgium, or England; some men obtained passes to allow them to go on boat trips up and down the Rhine River. Thus, by and large, the men of the 26th passed their time while on occupation duty. In July, plans were made to withdraw the American divisions in the Rhine bridgehead and substitute the newly formed American Forces in Germany. On August 15, 1st Division units began the long train ride from Coblenz through Belgium to Brest, the port of embarkation.[88]

The 1st Division was the last US Army combat division to return home and among the last troops of the AEF to leave Europe before the AEF was officially disbanded.

Brigadier General Frank Parker near Neuville, November 8, 1918. (Courtesy Colonel Robert R. McCormick Research Center.)

Brigadier General Frank Parker (third from left, looking at French civilians) and his staff with French refugees returning to their homes, November 9, 1918. (Courtesy Colonel Robert R. McCormick Research Center.)

1st Division headquarters, Calaret Farm near Verdun November 16, 1918. (Courtesy Colonel Robert R. McCormick Research Center.)

Another view of 1st Division headquarters, Calaret Farm near Verdun November 16, 1918. (Courtesy Colonel Robert R. McCormick Research Center.)

Left to right: Brigadier General Frank Parker, General Marshall (French Army), Lieutenant Colonel Theodore Roosevelt, Jr., Captain H. M. Lano, and Major Thomas R. Gowenlock, Etain, France, November 17, 1918, as the 26th Infantry Regiment crossed the armistice line. (Courtesy Colonel Robert R. McCormick Research Center.)

German officers and guards who transferred German army guns and ammunitions to the American army, in front of 1st Division headquarters, Landres, Meurthe et Moselle, France, November 18, 1918. (Courtesy Colonel Robert R. McCormick Research Center.)

Lieutenant Colonel and Mrs. Theodore Roosevelt, Jr., Romagne, France, November, 1918. Mrs. Roosevelt was a YMCA worker in France. (Courtesy Colonel Robert R. McCormick Research Center.)

Brigadier General Frank Parker joins Lieutenant Colonel and Mrs. Theodore Roosevelt, Jr., Romagne, France, November, 1918. (Courtesy Colonel Robert R. McCormick Research Center.)

Brigadier General Frank Parker, Treves, Germany, December 1, 1918. (Courtesy Colonel Robert R. McCormick Research Center.)

The 26th left in late August 1919, arriving in the US in early September. The regiment paraded with the division in New York on September 10; the grateful New Yorkers "yelled themselves hoarse in admiration." After this the regiment went with the division to Washington, DC, where, on September 17, they again paraded before cheering citizens. Finally, the regiment went to Camp Meade, Maryland; since the 26th Infantry Regiment and the 1st Division were Regular Army units, they would remain in existence. However, all the men who had joined or been drafted for the national emergency were to be demobilized and discharged from the service. From Camp Meade contingents of drafted men departed regularly for the various camps located near their homes; once they arrived at those camps, the men were given their final pay and discharged from the Army. By the end of September 1919, the 26th Infantry Regiment, as constituted during the Great War, had ceased to exist.[89]

So impressive had the 1st Division's accomplishments during the Meuse-Argonne Offensive been that on November 19 Gen. Pershing, Commander in Chief, issued General Orders Number 201; these orders were unique in that the 1st Division was singled out for commendation, the first and only time such a thing occurred in the AEF. Referring specifically to the period from October 4 through 11, Gen. Pershing wrote, in part, "The Commander-in-Chief has noted in this division a special pride of service and a high state of morale, never broken by hardship nor battle."[90]

The war was over, but the suffering of some of those who were wounded would never end. Likewise, the pain experienced by the families of those who were killed continued. Even those with loved ones who were wounded suffered the anxiety of not knowing the fate of their soldier.

It often took a great deal of time for word of a soldier's fate, whether good or bad, to reach his loved ones in the United States. Lieutenant Mansfield's parents did not receive word that their son was wounded on October 4 until they received a letter from him on November 9.[91] More striking still is the case of PFC Earl Eugene Waldvogle of Company F. A replacement who joined the company in August, Waldvogle was killed in action on October 4, the first day of the advance. In late November, he was listed among those who had died of disease, but Waldvogle's parents in Iowa never received word of this; they continued to hope to hear from their son. It wasn't until April 17, 1919, however, that Waldvogle's mother received an official telegram stating that her son had been killed in action.[92] In another example, Pvt. Domenico Dirigo of Company E was listed as missing in action October 1-11; it wasn't until November 28 that his status was changed to severely wounded October 2. However, two days later, under the poignant title "Italian Boy in 26th Infantry Among the Missing," his hometown newspaper displayed his military photograph with the news that he was still missing. There is no information recorded as to when his family was notified of his actual status; Dirigo returned home in September, 1919.[93]

The human cost of the war went far beyond those men killed, wounded, missing, or maimed. The families of these men suffered in other ways, sometimes for years. Corporal Fred L. Brooks of Company C was killed in action on October 5; it wasn't until December that his mother, Dora Brooks of Youngstown, Indiana, was notified.

Upon receipt of this sad news, Mrs. Brooks' health began to fail. Despite the efforts of her other children to cheer her, Mrs. Brooks' health continued to decline until her death in mid-April 1920. One of those killed on October 4 was Inman Gillen of Headquarters Company. Gillen was one of three sons of D. Pink and Mary Jane Gillen of Leesville, Indiana. Tragically, all three of the Gillen boys died in military service during the war. Inman and one of his brothers died as a result of combat while the third brother died from disease.[94] These were tragic stories that must have played out in innumerable homes across the United States in the ensuing years.

The case of Cpl. Gustav A. Erickson of Company E vividly illustrates the anguish those at home felt. Erickson was killed in action on October 4 and buried on the battlefield near Exermont. Erickson's brother, Sgt. Carl W. Erickson, assigned to a Provisional Motor Supply Train, also died in France during the war. After the war, the boys' grieving parents and sister wrote to the Graves Registration Service of the Quartermaster Corps to request that the boys' bodies be returned to the US together for interment, side by side, in Arlington National Cemetery. The Ericksons wrote:

> Could it be possible to have the two Sons remains burried *Side* by *Side* in Arlington Cemetery. As our Boys was together all their life in our Home and in Camp untill arriving in France they were parted and could never locate each other anny more. We would rejoice in our Sorrow to know that we could find the remains of our boys resting *together* in American Soil [*sic*].[95]

On December 22, 1921, the Erickson brothers were laid to rest, side by side, in Arlington National Cemetery.

Jessie Skilling, widow of battalion surgeon 1st Lt. John G. Skilling, who was killed in action on November 6, became impatient with the War Department's various early reports of her husband's death. Her impatience and anger was vented in an April 3, 1919, letter to the Army Adjutant General:

> Your information has been most cold and cruel and besides the crushing blow of death your Department causes those left to mourn, to die over and over again, as a result of your incompetent, unsystematic manner of giving out data to those people who gave and lost their all.

Skilling's body was recovered and reburied in an American cemetery in France.

Not every family received word of the burial of their loved ones. As late as mid-1920s there were approximately 100 to 150 men of the 26th who had died in France and who remained unaccounted for. Second Lieutenant Eric H. Cummings, killed while commanding a connecting patrol on October 4, was one such man. Despite strenuous efforts to locate Cummings's body through the mid-1920s, his remains were never found. The pain that this caused his mother Eliza is evident in the letter she wrote to the Graves Registration Service in 1921: "We never received any of his effects, and we are trying to find whether he was really killed or shell shocked or

Giorno, Antonio 2825621
Pvt. Co E 26th Inf.

Cited in GO 13, Hq 2d Inf. Brig. Camp Zachary Taylor, Ky., Dec. 31, 1919, for gallantry in action and devotion to duty during the operations of the 2d Inf. Brig. in the first phase of the Meuse-Argonne Offensive Oct 1 to 12, 1918.

vc 2-18-25

Award card showing the citation and authorization for a silver citation star (subsequently the Silver Star medal) for Antonio Giorno, Company E, 26th Infantry Regiment. Dozens of men of the regiment were cited in brigade and division orders "for gallantry in action" during the Meuse-Argonne Offensive. (Courtesy Wisconsin Adjutant General's Office, via Wisconsin Veterans Museum.)

blinded and in some hospital or even worse a prisoner, or lost identity [*sic*]." And in a letter to the officer in charge of the American cemetery in Romagne, Eliza wrote: "Our Gov. has misinformed us seems as to get us to give up the search which I never can [*sic*]."[96]

The War Department in Washington and AEF headquarters in Europe expended great efforts to find the missing men and answer anxious inquiries from relatives. At the other end of the chain, Lt. Fullerton, regimental adjutant, reported on the difficulties that descended on the record keepers and officers at the regimental level:

> Nearly 10,000 men and more than 300 officers have passed through this outfit [the 26th Infantry Regiment] since June, 1917. Just imagine the inquiries that come in about their wounds, their death, their place of burial, their efforts. It would drive a strong man to drink.[97]

And in March 1919, Lt.Col. Roosevelt, by then back in the US, sent Fullerton "a raft of letters that have been forwarded to me from various places, asking about men who have been killed, are missing, etc." and asking for Fullerton's assistance in researching and answering these heart-rending letters. Little wonder, then, that Fullerton lamented, "if I stay in the Army much longer as a Regimental Adjutant I will probably take my place among the 'most hated.' It is an undesirable job but I must see it through."[98]

Another unusual case, but with a happier ending, is that of Pvt. Sam Herzog. Herzog, of Company C, was gassed and evacuated during the battle; somehow his

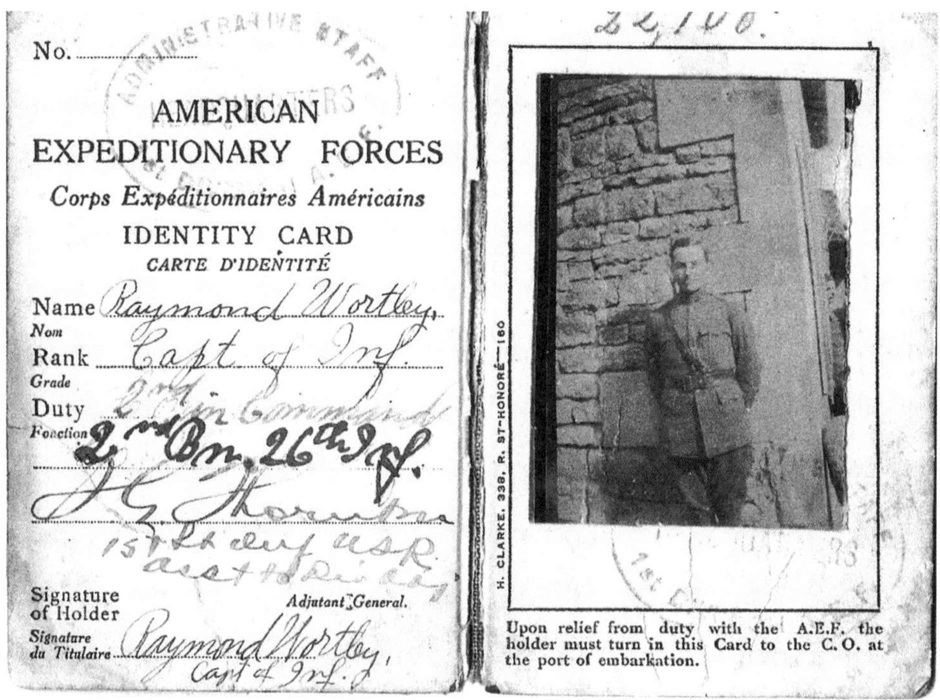
No. ....

AMERICAN
EXPEDITIONARY FORCES
Corps Expéditionnaires Américains
IDENTITY CARD
CARTE D'IDENTITÉ

Name Raymond Wortley.
Nom
Rank Capt of Inf.
Grade
Duty 2nd Bn Command
Fonction 2nd Bn. 26th Inf.

Adjutant General.

Signature of Holder
Signature du Titulaire Raymond Wortley, Capt of Inf.

22,100.

H. CLARKE, 338, R. ST-HONORÉ—180

Upon relief from duty with the A.E.F. the holder must turn in this Card to the C.O. at the port of embarkation.

AEF identity card for Captain Raymond D. Wortley, commander of the 2nd Battalion, 26th Infantry Regiment; Captain Wortley was killed in action, October 4, 1918. (Courtesy Janice Buchanan.)

records showed that he had died a prisoner of war in Germany. At his home in San Francisco years after the war, Herzog, unaware of that particular version of his wartime service, was surprised to receive an official letter of inquiry from the War Department in April 1921, asking about the report of his death in Germany. Herzog replied that, "the report was exaggerated."[99]

It would take weeks to resolve yet another kind of missing in action report: those men who had been taken prisoner. Wilfrid Hocking, a member of Company G, was wounded early in the battle, and he "spent an entire night on the battlefield with an arm and leg shattered by German bullets" before he was picked up by the Germans and taken prisoner.[100] Private William Litch was captured on October 4 and taken to a prison camp near Baden, Germany. A few days before the armistice, Litch bribed a guard with "a piece of soap not much larger than his thumb." The guard looked the other way, and Litch left the stockade, making his escape good.[101]

The end of the war brought another kind of accounting and reckoning as officers wrote citations for men who had performed bravely but had not been recommended for the Distinguished Service Cross. The 1st Division and both infantry brigades published such citations in official orders. Many men, such as Pvt. Antonio Giorno of Company E, were cited for "gallantry in action and devotion to duty" for the period 1 through 12 October. In Giorno's case, and no doubt in many others, the citation is brief and general. The record of his specific deeds among the nightmarish hills and woods so long ago has passed with the sands of time. Such citations allowed the recipient to affix a small silver star device to the ribbon of their Victory Medal. In 1932, Congress authorized the creation and award of the Silver Star medal, then, as now, the nation's third highest award for battlefield valor. These same citations were authorization for the Great War Doughboys to apply for and receive the new Silver Star medal. There is no record that Giorno ever applied for or received the medal; perhaps he, like others, felt that their deeds during the battle were in the past and there was no need to rehash the memories.[102]

Ten:

ANALYSIS

Postwar analysis by many participants revealed some interesting conclusions about the role of the 26th during the Meuse-Argonne Offensive. Major Frasier felt that the regiment's, and indeed the division's, success would have been achieved more quickly and with less bloodshed if they had been allowed to attack on October 1, upon getting into position. He felt that the three-day delay allowed the enemy time to rest and to regain some balance and some reinforcements.[1] Lieutenant Forster questioned the choice to use the 1st Battalion to lead the assault. The 1st Battalion had lain three full days on the jump-off line under fire while also sending out patrols. Although the other battalions had been exposed equally as long just back of the jump-off line and had lost men during artillery and gas attacks, it is certain that the 1st Battalion was the least rested battalion prior to the attack.[2]

The heavy losses of the division (nearly 8,500 men) and the regiment were attributed to the stubbornness of the resistance. In addition, even with artillery preparation, the infantry faced well-prepared positions, heavily interspersed with machine gun nests. Too, on the first day the 26th advanced through two deep ravines, Rau de Mayache and Exermont Ravine, without room to maneuver. The support and reserve battalions advanced too closely upon the lead battalion in this instance, and as a result they suffered heavy casualties. Mostly these losses fell upon the infantrymen. As Maj. Legge, writing for the Infantry School Advanced Officers' Class in 1922, said: "As we are all infantrymen it is scarcely necessary for me to say where the brunt of the battle was borne."[3]

Still, losses were not as great as they might have been. Analysts credited the thick fog that greeted every morning attack with allowing the Doughboys to advance farther with fewer casualties than might have been the case if enemy machine gunners and artillery observers would have been able to see the advancing lines.[4]

Analysts generally praised the artillery support. Major Legge, in commenting about the artillery support to the division as a whole, stated that the support "was always close and particularly successful."[5] The operations report written immediately after the first battle, on October 18, stated the artillery support was excellent.[6] Major

Frasier said that the artillery support "was about what might be expected in future actions," and that infantry should be prepared to "advance under its own fire when necessary." Writing from bitter experience still vivid in his memory, Frasier said that for the infantry to successfully advance following a rolling barrage, that barrage must be "sufficiently thick in proportion to the resistance offered by the enemy." Still, Frasier said that the artillery, "cooperated with us to the limit of its ability."[7] For their part, the 7th Field Artillery, which supported the 26th Infantry, felt they had supported the infantry to the best of their ability and very effectively. During the infantry assaults on Hill 212, Hill 272, and Arietal Farm, the artillery regiment played "a stream of shells up the valleys and around the hills under the guidance of reports from their liaison officers with the infantry – Lieutenants [Charles L.] Camp, [Lansing] McVickar, [Thomas F.] Furness, and [Harry T.] Madden." Such cooperation between the infantry and artillery was necessary for success in any attack.[8]

Accuracy of artillery fire seems to have been a problem on at least four occasions when "short" rounds fell on American soldiers. In addition to the American artillery fire that caused casualties in Company K on October 5, the short 155mm rounds reported by the 1st Battalion on October 6, and the short rounds that exploded in the trees above the heads of Company F on October 9, it appears that some American rounds fell on Company C just before jump off on October 4. Pvt. Carmine Ferritto reported that the rounds "fell short causing us many casualties at the same time the Germans put their barrage on top of us causing us many more casualties, we were pretty badly shot up before we got started."[9]

Both Legge and Frasier declared the use of an "accompanying gun" (i.e., a 75mm fieldpiece that accompanied a battalion during an assault, instead of staying behind with the rest of the artillery regiment) to be "of doubtful value."[10] These guns were too far forward at jump-off and were thus easily subject to enemy artillery fire. Once observed, even concealment could not save these guns. Furthermore, being horse-drawn, it was difficult for them to keep up with the advancing riflemen. Rexmond Cochrane, who made an extensive study of the division artillery's performance during the battle, felt that the assault guns provided "some psychological, if not actual, benefit."[11] Major Frasier, though, felt that placing a gun in an advanced position, under the command of "an able and aggressive artilleryman," would be "of the utmost assistance" if it could follow the infantry advance with its fire.[12] This idea, basically an artillery piece in an advanced position but not directly accompanying the assault waves, seems to have worked later in the battle.

Of interest is the view of Maj. Oscar I. Gates, commander of the 2nd Battalion, 7th Field Artillery Regiment, which supported the 26th Infantry. Major Gates, writing after the war, said that the "accompanying guns were of no assistance, neither [one] firing a single round and our suffering casualties amounting to 90% animals and 70% men.[13] He concluded that the use of horse-drawn guns in this manner was impractical, due to its vulnerability and the ruggedness of the terrain.[14]

Likewise, analysts praised the use of machine guns during the battle. Noting that the guns had been used for "overhead fire and for covering gaps in the line," Maj. Legge called their use "intelligent."[15] Major Frasier mentioned the "tremendous power" of the guns in assisting advancing infantrymen and in breaking up counterattacks. He also praised "long range indirect fire," whereby the guns fire over high terrain, obstacles, or friendly forces at the enemy who is, to the machine gunners, unseen.[16]

Both Legge and Frasier praised the 37mm gun performance. These guns, assigned to Headquarters Company, advanced with the assault waves and performed very well against machine gun nests. Lieutenant Forster stated that the "value of the 37mm gun as an accompanying weapon was fully justified by its performance in the attack." Frasier also said that the three-inch light Stokes mortars were properly used, but Legge, in speaking of the division as a whole, felt that these guns "could not be effectively supplied with ammunition."[17] The three-inch mortars were part of Headquarters Company and accompanied the assault battalion, while the larger six-inch mortars were assigned to the Trench Mortar Battery, part of the division artillery. The V.B. grenade, or rifle grenade, "proved itself an excellent weapon over hilly terrain."[18]

These infantry support weapons, especially machine guns, were crucial to an attacking wave of infantry. Properly employed, they could break up enemy strong points and machine gun nests, or suppress enemy riflemen forming for the inevitable counterattack. In order to do this, they needed to be fairly close to the leading edge of the battle. The tactics as employed during the Great War usually dictated that these weapons would follow immediately to the rear of the assault companies, some 400 yards behind the leading elements of the assault. They simply could not advance with the leading infantry platoons; their heavy loads would have prevented them from keeping up, and their slow movement would have made them ideal targets for German artillery and machine guns. When, as always happened, the leading infantry became hung up, it was very difficult for the machine gunners, cannoneers, and mortar men to advance to their support. According to one 1st Division machine gunner, "each man carried in addition to his full pack, helmet, gas mask, pistol, belt and pistol ammunition, a machine gun or tripod or two boxes of machine gun ammunition each containing 250 rounds – total weight from 80 to 100 pounds."[19]

These men had to struggle with their heavy, cumbersome loads over muddy, shell-torn ground before they could be of material assistance to the advancing infantry. To resupply them with ammunition, especially during an advance, was extraordinarily difficult, yet in order for an attack to succeed, that is precisely what was required, an overwhelming amount of firepower delivered at the right place, at the right time. [20]

The great depth of the 26th, especially during the initial attack, was a boon to supply and flank protection. The regiment, with all three battalions advancing, was almost a mile in depth. Although the regiment received heavy machine gun and artillery fire from the right, outside of the division's zone, throughout the battle, they were not seriously subjected to infantry attack from that direction, even though hostile troops were always at hand on the right. The great depth of the regiment dissuaded any attack.

Liaison between and among companies, battalions, and with regimental headquarters was rated as very good. Commanders relied on telephone and runners; communications as far back as regimental headquarters was difficult but effective. Major Frasier noted the "excellent cooperation between companies, battalions and regiments, and between divisions." Likewise, he lauded the cooperation between the rifle companies and their supporting machine gun companies.[21] The operations report of October 18 declared liaison "remarkably good." The report singled out the work of the signal personnel as "especially commendable." Due to the overall good communications, the report said, Col. Erickson was able to stay in constant touch with the assaulting battalions and "was able to direct operations personally."[22] Also to be taken into account is the large gap between the time a message was sent and the time when it was received, as evident on many extant field messages.

Treatment and evacuation of the wounded seems to have suffered from a lack of adequate manpower to attend to these functions. The rugged terrain and appalling weather, combined with enemy shellfire even in the rear areas, made it difficult to move wounded men farther to the rear. Two aid men per company were insufficient to help the large number of wounded men during the drive. Casualties among the medical officers and men further depleted the available help. Detailing riflemen as stretcherbearers caused a decrease in combat effectiveness for the regiment, and Maj. Frasier noted the tendency of able-bodied men to linger in the rear areas after helping the wounded to the aid stations. The men improvised, using machine gun and ammunition carts to haul men back on their return trips to the rear. The situation was summed up eloquently by Capt. Edgarton, both of whose aid men had survived the entire battle: "Two men per company and no stretcher bearers is not enough. The fields we went over are soaking with the blood of American soldiers who bled to death without aid."[23]

Supply of food and ammunition for the front line companies was barely satisfactory. Carrying such items over rugged terrain in the pitch dark under shellfire was always extremely difficult and hazardous. The men sometimes went without food, especially during the days of attack in early October, but this is not surprising. When an incompetent officer was removed from this duty, it fell upon a senior NCO, who then carried it out at least satisfactorily. In the field messages, there is at least some mention of an ammunition shortage, but it's not known how severe or widespread this shortage was; it might simply have been a "routine" request for resupply. At least one 26th Doughboy commented on the support rendered by the YMCA. Charles Evans stated that the charitable agency "braved the fiercest fire to bring cigarettes and chocolate to the men." Evans had "nothing but greatest praise for these tireless workers."[24]

The 26th's handling of enemy prisoners seems to have been satisfactory. The 1st Division had orderly procedures in place to handle prisoners of war. According to Field Order 47, 1st Division AEF, October 2, 1918, prisoners of war were to be escorted by a military police (MP) detachment to the divisional prisoner of war enclosure (PWE) at Cheppy. From there, MPs were to escort prisoners to the corps enclosure at Raucourt. The Field Order contained other particulars related to the registering, counting, and interrogation of prisoners; an annex to the order declared that prisoners were not to be molested or deprived of their personal property.[25]

However, the exigencies of combat precluded following these directives to the letter. It appears the 26th, as did other regiments, sometimes used riflemen to escort prisoners from the firing line to regimental headquarters. From there, headquarters used division military police to escort prisoners to division headquarters farther to the rear. Some of the other regiments in the division, however, sent riflemen from the line to escort prisoners all the way back to division headquarters. Colonel Greely, chief of staff of the 1st Division, later recalled that, "it seemed to me that the guards selected by the front line units were usually amongst the smallest men they had and not infrequently were 'Warps.'" The colonel possibly meant to use the word "Wops," a derogatory term then common used to refer to Italian Americans, hundreds of whom were in the 1st Division; no doubt other immigrant groups, most of which were well-represented in the 26th's ranks, could also have been identified by this term.[26]

In any event, the 26th was able to, on at least one or two occasions, elicit important military information from prisoners taken by them. Captain Thomas, regimental intelligence officer, relayed this information up the chain of command; what impact this had on operations is hard to determine. On the other hand, many of the Germans whom the Doughboys of the 26th were likely to come into contact with were machine gunners who typically fought to the death as rear guards. Those who did surrender were fortunate to be taken alive. As Lt. Fullerton wrote, "We didn't take many [prisoners], they were all machine gunners. Sufficient said."[27]

The regimental officers performed well and showed initiative. On October 4, when the 1st Battalion became hung up in Rau de Mayache, Capt. Youell, commander of the 2nd Battalion in support, moved forward to converse with Maj. Legge, 1st Battalion commander. The two agreed to have the 2nd Battalion pass through the 1st Battalion; this idea was relayed to Col. Erickson, the regimental commander, who readily assented. On October 5, Maj. Frasier, commanding the 3rd Battalion in reserve, found the lead battalions virtually in line to his front. He re-deployed his battalion to better secure the flank and rear, and once again Col. Erickson agreed to this plan. These are but two examples of regimental officers exercising initiative in the heat of battle when conditions required immediate action and communication to the rear was delayed. Captain Cornish applauded the "high type of leadership displayed by the officers."[28] Lieutenant Forster praised Col. Erickson, who kept his PC close to the lead battalions' PCs. Erickson also "made his presence felt by frequent messages to the front lines."[29]

Some of the 26th's company grade officers – captains and lieutenants – had seen military service before the war. For example, Lt. Willis C. Conover of Company C served in the US Navy from 1911 to 1914, having enlisted at the age of seventeen. Following his discharge, Conover enlisted in the New York National Guard and then saw service in the Regular Army before being commissioned in July 1918. Captain Raymond Wortley, 2nd Battalion commander at the start of the offensive, had served as an enlisted man in the California National Guard before the war and had received a Regular Army commission by 1916. Likewise, 2nd Lt. Charles Fullerton had joined the Illinois National Guard in 1903 at the age of sixteen. In 1916, he attended an officers training camp and was commissioned in 1917. Captain Ethelbert Van Ness Burrell, commander of Company B, had prior enlisted service as far back as the Spanish American War. And Maj. Rice Youell, Captains George Cornish, Hamilton Foster, Paul Starlings, and James Manning were all Regular Army officers by 1916.[30]

Other junior officers, however, were not professional soldiers. Rather, most of them were products of the various officer training camps started in 1917 at places like Plattsburgh, New York, and Fort Sheridan, Illinois. Many of the officers had been commissioned for less than a year. Yet almost all of them had, by this time, seen combat, and they had learned lessons in what historian Richard S. Faulkner calls "the school of hard knocks." The men had, to some degree, learned what part of official AEF tactical doctrine to retain, what part to discard, and what part to modify.

It will be recalled that on October 4 Lt. Mansfield of Company E watched his men advance and remarked that the waves looked like men moving forward as if on maneuvers. Such a formation, while visually splendid and inspiring, was unlikely to be effective against machine gun nests. Later that day the 2nd Battalion would move forward in small groups, by rushes and bounds, and on October 10 the same battalion advanced in small bounds until the objective was reached. Likewise, the 3rd Battalion, at dawn on October 4, began to use the natural cover of the terrain as they moved forward. Such adaptations to the realities of combat were signs of a painful learning curve.

Although it might be fairly argued that the high number of casualties suffered by the regiment indicates that the junior officers had not yet fully learned their lessons, it must also be borne in mind that these officers were still constrained by the physical limitations of the Great War battlefield. They fought under a paradigm for which they were not responsible and which they were powerless to change. Despite it all, they, for the most part, performed their difficult duties well.

Likewise, the men performed very well, as all analysts agreed. Major Legge commented on their "aggressiveness and willingness to go forward," while Capt. Cornish noted their, "will to conquer which implied high morale."[31] Major Frasier called the men "brave and stubborn," and said they were "at all times full of the offensive spirit."[32] Lieutenant Forster felt that the previous successes of the regiment, especially in the St. Mihiel Offensive, encouraged "high morale and fighting determination and efficiency."[33]

Many of the men in the 26th were fairly new replacements, coming to the regiment in mid-to-late-August, fresh from the United States and with minimal training. Lieutenant Forster commented upon the "division spirit" that was prevalent throughout the division and was developed and fostered by successes on the battlefield; the replacements that came into the division in August "had heard of the division in the rear and were willing to accept the help of the seasoned veterans. Their word to the newcomer was law."[34] That the regiment sufficiently imbued in these new men the spirit and pride associated with the 1st Division and adequately prepared them for combat is evident in the results.

While the regiment, and division, suffered great casualties, it also made great gains. True, it did not achieve its initial objectives on schedule, but all conditions must be taken into account. Most of the time, the regiment performed while "insufficiently fed and with practically no sleep."[35] Lieutenant Forster, speaking of the combat that ended on October 12, recalled that the men had "lived in the open for twenty days with no cover except their shelter halves which were never pitched [i.e., made into tents]."[36] It is difficult to compare regiments, even within the same division. Differences in terrain, enemy resistance and fortifications, and weather, to name just three factors, render any such comparisons as "apples to oranges" at best. The German soldiers facing the regiment, some of whom were rated as first-class troops, showed a marked inclination to stay and fight throughout most of the campaign; their resistance was characterized as stubborn and desperate.[37] All things considered, the 26th Infantry Regiment performed very well under harsh conditions against a determined enemy in well-fortified and defended positions.

Appendix A:

ROLL OF HONOR, 26TH INFANTRY REGIMENT, SEPTEMBER 26 TO NOVEMBER 30, 1918.

It is difficult to compile a complete list of those men who were killed in action, died of wounds, or missing in action for the Meuse-Argonne Offensive. There are two extant lists of members of the 26th Infantry Regiment who died during the war. The list in *History of the First Division During the World War, 1917-1919* (Philadelphia: The John C. Winston Company, 1922) shows cause of death (killed, died of wounds, died of disease, died while a prisoner of war), but does not give date of death. The list in Bushnell Fullerton's *The Twenty-Sixth Infantry in France* (Martin Flock & Co., Frankfort, Germany, 1919) does give date of death but purports to include only those killed or died of wounds. When the two lists are compared, some discrepancies come to light. Some men listed as killed in action or died of wounds in Fullerton are listed as having died of disease in *History of the First Division*. At least one man who was wounded but survived the war is listed as having died while a prisoner of war in *History of the First Division*. And some men are omitted from both lists. I have chosen to include all those in Fullerton's list who died sometime between the start of the offensive and the end of November 1918, coupled with the additions found in other records. The list includes some men who died of disease during that period, on the theory that the rough campaigning might have contributed to their sickness. Some men died after the end of November, and it's certainly possible that they died as a result of wounds suffered during the battle, but it is more likely that they died of disease not directly related to the campaign. I have corrected any known misspellings.[1]

Captains

Roll of Honor Chart

NAME	COMPANY	DATE OF DEATH
CAPTAINS		
Foster, Hamilton K.	A	Oct. 2
Wortley, Raymond D.	2nd Batt.	Oct. 4
FIRST LIEUTENANTS		
Sands, Walter A.	H	Oct. 4
Skilling, John G.	Med. Det.	Nov. 6
SECOND LIEUTENANTS		
Amory, Thomas D.	D	Oct. 3
Anderson, Morgan M.	I	Oct. 5
Brown, Bayard	K	Oct. 10
Cummings, Eric H.	C	Oct. 1-11
Dillon, Harry	C	Oct. 4
Gholson, Samuel G.	MG	Oct. 4
Reed, George A.	MG	Oct. 4
Sheridan, Phillip B.	L	Oct. 9
SERGEANTS		
Barton, Roy W.	B	Oct. 9
Carroll, Morris	A	Oct. 4
Deighan, Harold	F	Oct. 6
Jenson, Ejner C.	C	Oct. 5
Koerner, Herman	G	Oct. 5
Monty, Arthur	A	Oct. 4
Mullins, Denver S.	I	Nov. 8
Neathery, Roy A.	H	Oct. 7
Powell, Thomas	D	Oct. 7-8
Ripperdon, Sherman	G	Oct. 2-12
Roob, Raymond	I	Oct. 20
Shenk, Alfred H.	MG	Nov. 6
Stallings, Al. H.	A	Oct. 3
Steinbacher, Royal P.	L	Oct. 9
CORPORALS		
Allen, Arthur	A	Oct. 4
Baranski, William	F	Oct. 6
Benson, Walt F.	M	Oct. 9
Berghus, William J.	G	Oct. 2-12
Bohn, Henry	H	Oct. 4-11

Brabo, Henry F.	H	Oct. 10
Bradford, Ray S.	F	Oct. 4
Brenton, Frank H.	B	Oct. 9
Brooks, Fred L.	C	Oct. 5
Brown, Oscar E.	A	Oct. 1-11
Buckles, Robert A.	F	Oct. 5-11
Clayton, John N.	D	Oct. 5
Daniel, Nick	F	Oct. 5
Dean, Percy A.	L	Oct. 7
Egan, Charles	H	Oct. 4
Erickson, Gustav A.	E	Oct. 4
Erickson, Virgil	MG	Oct. 2
Evering, Walter C.	HQ	Nov. 8
Fenton, Neal D.	Med. Det.	Oct. 9
Gagnon, Armand A.	A	Oct. 4-11
Hall, Eugene	B	Oct. 9
Hatfield, John D.	E	Oct. 9
Hopkins, Frederic B.	MG	Oct. 4
Hrenko, Mike	B	Oct. 5
Kelly, John	A	Oct. 2
Kurland, Benjamin	K	Oct. 4
Leander, Axel	C	Oct. 12
Lee, William F.	L	Oct. 5
Matthews, Harry A.	MG	Nov. 6
Montgomery, Sidney	A	Oct. 8
Moore, Leslie	A	Oct. 4
Nauss, Jacob	C	Oct. 6
Prout, William L.	MG	Oct. 5
Quilty, Edward W.	H	Oct. 4
Robinson, Cloy M.	L	Oct. 5
Sezenski, Walter	D	Oct. 6
Sheppard, Edward O.	D	Oct. 7
Skitarelich, George	G	Oct. 5
Stevenson, James L.	L	Oct. 10
Tyrus, Mathew F.	E	Oct. 9
Zak, Harry	D	Oct. 7. 18

MECHANICS		
Swan, John	K	Oct. 7. 18
Wooten, John	F	Oct. 4-11
COOKS		
Gustafson, Leon E.	E	Oct. 1-11
BUGLERS		
Billings, John A.	A	Oct. 7
PRIVATES FIRST CLASS		
Brandt, Henry A.	M	Oct. 3
Brock, Frank T.	C	Oct. 8-18
Buchalski, Stanley	A	Oct. 5
Ciranny, Louis	Med. Det.	Oct. 7
Colantoni, Antino	D	Oct. 5
Collier, Frank V.	A	Oct. 4
Crow, Charles C.	HQ	Oct. 6
Dougan, Francis E.	MG	Nov. 6
England, Richard	M	Oct. 3
Gesinski, Charles	HQ	Oct. 6
Houston, William M.	C	Oct. 1
Irving, William P.	A	Oct. 5
Johnson, Orland E.	F	Oct. 1-11
Jones, David O.	MG	Oct. 6
Kevill, De Forest	H	Nov. 24
Lieberman, Harry L. Sup.	Oct. 2	
Margeas, Bill	D	Oct. 6
Mincey, Fayette	A	Oct. 1-11
O'Keefe, Thomas J.	H	Oct. 5
O'Neill, Robert D.	MG	Oct. 8
Phillips, Haskell	F	Oct. 18
PRIVATES		
Abrams, Harry	D	Sep. 27
Adams, Will-am H.	I	Oct. 6
Allein, William	HQ	Oct. 6
Allengham, Jesse F.	C	Oct. 8
Armstrong, John	A	Oct. 6-8
Arneman, Rudolph	B	Oct. 6
Arthur, McKinley	B	Oct. 6
Baggett, Joseph B.	A	Oct. 6

Barryman, Clifford W.	A	Oct. 2
Barton, Alva R.	F	Oct. 18
Baylor, Fred C.	B	Oct. 5
Bengston, Eugene	E	Oct. 1-11
Bennett, William	E	Oct. 9
Berghoefer, Arthur A.	H	Oct. 1-11
Bernard, William P.	D	Oct. 5
Berndt, Frank C.	D	Oct. 5
Betson, Ira G.	A	Oct. 6
Bican, Joe	A	Oct. 6
Bloetcher, Fred	A	Oct. 30
Bonkowski, Eugene	D	Oct. 5
Bonnett, John A.	E	Oct. 1-11
Boricki, Paul	B	Oct. 7
Bottino, Chauncey	B	Oct. 5
Bouts, Walter E.	B	Oct. 9
Boyce, Joseph W.	HQ	Oct 5
Boyd, John R.	A	Oct. 5
Boyd, Sandy	E	Nov. 8
Bramblett, John E.	E	Oct. 1-11
Briggs, Ralph S.	F	Oct. ?
Brown, William	A	Oct. 5
Bruner, Earl L.	F	Oct. 7
Bullers, Frederick	D	Oct. 3
Bunck, Henry	B	Oct. 5
Bundy, Elmer	F	Oct. 6
Burwell, James A.	I	Oct. 9
Cala, Piote	F	Oct. 1-11
Carter, William B.	B	Oct. 6
Caspary, Steven H.	F	Oct. 4
Cater, Ira	A	Oct. 16
Chambers, William E.	C	Oct. 1
Chiesa, Carmelo	B	Oct. 7
Clementson, Artur	A	Oct. 6
Cohen, Albert Jr.	H	Oct. 4-11
Compney, Ronald C.	L	Oct. 5
Conboy, Peter	E	Oct. 23
Crammer, Ralph	B	Oct. 7-8
Crandall, Louis	C	Oct. 6
Cuchick, Charles	B	Oct. 8

Dallison, James A.	E	Oct. 9
Dawn, John R.	L	Oct. 7
Davis, Jacob A.	B	Oct. 8
Davis, Stanley L.	I	Oct. 6
Deitrick, George W.	MG	Nov. 6
Denton, Lesley	Med. Det.	Oct. 8
De Pialo, Calegero	E	Oct. 8
Dingler, Luther	D	Oct. 4
Dixon, William	C	Oct. 8
Dodge, Edward	A	Oct. 4
Donnelly, Thomas	C	Oct. 4
Donnelly, William B.	I	Oct. 5
Dorsey, Harry H.	E	Oct. 4
Downs, Oliver H.	MG	Oct. 9
Dugan, Frank	H	Oct. 26
Elliot, Judge D.	C	Oct. 10
Ellis, Frank	C	Oct. 8
Emerick, Lester	A	Oct. 5
Enright, Thomas J.	I	Nov. 23
Erickson, Thomas	K	Oct. 5
Feeback, Gilbert	E	Oct. 4
Filice, Giovanni	MG	Oct. 4
Fisher, Fred F.	A	Oct. 4
Franks, John	A	Oct. 5
French, Clinton	K	Oct. 7
French, Ross E.	B	Oct. 2
Frizell, James B.	B	Oct. 8
Fugo, Ernest	A	Oct. 5
Fuller, A. A.	MG	Oct. 7
Gaines, Warren J.	G	Oct. 1-11
Gallagher, Phillip	D	Oct. 2
Gannon, Oscar	MG	Oct. 4
Garufi, Giovani	D	Oct. 7
Gavin, John	MG	Oct. 4
Gechas, Charles A.	L	Oct. 5
Gensler, Arthur	D	Oct. 4
Gerson, Raoul	B	Oct. 12
Gibson, Gail	D	Oct. 7
Giesken, Harry A.	MG	Oct. 6
Gonzales, Marcelo	C	Oct. 6

Gorbso, Frank	A	Oct. 1-11
Gosecky, Bolek	K	Oct. 4
Graham, Kenneth	D	Oct. 7
Gramoukos, Antino	D	Oct. 7
Greenfield, Samuel	B	Oct. 2
Greer, Harold C.	MG	Oct. 4
Griffin, Harrison	B	Oct. 6-9
Gross, Joseph	F	Oct. 1-11
Grover, Willard	A	Oct. 4
Haas, Edward H.	MG	Oct. 6
Hack, William J.	D	Oct. 9
Hamilton, Carl	A	Oct. 4
Hanley, Michael	E	Oct. 1-11
Hanson, Louis A.	D	Oct. 5
Harlan, Ruby B.	F	Oct. 1-11
Harold, Cornelius	G	Oct. 9
Healy, Dennis	B	Oct. 1-11
Heffron, Daniel J.	E	Oct. 1-11
Heller, Cyril L.	D	Oct. 5
Hensel, Earl L.	D	Oct. 5
Hilbreath, Dewey	MG	Oct. 4
Hilton, Ray C.	D	Oct. 9
Hoar, Emery F.	D	Oct. 1-11
Hollis, Thomas B.	D	Nov. 13
Horr, Burton G.	I	Oct. 13
Howard, John W.	C	Oct. 8
Hudson, Horace J.	A	Oct. 6
Jacobs, Harry I.	C	Oct. 1-11
Jenkins, Homer	C	Oct. 9
Jennings, Leonard H.	D	Oct. 6
Johnson, Porter W.	F	Oct. 4-7
Jones, Ernest W.	MG	Oct. 9
Kamp, Andrew W.	E	Oct. 11
Kellogg, Thomas H.	A	Oct. 5
Kelly, Ray C.	MG	Oct. 4
Kindell, Oscar	F	Oct. 1-11
Kleile, Glen F.	B	Oct. 9
Komsteller, Louis H.	E	Oct. 1-11
Konieczka, Dominick	E	Oct. 9
Kopke, Edwin F.	H	Oct. 4-11

Korkotselos, Dimitrios	G	Oct. 2-12
Kracmer, Frank	L	Oct. 5
Kucharski, Casimir	E	Oct. 4
Kuhne, Fred	L	Oct. 6
Landis, Mike H.	K	Oct. 5
Laughlin, Nicholas B.	G	Oct. 2-12
Leach, William G.	A	Oct. 6
LeSage, Clifford	H	Oct. 4-11
Lewis, Albert B.	A	Oct. 6
Lonika, John	E	Oct. 1-11
Lowyre, Garfield	B	Oct. 6
Luedtke, Albert R.	I	Oct. 5
Lukowski, Joseph A.	G	Oct. 2
Mahan, Grover C.	H	Oct. 4-11
Mann, Francis A.	D	Nov. 27
Manwaring, Ralph	MG	Oct. 9
Marcellous, Jesse J.	F	Oct. 1-11
Matejack, Edmund	B	Oct. 8
McGeough, Clement	F	Oct. 1-11
McKnight, Stanley	L	Oct. 29
McNeil, Donald	H	Oct. 9
McNitt, Shirley	M	Oct. 1-11
McWilliams, John	C	Oct. 6
Mehelas, James	A	Oct. 5
Meinen, Everett	HQ	Nov. 8
Metiviezuk, Afanasi	A	Oct. 6
Mew, Joseph W.	H	Sep. 30
Meyer, Harry	A	Nov. 18
Meyers, Joseph J.	L	Oct. 13
Mikolajcsak, Frank	F	Nov. 5-8
Milbaur, Saul	I	Oct. 5
Milford, James R.	K	Oct. 1-11
Milham, Donald F.	A	Oct. 4
Miller, Henry	A	Oct. 5
Mintz, Edward	H	Oct. 4-11
Mollineaux, George H.	I	Oct. 5
Morken, Edwin	A	Oct. 6
Morter, Harry E.	I	Oct. 4
Municheas, George K.	H	Oct. 4
Naill, John C.	MG	Oct. 4

Nicodemus, John	F	Oct. 1-11
Oberski, Tony J.	H	Oct. 7
Oestreich, Ezra H.	F	Oct. 1-12
Olchick, Alexandrine	E	Nov. 8
Olson, Christian	D	Oct. 5
O'Neil, James	F	Oct. 1-11
Oney, John W.	E	Oct. 1- 11
Orman, Carl C.	MG	Nov. 6
Page, Willie E.	HQ	Nov. 8
Palmer, Tony	E	Oct. 9
Parsons, Jesse	I	Oct. 10
Pavluk, Sarge C.	E	Oct. 1-11
Perkins, Albert E.	MG	Oct. 4
Peterson, Harry	M	Oct. 6
Pettingill, Leo H.	A	Oct. 1-11
Priester, Francis J.	D	Oct. 9
Rathburn, Lee	A	Oct. 5
Rathwisch, Herman K.	H	Oct. 1-11
Rawleigh, Martin F.	G	Oct. 7
Raza, Hypolite	F	Oct. 1-11
Richardson, James W.	A	Oct. 7
Rintala, Sam E.	A	Oct. 6
Robinson, Thomas L.	D	Oct. 7
Rogan, Carl E.	L	Oct. 5
Rolisch, Stanley	I	Oct. 8
Rosplack, John	B	Oct. 5
Rouse, Fay, E.	I	Oct. 5
Saboe, Thomas H.	D	Oct. 6
Sabol, John A.	D	Oct. 7
Santino, Antonio	C	Oct. 11
Sanders, John E.	I	Oct. 5
Sasamowicz, Harry	E	Oct. 1-11
Schaap, Glen F.	L	Oct. 6
Scherer, William	HQ	Oct. 1
Schildknecht, Henry	D	Oct. 7
Schlegel, Rudolph	C	Oct. 8
Schnell, Edward H.	K	Oct. 4
Shaver, Clifford L.	MG	Oct. 7
Sheridan, Robert	L	Oct. 20
Sheveland, Barney	D	Oct. 4

Silker, Wyatt	M	Oct. 1
Sims, Early R.	L	Oct. 6
Sirgusa, Joseph	A	Oct. 4
Skinner, Arthur	L	Oct. 1-11
Skinner, Charles	E	Oct. 1-11
Slack, Joseph	B	Oct. 8
Smith, Fred W.	H	Nov. 6
Smith, Lyle C.	E	Oct. 1-11
Spencer, John C.	D	Oct. 6
Spencer, Leroy	A	Nov. 9
Spike, William	B	Oct. 6
Starkey, Charles L.	E	Oct. 4
Stephens, Fred L.	D	Oct. 7
Stockwell, George	M	Oct. 1-11
Stoddard, Clement	B	Oct. 9
Stouder, Harvey R.	H	Oct. 1-11
Strauser, Ernest	H	Oct. 4-11
Taylor, Harvey	A	Oct. 5
Terrill, Vernon H.	M	Oct. 9
Tettamanti, Agostino	M	Oct. 9
Thibodeau, Ignace	E	Oct. 1-9
Thomas, Joshua W.	C	Oct. 9
Thompson, Clarence	D	Oct. 6
Thompson, LeRoy E.	M	Nov. 4
Thorn, Raymond	A	Oct. 4
Towslee, Frank W.	L	Oct. 24
Tumbarello, Giacomo	A	Oct. 6
Turner, Oscar A.	C	Oct. 11
Upson, Ray S.	B	Oct. 8
Van Voorhes, Leslie	L	Oct. 1-11
Vaughn, Albert	HQ	Nov. 8
Veronovicz, Alex	E	Oct. 1-11
Voltz, Clarence V.	F	Oct. 1-11
Waldvogle, Earl M.	F	Oct. 1-12
Walsh, James L.	H	Oct. 11
Walters, John	HQ	Oct. 6
Weiglenda, George	M	Oct. 9
Williams, Marion	B	Oct. 5
Wilson, Arvie R.	L	Oct. 6
Wilson, David W.	I	Nov. 24

Wilson, Irvin	K	Oct. 7
Wilton, Raymond K.	K	Oct. 6
Winders, William N.	E	Oct. 1-11
Wolkowski, Joseph	C	Oct. 6
Wood, Walter	I	Oct. 5
Yianeles, John	E	Oct. 1-9
Zear, Leon A.	Med. Det.	Oct. 3

Appendix B:

GENERAL HEADQUARTERS, AEF, GENERAL ORDERS NO. 201

GHQ, American Expeditionary Forces, General Orders No. 201, France, Nov. 10, 1918.

1. The Commander-in-Chief desires to make of record in the General Orders of the American Expeditionary Forces, his extreme satisfaction with the conduct of the officers and soldiers of the 1st Division in its advance west of the Meuse, between October 4 and 11, 1918. During this period the division gained a distance of seven kilometers over a country which presented not only remarkable facilities for enemy defense but also difficulties of terrain for the operation of our troops.

2. The division met with resistance from elements of eight hostile divisions, most of which were first class troops and some of which were completely rested. The enemy chose to defend its position to the death, and the fighting was always of the most desperate kind. Throughout the operations the officers and men of the division displayed the highest type of courage, fortitude and self-sacrificing devotion to duty. In addition to many enemy killed the division captured one thousand four hundred and seven of the enemy, thirteen 77mm field guns, ten trench mortars and numerous machine guns and stores.

3. The success of the division in driving a deep advance into the enemy's territory enabled an assault to be made on the left by the neighboring division against the northeastern portion of the forest of Argonne, and enabled the 1st Division to advance to the right and outflank the enemy's position in front of the division on that flank.

4. The Commander-in-Chief has noted in this division a special pride of service and a high state of morale, never broken by hardship nor battle.

5. This order will be read to all organizations at the first assembly formation after its receipt.

By Command of General Pershing: James W. McAndrew, Chief of Staff; Official: Robert C. Davis, Adjutant General.[1]

NOTES

Introduction

1. Edward G. Lengel, *To Conquer Hell, The Meuse-Argonne, 1918: The Epic Battle That Ended the First World War* (New York: Henry Holt and Company, 2008), pp. 49, 57.
2. Ibid., pp. 57-62.
3. Ibid., pg. 4.

Chapter 1: Overview; The 26th Infantry Regiment from 1901 to 1918

1. The Society of the First Division, *History of the First Division During the World War, 1917-1919* (Philadelphia: The John C. Winston Company, 1922), pg. 1 (hereafter cited as *History of the First Division*).
2. Jonathan Gawne, "The WWI Squad, Section and Platoon," *The G.I. Journal*, Vol. 1, Number 3, Fall, 1996, pp. 10-11.
3. Capt. G. R. F. Cornish, "The Twenty-Sixth Infantry (U.S.) in the Meuse-Argonne Offensive" (The Command and General Staff School, Fort Leavenworth, Kansas, 1931); Maj. P. A. Hodgson, "A Critical Analysis of the Infantry Scheme of Maneuver of the 1st Division at the Battle of St. Mihiel" (Command and General Staff School, Fort Leavenworth, Kansas, n. d.), pg. 4.
4. William G. Dooly, Jr., *Great Weapons of World War I* (New York: Walker and Company, 1969), pg. 109; Richard S. Faulkner, *The School of Hard Knocks: Combat Leadership in the American Expeditionary Forces* (College Station, TX: Texas A&M University Press, 2012), pg. 253.
5. Dooly, *Great Weapons of World War I*, pg. 91; Faulkner, *The School of Hard Knocks*, pp. 253-254.
6. Dooly, *Great Weapons of World War I*, pp. 84-85; Faulkner, *The School of Hard Knocks*, pg. 244.
7. Faulkner, *The School of Hard Knocks*, pp. 247-248.
8. Dooly, *Great Weapons of World War I*, pg. 95; Faulkner, *The School of Hard Knocks*, pg. 248.
9. Dooly, *Great Weapons of World War I*, pp. 11-12.

10. Ibid., pg. 17.
11. Ibid., pp. 100-101.
12. Ibid., pg. 73; Capt. Alban B. Butler, Jr., *"Happy Days!" A Humorous Narrative in Drawings of the Progress of American Arms, 1917-1919* (Washington, D.C.: Society of the First Division, A.E.F., 1928), pg. 81.
13. Ibid., pg. 109.
14. Rexmond C. Cochrane, "The 1st Division Along the Meuse, 1-12 October 1918" (Gas Warfare in World War I, Study Number 8, US Army Chemical Corps Historical Studies. U.S. Army Chemical Corps Historical Office, Army Chemical Center, Maryland, 1957), pg. 9.
15. Lengel, *To Conquer Hell*, pg. 76.
16. Byron Farwell, *Over There: The United States in the Great War, 1917-1918* (New York: W. W. Norton & Company, Ltd., 1999), pp. 44-45, 304-305.
17. Bushnell Fullerton, *The Twenty-Sixth Infantry in France* (Martin Flock & Co., Frankfort, Germany, 1919), pp. 3-5, http://webpages.charter.net/gallison2b/History%20of%2026th%20Regiment%20in%20WWI.pdf (the pagination for this online version differs from the print version and other online versions).
18. Fullerton, *The Twenty-Sixth Infantry*, pg. 5; *History of the First Division*, pp. 6-7.
19. Faulkner, *The School of Hard Knocks*, pp. 142-143.
20. Fullerton, *The Twenty-Sixth Infantry*, pg. 6.
21. Ibid., pg. 7.
22. Ibid., pg. 8.
23. Ibid., pp. 9-11.
24. Ibid., pp. 12-13.
25. Ibid., pg. 13.
26. Ibid., pp. 13-22.
27. Ibid., pp. 23-28.
28. Ibid., pg. 27.
29. Maj. Walter R. McClure, "Operations of Company M, 26th Infantry (1st Division) in the St. Mihiel Offensive, September 12 – September 16, 1918" (The Infantry School, Advanced Course, 1932-1933, Fort Benning, Georgia), pp. 2-3.
30. Fullerton, *The Twenty-Sixth Infantry*, pg. 33.
31. Ibid.
32. McClure, "Operations of Company M," pg. 6.
33. Ibid., pg. 34.
34. Ibid., pg. 35.
35. McClure, "Operations of Company M," pp. 13-14; James H. Hallas, *Squandered Victory: The American First Army at St. Mihiel* (Westport, CT: Praeger, 1995), pp. 173-174.
36. McClure, "Operations of Company M," pg. 15; Hallas, *Squandered Victory*, pp. 173-174.

37. Fullerton, *The Twenty-Sixth Infantry*, pg. 35-36. Figures for losses per company can be reconstructed from morning reports. For example, Company E reported at least two men killed or died of wounds, 12 men wounded, and three men missing in action. Company F, also in the 2nd Battalion, reported at least one man killed by shellfire and at least 10 men wounded by shell fire; also, at least four men from that company were reported as missing in action. See Record Group 120, Folder 33.6, Box 81, 1st Division Historical File, Records of the American Expeditionary Forces, 1917-1923, National Archives and Records Administration (NARA), College Park, Maryland (hereafter cited as RG 120).
38. McClure, "Operations of Company M," pg. 18
39. Fullerton, *The Twenty-Sixth Infantry*, pg. 41.

Chapter 2: "Grueling days," September 26 through October 3

1. Cochrane, "The 1st Division Along the Meuse," pg. 5.
2. Lt. Col. Theodore Roosevelt, *Average Americans*, (New York: G. P. Putman's Sons, 1920), pg. 194, http://books.google.com.
3. Cornish, "The Twenty-Sixth Infantry," pg. 3; for Capt. Wortley, e-mail from Janice Buchanan to the author, October 20, 2013. Ms. Buchanan is a distant cousin of Capt. Wortley.
4. Capt. Lyman S. Frasier, "Operations of the Third Battalion, 26th Infantry, First Division, in the Second and Third Phases of the Meuse-Argonne Offensive" (The Infantry School, Fort Benning, Georgia, 1926-27), pg. 2. Although Frasier was a major during the battle, he reverted to the rank of captain after the war, and that was his rank when he wrote his monograph.
5. Fullerton, *The Twenty-Sixth Infantry*, pg. 42
6. *The Story of the Twenty-Eighth Infantry in the Great War*, (N.p., n.d., but Germany, 1919), not paginated.
7. "WWI Anniversary Kindles Memories for City's 'Yankee Doodle Dandies,'" *Zanesville Times Recorder*, Zanesville, Ohio, June 26, 1977, page 12-A, column 1, http://newspaperarchive.com/.
8. Capt. Albert B. Helsley, "Operations of the Machine Gun Company, 16th Infantry (1st Division), During the Second Phase of the Meuse Argonne Offensive, September 30 - October 12, 1918" (The Infantry School, Advanced Course, Fort Benning, Georgia, 1930-1931), pg. 15.
9. Cornish, "The Twenty-Sixth Infantry," pg. 3; Record Group 117, Entry E, Box 188, Records of the American Battle Monument Commission, NARA (hereafter cited as RG 117), map annotations by Thomas Cornell and David Meeker.
10. Cornish, "The Twenty-Sixth Infantry," pg. 3; Frasier, "Operations of the Third Battalion," pg. 7.
11. Cornish, "The Twenty-Sixth Infantry," pg. 2.
12. Ibid., pg. 4.
13. Cochrane, "The 1st Division Along the Meuse," pg. 6.

14. Cornish, "The Twenty-Sixth Infantry," pg. 3; *History of the First Division*, pg. 180.
15. Handwritten notes by Maj. Legge in Cornish, "The Twenty-Sixth Infantry."
16. Handwritten notes by Maj. Legge in Cornish, "The Twenty-Sixth Infantry"; RG 120, Field Messages. These field messages, communication slips sent to and from regimental headquarters, were written by officers during the heat of battle. Those originating at regimental headquarters were written by Colonel Erickson or someone on the regimental staff, and those from the battalions were written by battalion commanders. The copies at NARA bear numerous times and notation numbers, and I've chosen to omit these in the notes.
17. RG 120, Field Messages.
18. RG 117, letter and map annotations by Conover, February 21, 1929.
19. RG 117, letter from Conover, February 21, 1929; RG 120, Field Messages.
20. RG 120, Field Messages.
21. Ibid.
22. Ibid. Early drafts of the American Battle Monuments Commission's *1st Division Summary of Operations in the World War* (Washington, D.C.: United States Government Printing Office, 1944) indicated that the 363rd Infantry Regiment was directly in front of the 1st Battalion, 26th Infantry Regiment, and disallowed the claim that there were no friendly troops in front of the 1st Battalion. This interpretation was probably derived from field messages to the effect that the 363rd Infantry had advanced ahead of the 1st Battalion's line. In reality the 363rd was to the right of, and in advance of, the 1st Battalion; there were, indeed, no friendly troops directly in front of the 26th Infantry Regiment.
23. RG 120, Field Messages; RG 120, Entry 1241, Box 50, Folder 201-33.1, Operation Report, October 1, 1918; RG 117, letter and annotated map from Cornell, June 27, 1927.
24. Cornish, "The Twenty-Sixth Infantry," pg. 3; *History of the First Division*, pg. 180.
25. RG 120, Field Messages.
26. Fullerton, *The Twenty-Sixth Infantry*, pg. 43; see also Cornish, "The Twenty-Sixth Infantry," and Frasier, "Operations of the Third Battalion."
27. Cornish, "The Twenty-Sixth Infantry," pg. 3; Frasier, "Operations of the Third Battalion," pg. 8.
28. Frasier, "Operations of the Third Battalion," pg. 54.
29. RG 120, Daily Operation Reports, October 2, 1918.
30. Frasier, "Operations of the Third Battalion," pg. 7.
31. Ibid., pp. 8-9.
32. Alan Tallis, "Diary of a Shavetail." http://www.tallisfamily.co.uk/ShavetailDiary.htm, used courtesy of Alan Tallis, United Kingdom; (hereafter cited as "Diary of a Shavetail").
33. Cochrane, "The 1st Division Along the Meuse," pp. 16-18.
34. Ibid., pg. 1.

35. "Over the Top 17 Times in 6 Months of Action," *McKean Democrat*, Smethport, Pennsylvania, May 23, 1919, page 1, column 1, http://newspaperarchive.com/.
36. RG 120, Field Messages.
37. RG 117, letter from Meeker, August 30, 1926.
38. For the patrol on October 2, see: *Infantry in Battle* (Washington, D.C.: The Infantry Journal, Inc., 1939), pp. 340-343; RG 117, letter from Meeker, August 30, 1926; Roosevelt, *Average Americans*, pp. 191-192; and Distinguished Service Cross citation for Lt. Amory at Military Times Hall of Valor, http://projects.militarytimes.com/citations-medals-awards/recipient.php?recipientid=10430 (hereafter cited as Hall of Valor). After the war there was some difficulty in locating Lt. Amory's body. Even Amory's brother, 1st Lt. George S. Amory, Company L, 303rd Infantry Regiment, attempted to ascertain the grave's location. George Amory provided descriptions of what appears to be two different grave locations: one "on the high ground that lies between the Rau de Mayache and the Rau de Gauffre (Exermont Ravine), overlooking the Neuville le Comte Farm," and another that places the grave north of Eclisfontaine, outside the 26th's zone. Sergeant Charles W. O'Connor, who buried Amory, provided a detailed sketch that appears to support the Eclisfontaine location, although the site of the patrol was actually on the high ground between Rau de Mayache and Exermont Ravine, approximately 2,700 yards away from the grave as indicated by O'Connor. O'Connor indicates that he buried Amory just a short distance from where he fell. It is possible that O'Connor's sketch refers to a location in the Rau de Mayache/Exermont Ravine area that might be similar in appearance to the Eclisfontaine area. The only other option is that Amory and Meeker became utterly confused and mistook the Eclisfontaine area as the intended target of their patrol; in other words, the patrol went to the wrong area and no one ever realized the mistake. I think that scenario is unlikely. Amory's body was eventually found after much exhaustive searching on the part of engineer troops still in the area in 1919. The initial grave's location is not found in the burial file. See RG 92, Thomas Amory, Burial Information File, various correspondence.
39. RG 120, Field Messages.
40. Fullerton, *The Twenty-Sixth Infantry*, pg. 43; Cornish, "The Twenty-Sixth Infantry," pg. 4; Capt. Barnwell R. Legge, "The First Division in the Meuse Argonne, September 26 - October 12, 1918" (The Infantry School, Fort Benning, Georgia, 1922-1923), pg. 10 (although Legge was a major during the battle, he reverted to the rank of captain after the war and that was his rank when he wrote his monograph); RG 120, Field Messages; "University Student Cited For Gallantry," *Fayetteville Democrat*, Fayetteville, Arkansas, June 26, 1920, page 1, column 6, http://newspaperarchive.com/.

41. Hall of Valor, Silver Star citation for Lt. Meeker, and Distinguished Service Cross citation for Pvt. McEntee. In July 1918, Congress authorized the award of a small silver star device to be affixed to the ribbon of any service or campaign medal for each act of gallantry for which a person might be cited in orders. Called the Silver Citation Star, it was, in August 1932, changed to the current Silver Star medal, the nation's third highest award for valor. See David Borthick and Jack Britton, *Medals, Military and Civilian, of the United States*, Tulsa, OK: Military Collectors' News Press, 1984, pg. 147.
42. RG 120, Field Messages.
43. Ibid.
44. RG 117, letter from Meeker, August 30, 1926.
45. RG 120, Field Messages.
46. *History of the First Division*, pg. 185.
47. Tallis, "Diary of a Shavetail."
48. Information on Capt. Wortley from e-mail, Janice Buchanan to the author, October 20, 2013. Includes a transcript of one page of a letter written by a regimental chaplain to Capt. Wortley's mother sometime after the war. Captain Wortley was Ms. Buchanan's distant cousin. See also http://www.arlingtoncemetery.net/raymond-wortley.htm.
49. Table of Organization in Gawne, "The WWI Squad, Section and Platoon," pg. 11; Company rosters, September 30, 1918, courtesy Colonel Robert R. McCormick Research Center, First Division Museum at Cantigny, Wheaton, Illinois. The table reflects only those officers actually on duty in each rifle company; a few officers were detailed to various duties, such as duty with Supply Company or battalion headquarters, and they are not reflected in these totals. Company E's roster is missing, and the numbers here are based upon my research in other sources. Company G's roster is unclear, and the numbers here are my best interpretation of the information on the roster.

Chapter 3:
"The fire in front was withering," October 4

1. Tallis, "Diary of a Shavetail." Regarding the identity of "Sergeant O," Sgt. John T. O'Keefe was the only sergeant whose surname begins with the letter "O" on Company E's August, 1918, roster; the September 1918, roster is missing, and he does not appear on the October, 1918, roster.
2. Ibid.
3. Ibid.
4. Frasier, "Operations of the Third Battalion," pg. 9.
5. Record Group 92, Records of the Office of the Quartermaster General, National Archives and Records Administration, Giovanni Filice, Burial Information File (hereafter cited as RG 92); RG 92, Samuel Gholson, Burial Information File; RG 92 George Reed, Burial Information File.
6. Handwritten notes by Maj. Legge in Cornish, "The Twenty-Sixth Infantry."

7. Capt. George J. Forster, "Operations of the 37-mm Gun Platoon, 26th Infantry, 1st Division, October 1-12, 1918." The Infantry School, Advanced Course, Fort Benning, Georgia, 1931-1932, pg. 3.
8. Cornish, "The Twenty-Sixth Infantry," pg. 4; RG 92, Eric H. Cummings, Burial Information File.
9. RG 117, letter from Meeker, August 30, 1926.
10. RG 120, Field Messages, including hand-drawn map.
11. Tallis, "Diary of a Shavetail."
12. Ibid.
13. Cochrane, "The 1st Division Along the Meuse," pg. 22
14. Tallis, "Diary of a Shavetail."
15. Cochrane, "The 1st Division Along the Meuse," pp. 21-22; Cornish, "The Twenty-Sixth Infantry," pg. 5; RG 92, Eric Cummings Burial Information File. It is difficult to ascertain the precise date and circumstances of Lt. Cummings's death. He was originally listed as missing in action as of October 8, 1918. Several other men from Company C are listed as missing in action on that date, but this is not surprising since it was the first day on which the 1st Battalion had time to regroup, reorganize, and attempt an accurate head count. In 1921, Cummings's mother, Eliza, seeking information about her son, wrote to War Department officials indicating that Lt. Cummings had been in command of a liaison group between the 1st and 32nd Divisions, which would have been on October 4. In 1926, a fellow member of Company C, Sgt. Paul Braun, wrote indicating his opinion that Cummings had probably been a part of the patrol that was wiped out early in the fighting. In 1930, a letter from the War Department indicates that previous reports were in error and that Cummings had been officially listed as killed in action on October 4, 1918.
16. Hall of Valor, Distinguished Service Cross citation for Pvt. Lundegard.
17. RG 92, Hamilton K. Foster, Burial Information File, testimonies of Lt. P. R. Caruthers, Cpl. George Whitson, and Pvt. Lewis Sowards, Company A; Roosevelt, *Average Americans*, pg. 192.
18. Hall of Valor, Distinguished Service Cross citation for Lt. Baxter.
19. Forster, "37-mm Gun Platoon," pg. 3.
20. Ibid.
21. Tallis, "Diary of a Shavetail."
22. RG 117, letter from Edgarton, June 29, 1926; see also Fullerton, *The Twenty-Sixth Infantry.*
23. RG 92, Walter H. Sands, Burial Information File, testimony of Pvt. Francis McDonald, Company H; e-mail from Janice Buchanan to the author, October 20, 2013.
24. Tallis, "Diary of a Shavetail;" For a discussion of American tanks during the Meuse-Argonne Offensive, see Capt. Dale E. Wilson, *Treat 'em Rough! The Birth of American Armor, 1917-20* (Novato, CA: Presidio Press, 1990), pp. 156-174. The tanks mentioned by Lt. Mansfield might have been those crewed by Sergeants Harold J. Ash and Harley R. Nichols, and Cpl. Albert J. Zimborski (see Wilson, *Treat 'em Rough!*, pp. 159-161.)

25. For information on Brown and Anderson, see Fred Girton and Myron E. Adams, *The History and Achievements of the Fort Sheridan Officers' Training Camps* ([Chicago?]: The Fort Sheridan Association, 1920), pp. 52 and 40, respectively, http://babel.hathitrust.org; Frasier, "Operations of the Third Battalion," pg. 9.
26. Cochrane, "The 1st Division Along the Meuse," pp. 23.
27. RG 92, Giovanni Filice, Burial Information File; RG 92, Samuel Gholson, Burial Information File, testimony of Sgt. Clinton Allen; RG 92 George Reed, Burial Information File.
28. Cornish, "The Twenty-Sixth Infantry," pg. 5.
29. RG 117, letter from Edgarton, June 29, 1926.
30. Frasier, "Operations of the Third Battalion," pg. 10.
31. Hall of Valor, citations for Sgt Dobbs, Sgt. Pusitz, Cpl. Crist, Pvt. Lindsay, and Pvt. Victor.
32. Quoted in Forster, "37-mm Gun Platoon," pg. 5; see also RG 120, Field Messages.
33. RG 120, Field Messages.
34. Girton and Adams, *The Fort Sheridan Officers' Training Camps*, pg. 72, http://babel.hathitrust.org; *The Wisconsin Alumni Magazine*, Volume 25, Number 1 (November 1923), http://digicoll.library.wisc.edu/.
35. Carmine Ferritto Collection (AFC/2001/001/49562), Veterans History Project, American Folklife Center, Library of Congress, Washington, D.C. Ferritto dictated his diary to Cpl. Albert Phillips in Germany in 1919. The original has many misspellings, and I have corrected them to ease readability (hereafter cited as Ferritto Collection, LOC).
36. Quoted in Forster, "37-mm Gun Platoon," pg. 5; see also RG 120, Field Messages.
37. Michigan Genealogy Trails, http://genealogytrails.com/mich/news1919.html.
38. RG 120, Field Messages.
39. Quoted in Forster, "37-mm Gun Platoon," pg. 6; see also RG 120, Field Messages.
40. Capt. Carl Hanton, et al., *The 32nd Division in the World War, 1917-1919* (Madison, WI: Wisconsin War History Commission, 1920), pg. 98, 100.
41. Cornish, "The Twenty-Sixth Infantry," pg. 3, 5, and handwritten notes by Maj. Legge; Hall of Valor, Silver Star citation for Capt. Wortley and Distinguished Service Cross citation for Maj. Youell; RG 117, letter from Edgarton, June 29, 1926; RG 92, Raymond Wortley, Burial Information File.
42. Tallis, "Diary of a Shavetail."
43. Forster, "37-mm Gun Platoon," pg. 7.
44. Virginia Military Institute, *Record of Service in the World War of V.M.I. Alumni and their Alma Mater* (Richmond, VA: The Richmond Press, 1920), pg. 152, http://babel.hathitrust.org.
45. RG 92, Raymond Wortley, Burial Information File, testimony of PFC Alex Mears, Company H; e-mail from Janice Buchanan to the author, October 20, 2013; see also Frasier, "Operations of the Third Battalion."
46. RG 117, letter from Edgarton, June 29, 1926.
47. Cornish, "The Twenty-Sixth Infantry," pg. 5.
48. Forster, "37-mm Gun Platoon," pp. 6-7.

49. Tallis, "Diary of a Shavetail."
50. Forster, "37-mm Gun Platoon," pg. 7.
51. Ibid., pp. 7-8.
52. Tallis, "Diary of a Shavetail."
53. Ibid.
54. Hall of Valor, Distinguished Service Cross citation for Maj. Youell.
55. RG 117, letter from Edgarton, June 29, 1926; handwritten notes by Maj. Legge in Cornish, "The Twenty-Sixth Infantry." Lieutenant Mansfield wrote that the 2nd Battalion passed the 1st Battalion beginning at 1100, about four hours earlier than the time suggested by Maj. Legge, 1st Battalion commander. Lieutenant Forster said that the passage was approved just after noon. Probably the 2nd Battalion passed the 1st sometime after 1100, but before 1500, in the high ground between Rau de Mayache and the Exermont Ravine. See Tallis, "Diary of a Shavetail" and Forster, "37-mm Gun Platoon."
56. Hall of Valor, Distinguished Service Cross citations for Cpl. Echols and Cpl. O'Keefe.
57. Frasier, "Operations of the Third Battalion," pp. 10-11.
58. Cochrane, "The 1st Division Along the Meuse," pg. 23; see also Fullerton, *The Twenty-Sixth Infantry.*
59. Fullerton, *The Twenty-Sixth Infantry*, pg. 44.
60. Forster, "37-mm Gun Platoon," pg. 8.
61. Cochrane, "The 1st Division Along the Meuse," pg. 25; see also Fullerton, *The Twenty-Sixth Infantry*, pg. 44. According to the field messages, at one point Capt. James A. Edgarton, commander of Company F, the left assault company of the 2nd Battalion, reported that his company had reached Hill 212 and that Company E, to his right, had not yet advanced as far. Edgarton does not mention this in his postwar letter to the American Battle Monument Commission. Instead, he indicates his final position by nightfall on October 4 as just north of Exermont Ravine. See RG 120, Field Messages, and RG 117, letter from Edgarton, June 29, 1926. Captain Shipley Thomas, 26th Infantry Regiment intelligence officer, claimed that the 26th did not take the high ground north of Exermont Ravine until the following day, October 5, but this is certainly an incorrect recollection; Thomas also claimed that during October 4 and 5, the strength of the 2nd Battalion went from thirty officers and 1,000 men down to six officers and 285 men. Interestingly, Thomas "served continuously with this regiment throughout every engagement in which the 1st Division took part, and was never wounded or evacuated from the front for any cause." He was "the only combat officer of this regiment holding this record." See Capt. Shipley Thomas, *The History of the A.E.F.* (New York: George H. Doran Company, 1920), pp. XII, 300-301, https://archive.org/details/historyaef00thomgoog.
62. Cornish, "The Twenty-Sixth Infantry," pg. 6.
63. Frasier, "Operations of the Third Battalion," pg. 11.
64. Forster, "37-mm Gun Platoon," pp. 8-10.
65. Cornish, "The Twenty-Sixth Infantry," pg. 5; Frasier, "Operations of the Third Battalion," pg. 11.

66. Cornish, "The Twenty-Sixth Infantry," pg. 6.
67. RG 117, letter from Edgarton, June 29, 1926.
68. Frasier, "Operations of the Third Battalion," pg. 11.
69. RG 117, letter from Conover, February 21, 1929.
70. Fullerton, *The Twenty-Sixth Infantry*, pg. 79.
71. Hall of Valor, Distinguished Service Cross citations for Maj. Legge.
72. Roosevelt, *Average Americans*, pp. 176.
73. Frasier, "Operations of the Third Battalion," pg. 25.
74. Ibid.
75. Ibid., pp. 25-26.
76. Handwritten notes by Maj. Legge in Cornish, "The Twenty-Sixth Infantry."
77. Hall of Valor, Distinguished Service Cross citation for Lt. Grant.
78. Frasier, "Operations of the Third Battalion," pp. 26-27.
79. Ernest L. Wrentmore, *America's Youngest Soldier: On the Front Lines in World War One* (Steve W. Chadde, 2014), pg. 44. Originally published as *In Spite of Hell: A Factual Story of Incidents that Occurred During World War I, as Experienced by the Youngest Soldier to Have Seen Combat Duty With the American Expeditionary Forces in France – As a Member of the Famous Company I, 60th Infantry, Fifth (Red Diamond) Division*, New York: Greenwich Book Publishers, 1958.
80. Forster, "37-mm Gun Platoon," pg. 9.
81. Frasier, "Operations of the Third Battalion," pg. 27.
82. Forster, "37-mm Gun Platoon," pg. 21.
83. Ibid.

Chapter 4:
"Vicious in the extreme," October 5

1. Legge, "The First Division in the Meuse-Argonne," pg. 21.
2. Ibid., pp. 21-22.
3. Capt. Leonard R. Boyd, "The Operations of the 1st Battalion, 16th Infantry, in the Second Phase of the Meuse-Argonne," (The Infantry School, Company Officers' Course, Fort Benning, Georgia, 1924-1925), pp. 3-4.
4. Frasier, "Operations of the Third Battalion," pg. 12; Cornish, "The Twenty-Sixth Infantry," pg. 6.
5. Legge, "The First Division in the Meuse-Argonne," pg. 22.
6. Frasier, "Operations of the Third Battalion," pg. 12.
7. Legge, "The First Division in the Meuse-Argonne," pg. 22; Cornish, "The Twenty-Sixth Infantry," pg. 6.
8. Frasier, "Operations of the Third Battalion," pg. 12.
9. Ibid. Some sources say that tanks were not used during the second day.
10. Fullerton, *The Twenty-Sixth Infantry*, pg. 44; Cornish, "The Twenty-Sixth Infantry," pg. 5.

11. Three early references declare that the 1st Battalion reached Hill 212 quickly. *The Twenty-Sixth Infantry in France* (written by Capt. Bushnell Fullerton, regimental adjutant, in Germany in 1919) and *History of the First Division during the World War, 1917-1919* (written by a committee of division officers and reviewed carefully, 1919-1922), both stated that the 1st Battalion advanced quickly to Hill 212. Lieutenant Forster, who commanded the 37mm gun platoon, writing in 1931, stated that the 1st Battalion "advanced rapidly to Hill 212 about one kilometer in advance of the position of the night before. The battalion sent small groups forward and then advanced through the four paths cut in the wire." (see Forster, "Operations of the 37-mm Gun Platoon," pg. 10) However, Maj. Frasier, commander of the 3rd Battalion, who wrote the fullest account, indicates that the advance was difficult and heavily contested. By following the progress of the battle from the perspective of Maj. Frasier's 3rd Battalion, coupled with Lt. Forster's account and field messages, we can get an overall picture of the 26th's advance on October 5. The times reported here are a harmonization of all the various sources. Although Maj. Frasier's account is detailed and thorough, I feel that the times he recorded might be a bit later than the times of the actual occurrences.
12. Frasier, "Operations of the Third Battalion," pg. 13.
13. Ibid., pg. 16.
14. Ibid., pg. 13.
15. Hall of Valor, Distinguished Service Cross citations for Lt. Cornell and Pvt. Dugan.
16. "Letter Tells How Soldier Met Death," *The Racine Journal-News*, Racine, Wisconsin, April 16, 1919, page 1, column 5, http://newspaperarchive.com/.
17. Forster, "37-mm Gun Platoon," pg. 7; see also RG 120, Field Messages.
18. RG 120, Field Messages.
19. RG 117, letter and annotated map from Cornell, June 27, 1927.
20. Forster, "37-mm Gun Platoon," pg. 11.
21. Frasier, "Operations of the Third Battalion," pp. 13-14.
22. Hanton, et al., *The 32nd Division*, pp. 98-100.
23. Frasier, "Operations of the Third Battalion," pg 14.
24. Ibid., pg. 15.
25. Forster, "37-mm Gun Platoon," pg. 11.
26. Frasier, "Operations of the Third Battalion," pg 15.
27. Ibid., pp. 15-16.
28. Ibid., pg. 16, showing later times.
29. Ibid., pg. 16, showing later times; Forster, "37-mm Gun Platoon," pp. 11-12; RG 120, Field Messages.
30. RG 120, Field Messages.
31. Ibid.
32. Forster, "37-mm Gun Platoon," pg. 12.
33. Ibid., pp. 12-13.
34. Ibid., pg. 15.

35. Frasier, "Operations of the Third Battalion," pp. 16-17.
36. Ibid., pp. 17-18.
37. Hall of Valor, Distinguished Service Cross citation for Lt. Forster.
38. Forster, "37-mm Gun Platoon," pg. 13; see also RG 120, Field Messages.
39. Frasier, "Operations of the Third Battalion," pg. 16; *History of the Seventh Field Artillery (First Division, A.E.F.), World War, 1917-1919*, n.p., 1929, pg. 98, http://babel.hathitrust.org.
40. Forster, "37-mm Gun Platoon," pg. 13.
41. Ibid., pg. 14; RG 120, Field Messages.
42. Roosevelt, *Average Americans*, pp. 195.
43. Years later, Maj. Legge would characterize artillery support on October 5 as "weak." Capt. Cornish, however, in the same paper, wrote that "Excellent cooperation with the artillery marked the day." See Cornish, "The Twenty-Sixth Infantry," pg. 6.) Likewise, the 7th Field Artillery history stated that on this day "so close was the liaison maintained with the attacking infantry front line that at the request of the latter, special targets were picked up and destroyed." See *History of the Seventh Field Artillery*, pg. 97. Obviously the state of artillery cooperation and support was a matter of perspective.
44. Frasier, "Operations of the Third Battalion," pg. 18.
45. Ibid.
46. Ibid., pg. 19.
47. Legge, "The First Division in the Meuse-Argonne," pg. 23.
48. *History of the First Division*, pg. 196.
49. RG 92, Morgan Anderson, Burial Information File. In correspondence in the file, Capt. Starlings recalls Anderson's death as having occurred on October 4, but the type of offensive action described would have occurred on October 5. Anderson was cited for bravery in 1st Division orders, and Starlings, according to an investigator, recalled that he "died like a gallant officer leading his men." Frasier, "Operations of the Third Battalion," pp. 19-20; see also Cornish, "The Twenty-Sixth Infantry."
50. Legge, "The First Division in the Meuse-Argonne," pg. 24.
51. Frasier, "Operations of the Third Battalion," pg. 20.
52. Legge, "The First Division in the Meuse-Argonne," pg. 24.
53. Frasier, "Operations of the Third Battalion," pp. 21-22.
54. Ibid., pg. 22.
55. Ibid.; *Maryland in the World War, 1917-1919, Military and Naval Service Records*, vol. II (Baltimore: Maryland War Records Commission, 1933), pg. 1987, http://babel.hathitrust.org; Hall of Valor, Distinguished Service Cross citation for Cpl. McCoy.
56. Frasier, "Operations of the Third Battalion," pg. 22; RG 120, Field Messages.
57. Forster, "37-mm Gun Platoon," pg. 15; Butler, *"Happy Days!"* pg. 76.
58. RG 120, Field Messages.
59. Forster, "37-mm Gun Platoon," pg. 15; see also Cornish, "The Twenty-Sixth Infantry."

60. RG 117, letter from Manning, July 23, 1926.
61. Ibid.
62. Ibid.
63. Ibid.; Cornish, "The Twenty-Sixth Infantry," pg. 6.
64. Cornish, "The Twenty-Sixth Infantry," pg. 6.
65. RG 117, letter from Manning, July 23, 1926.
66. Cochrane, "The 1st Division Along the Meuse," pg. 28.
67. Handwritten notes by Maj. Legge in Cornish, "The Twenty-Sixth Infantry."
68. Shipley Thomas, *S-2 in Action* (Harrisburg, PA: The Military Service Publishing Co., c. 1940), unpaged Preface by Colonel Hjalmar Erickson, http://babel.hathitrust.org.
69. RG 120, Field Messages.
70. Frasier, "Operations of the Third Battalion," pg. 23.
71. Ibid.
72. Ibid., pp. 23-24.
73. Ibid., pp. 24-25.
74. Ibid. pg. 24.
75. Ibid.
76. RG 117, letter from Kennedy, October 12, 1928.
77. Morgan Anderson, Statement of Service Card, Wisconsin, Adjutant General's Office: Regimental Muster and Descriptive Rolls, World War I; see also information on-line, Find A Grave, http://www.findagrave.com/, and Girton and Adams, *The Fort Sheridan Officers' Training Camps*, pg. 40, http://babel.hathitrust.org.
78. Frasier, "Operations of the Third Battalion," pp. 27-28.
79. Cornish, "The Twenty-Sixth Infantry," pg. 6. As noted, the numbers for losses are estimates and don't always agree among the sources. Also, officers often made claims of having lost certain numbers of officers or NCOs, and these claims, too, sometimes conflict with other evidence. In the heat and confusion of battle, all men are not immediately accounted for; it might seem that there are "no NCOs" left at a given time, only to have some show up sometime thereafter. Letter from Lt. Fullerton to his brother Will, October 9, 1918, used courtesy of Patricia Fullerton Hamman.
80. Frasier, "Operations of the Third Battalion," pg. 28.
81. Ibid.
82. Although the general actions and movements or the 26th Infantry on October 5 are well known, the precise movements, positions, and timing of the battalions are open to question. For instance, we know that the 2nd Battalion, having passed the 1st Battalion and moved into the assault position early on October 4, occupied a position slightly ahead of the 1st Battalion on the morning of the 5th. Once the advance started, the 1st Battalion passed through the 2nd and led, with the 2nd in close support; soon the two battalions closed up and almost merged by mid-morning during the assault on Hill 212. Sometime around 1000, Col. Erickson, in an effort to organize his regiment, ordered the 2nd Battalion back to Hill 200 where, presumably, it would guard against a counterattack from the

rear and right-rear. By 1100 the 2nd Battalion was in position; nothing more is known of its activities or locations for the rest of the day. Also there is some discrepancy regarding the precise movements and timing of the other battalions. It's not clear at what point the 3rd Battalion passed the 1st and continued the assault. It probably occurred around 1315-1400 on the north slope of Hill 212, probably after the 1st Battalion reached the edge of the woods on the north slope (i.e., the first objective). Major Legge, 1st Battalion commander, states that this passage took place at the first objective at noon; Lt. Forster places it perhaps a little earlier. Major Frasier's narrative of the 3rd Battalion's advance states that, at the start of the advance, the men "moved down the slopes of Hill 212." (see Frasier, "Operations of the Third Battalion," pg. 18) The men then, under severe fire as described above, crossed the valley to the north on the way to Hill 272 and Arietal Farm, the second objective. The battalion took Arietal Farm sometime between 1430 and 1530.

83. Cornish, "The Twenty-Sixth Infantry," pg. 6; see also Fullerton, *The Twenty-Sixth Infantry,* and Cochrane, "The 1st Division Along the Meuse."
84. RG 120, Field Messages.
85. Cochrane, "The 1st Division Along the Meuse," pg. 31.
86. Ibid., pp. 31-32.

Chapter 5: "A rather sharp fight," October 6 through October 8, Notes

1. RG 120, Field Messages.
2. Ibid.
3. Frasier, "Operations of the Third Battalion," pp. 28-29.
4. Ibid., pg. 30.
5. Ibid.; *Infantry in Battle*, pg. 188.
6. RG 92, Bayard Brown, Burial Information File; Frasier, "Operations of the Third Battalion," pg. 30; Hall of Valor, Distinguished Service Cross citation for Lt. Brown. Brown's gravestone states that he was a member of Company K, and that he was "killed in the Argonne Oct 6, 1918." However, his citation for the Distinguished Service Cross does not give his company, but it states that on October 9 he assumed command after his company commander was killed. The commander of Company K, Dayton Sackett, was seriously wounded, not killed, on October 9. Sackett, in his correspondence (see RG 92, Burial Information File), declares that Brown was wounded on October 6 and died at the field hospital at 0100 on October 7. See http://www.findagrave.com/ and Girton and Adams, *The Fort Sheridan Officers' Training Camps*, pg. 52, http://babel.hathitrust.org.
7. Frasier, "Operations of the Third Battalion," pg. 30.
8. Cornish, "The Twenty-Sixth Infantry," pg. 7.
9. *Infantry in Battle*, pp. 189-190.
10. Frasier, "Operations of the Third Battalion," pg. 31; *Infantry in Battle*, pg 190.

11. Hall of Valor, Distinguished Service Cross citation for Cpl. Fenton.
12. Frasier, "Operations of the Third Battalion," pg. 31; *Infantry in Battle*, pg 190; see also Cornish, "The Twenty-Sixth Infantry."
13. Frasier, "Operations of the Third Battalion," pg. 32.
14. Frasier, "Operations of the Third Battalion," pg. 31; *Infantry in Battle*, pg 190.
15. Hall of Valor, Silver Star citation for Lt. Pool.
16. Frasier, "Operations of the Third Battalion," pg. 32; *Infantry in Battle*, pg 190.
17. Frasier, "Operations of the Third Battalion," pg. 33.
18. Ibid., pg. 34.
19. Ibid.
20. *History of the Seventh Field Artillery*, pg. 97.
21. Hall of Valor, Distinguished Service Cross citation for Maj. Frasier.
22. Hall of Valor, Distinguished Service Cross citation for Sgt. Blalock. Sergeant Blalock's award narrative gives the date of action as October 7, however the 26th's operations report states that this action occurred during the patrols against Hill 269 on October 6. See RG 120, "Report on the Operations of the 26th Infantry Northeast [*sic*] of Verdun, Sept. 30, 1918 to Oct. 11, 1918," October 18, 1918.
23. Fullerton, *The Twenty-Sixth Infantry*, pg. 45; Cornish, "The Twenty-Sixth Infantry," pg. 7.
24. Handwritten notes by Maj. Legge in Cornish, "The Twenty-Sixth Infantry."
25. Frasier, "Operations of the Third Battalion," pg. 34.
26. Ibid.
27. Ibid., pg. 35.
28. Ibid.
29. Cochrane, "The 1st Division Along the Meuse," pg. 34.
30. Frasier, "Operations of the Third Battalion," pg. 35; Cornish, "The Twenty-Sixth Infantry," pg. 7.
31. Cornish, "The Twenty-Sixth Infantry," pg. 7.
32. Forster, "37-mm Gun Platoon," pg. 16.
33. Ibid.
34. Frasier, "Operations of the Third Battalion," pg. 36.
35. Ibid.
36. Willliam C. Levere, *The History of Sigma Alpha Epsilon in the World War* (Published by the Fraternity, 1928), pg. 430, http://babel.hathitrust.org. See also Gordon B. Knowles, Statement of Service card, copy in the author's possession.
37. RG 117, letter from Edgarton, June 29, 1926.
38. RG 120, Field Messages.
39. RG 117, letter from Manning, July 23, 1926.
40. RG 120, Field Messages; Fullerton, *The Twenty-Sixth Infantry*, pg. 45; RG 117, letter from Manning, July 23, 1926.
41. RG 117, letter from Manning, July 23, 1926.
42. RG 120, Field Messages.
43. Hall of Valor, Distinguished Service Cross citation for Lt. Sisson. Lieutenants Jones and Williams performed burials, see RG 92, various files.

44. Letter from Fullerton to his mother, October 22, 1918, letter from Fullerton to his brother Will, October 9, 1918, and letter from Fullerton to "Louise," October 24, 1918, used courtesy of Patricia Fullerton Hamman.
45. Frasier, "Operations of the Third Battalion," pg. 36.
46. Thomas, *S-2 in Action*, unpaged Preface by Colonel Erickson.
47. Helsley, "Operations of the Machine Gun Company, 16th Infantry," pg. 31.
48. Frasier, "Operations of the Third Battalion," pg. 37.
49. Frasier, "Operations of the Third Battalion," pp. 37-39.
50. Ibid., pg. 38.
51. Legge, "The First Division in the Meuse-Argonne," pg. 26.
52. Frasier, "Operations of the Third Battalion," pg. 38.
53. Ibid.
54. Ibid.
55. Ibid., pg. 39.
56. Ibid.
57. Ibid., pp. 39-40.
58. Ibid., pg. 40.
59. Tallis, "Diary of a Shavetail."
60. Frasier, "Operations of the Third Battalion," pg. 40.
61. Forster, "37-mm Gun Platoon," pp. 17-18; see also RG 120, Field Messages.
62. Frasier, "Operations of the Third Battalion," pg. 41; see also Cornish, "The Twenty-Sixth Infantry."
63. Helsley, "Operations of the Machine Gun Company, 16th Infantry," pg. 41.
64. RG 120, Field Messages.
65. RG 117, letter from Richards, September 4, 1926.
66. Ibid.
67. RG 120, Field Messages.
68. Ibid.
69. Ibid.
70. Ibid.
71. Ibid.
72. *History of the First Division*, pg. 205.
73. Letter from Fullerton to his brother Will, October 9, 1918, used courtesy of Patricia Fullerton Hamman.
74. Ibid.

Chapter 6: "Machine gunners ... fought like wild men," October 9 and October 10

1. Cochrane, "The 1st Division Along the Meuse," pg. 38.
2. Cornish, "The Twenty-Sixth Infantry," pg. 7; letter from Fullerton to his brother Will, October 9, 1918, used courtesy of Patricia Fullerton Hamman.

3. *600 Days' Service: A History of the 361st Infantry Regiment of the United States Army* (n.p., n.d. but c1919), pp. 97-100; *The Story of the 91st Division* (San Francisco: 91st Division Publication Committee, 1919), pp. 44-45.
4. Frasier, "Operations of the Third Battalion," pp. 41-42.
5. Ibid.
6. RG 120, Field Messages.
7. Frasier, "Operations of the Third Battalion," pg. 42; see also Cornish, "The Twenty-Sixth Infantry."
8. Cochrane, "The 1st Division Along the Meuse," pg. 39; Forster, "37-mm Gun Platoon," pg. 18.
9. RG 117, letter from Richards, September 4, 1926.
10. Ibid.; for the engineers' version of the events on and around Hill 269, see *A History of the 1st US Engineers, 1st US Division* (Coblenz, Germany, 1919), pp. 42-46, http://babel.hathitrust.org/.
11. Legge, "The First Division in the Meuse-Argonne," pg. 31; Hall of Valor, Distinguished Service Cross citation for Lt. Richards and Silver Star citations for Sgt. Charles, Sgt. Lynch, Cpl. Johnson, PFC Jones, PFC Waldroop, Pvt. Downs, Pvt. Lozupone, Pvt. Manwaring, and Pvt. Townsend.
12. Handwritten notes by Maj. Legge in Cornish, "The Twenty-Sixth Infantry."
13. RG 120, Field Messages.
14. Roosevelt, *Average Americans*, pg. 193.
15. RG 117, letter from Edgarton, June 29, 1926.
16. Ibid.; Maj. Frasier, commander of the 3rd Battalion in support, stated that the 2nd Battalion jumped off at 0830, but this would contradict the divisional order that stated the 26th and 28th regiments would start at H+22 minutes. Also, Maj. Legge, commander of the 1st Battalion in division reserve, stated, in what was surely a typographical error, that the 1st Battalion led the assault on this day. The mistake was repeated by Capt. Cornish later, but it was also corrected by Maj. Legge in his hand-written notes included with Capt. Cornish's report. All other early sources are correct in stating that the 2nd Battalion led the assault on October 9. See RG 120, Field Messages, Frasier, "Operations of the Third Battalion," and Cornish, "The Twenty-Sixth Infantry," including Legge's handwritten notes.
17. Hall of Valor, Distinguished Service Cross citation for Lt. Sackett.
18. *Pierce County in the World War* (Red Wing, MN: Red Wing Publishing Company, 1919), pg. 114, http://books.google.com.
19. Frasier, "Operations of the Third Battalion," pp. 42-43.
20. Hall of Valor, Distinguished Service Cross citation for Sgt. Wilkinson.
21. Forster, "37-mm Gun Platoon," pp. 18, 23.
22. Frasier, "Operations of the Third Battalion," pg. 43.
23. *History of the First Division*, pg. 209.

24. RG 92, Phillip Sheridan, Burial Information File, testimony of Pvt. Kimel O. Wilson, Company L. Sheridan was still wearing identification tags with his former unit designation, 301st Machine Gun Battalion, 76th Division (a depot division). Such was the dearth of experienced combat officers that Sheridan, apparently trained as a machine gun officer, was placed into a rifle company as a platoon leader. Captain John Coonan, a member of Company L who commanded it in Germany after the war, called Sheridan "an officer of great courage." For Darkoski, see Hall of Valor, Distinguished Service Cross citation for Sgt. Darkoski.
25. RG 120, Field Messages.
26. Ibid.
27. Ibid.
28. Ibid.
29. Ibid.
30. Ibid.; Frasier, "Operations of the Third Battalion," pg. 43.
31. RG 120, Field Messages.
32. Ibid.
33. Frasier, "Operations of the Third Battalion," pp. 43-44.
34. Ibid., pg. 44.
35. RG 120, Field Messages.
36. Ibid.; Frasier, "Operations of the Third Battalion," pg. 44.
37. RG 120, Field Messages.
38. Ibid.
39. Forster, "37-mm Gun Platoon," pp. 18, 20.
40. RG 120, Field Messages.
41. Ibid.
42. Frasier, "Operations of the Third Battalion," pg. 44; Terry M. Bareither, editor, *An Engineer's Diary of the Great War* (West Lafayette, IN: Purdue University Press, 2002), pp. 102-103. By October 10, the front lines were about 2.5 miles north of Exermont, a village in Exermont Ravine at the junction of the 18th and 28th Infantry Regiments' zones; what Lt. Spring experienced might have been the fire from bypassed German machine guns in the woods and hills north of Exermont. But the rear areas weren't safe as late as October 13, a day after the 26th's relief. Cpl. Elmer W. Sherwood, 150th Field Artillery Regiment, 42d Division, reported on that day that, "'Fritz' is shelling [Exermont] now and a building topples over occasionally." See Elmer W. Sherwood, *The Diary of a Rainbow Veteran, Written at the Front* (Terre Haute, IN: Moore-Langen Company, 1929), pg. 177.
43. Frasier, "Operations of the Third Battalion," pg. 44.
44. Fullerton, *The Twenty-Sixth Infantry*, pg. 46.
45. Ibid.
46. Quoted in Cochrane, "The 1st Division Along the Meuse," pg. 42.
47. Handwritten notes by Maj. Legge in Cornish, "The Twenty-Sixth Infantry."
48. RG 117, letter from Edgarton, June 29, 1926; "Dr. Daniel Stedem Dies at Hospital He Helped Develop," *Tonawanda News*, January 9, 1963, http://fultonhistory.com.

49. Frasier, "Operations of the Third Battalion," pg. 45.
50. RG 120, Field Messages.
51. RG 117, letter from Edgarton, June 29, 1926.
52. Cochrane, "The 1st Division Along the Meuse," pg. 45; RG 120, Field Messages.
53. Cochrane, "The 1st Division Along the Meuse," pg. 45; RG 120, Field Messages.
54. RG 120, Field Messages.
55. Legge, "The First Division in the Meuse-Argonne," pg. 32.
56. Cornish, "The Twenty-Sixth Infantry," pg. 8.
57. RG 117, letter from Edgarton, June 29, 1926; Cochrane, "The 1st Division Along the Meuse," pg. 45.
58. RG 120, Field Messages.
59. Hall of Valor, Distinguished Service Cross citation for Pvt. Parent; for Capt. Acklin, see https://www.utoledo.edu/library/canaday/exhibits/acklin/williamacklin.html.
60. RG 120, Field Messages.
61. Ibid.
62. Ibid.
63. Ibid.
64. Ibid.
65. Ibid.
66. Ibid.; Frasier, "Operations of the Third Battalion," pp. 45-46.
67. Frasier, "Operations of the Third Battalion," pg. 46.
68. Hall of Valor, Distinguished Service Cross citation for Capt. McClure.
69. RG 120, Field Messages.
70. Legge, "The First Division in the Meuse-Argonne," pg. 33; RG 120, Field Messages.

Chapter 7: "It was wicked to order our men to attack again," October 11 and October 12

1. Frasier, "Operations of the Third Battalion," pg. 46; Cornish, "The Twenty-Sixth Infantry," pg. 8; RG 120, Field Messages.
2. Frasier, "Operations of the Third Battalion," pg. 46; RG 120, Field Messages.
3. Frasier, "Operations of the Third Battalion," pg. 46.
4. Quoted in Cochrane, "The 1st Division Along the Meuse," pg. 45; RG 120, Field Messages.
5. RG 120, Field Messages.
6. Ibid.
7. Quoted in Cochrane, "The 1st Division Along the Meuse," pg. 46.
8. Cornish, "The Twenty-Sixth Infantry," pg. 8; Legge, "The First Division in the Meuse-Argonne," pg. 33; RG 120, Field Messages.
9. Forster, "37-mm Gun Platoon," pg. 19; RG 120, Field Messages.
10. Frasier, "Operations of the Third Battalion," pg. 47.
11. RG 120, Field Messages.

12. RG 120, Field Messages; Forster, "37-mm Gun Platoon," pg. 19.
13. RG 120, Field Messages.
14. Ibid.
15. Forster, "37-mm Gun Platoon," pg. 19; RG 120, Field Messages.
16. RG 120, Field Messages.
17. Ibid.
18. Ibid.
19. Ibid.
20. Ibid.
21. Frasier, "Operations of the Third Battalion," pp. 47-48.
22. Ibid., pg. 49.
23. Ibid., pg. 48.
24. Ibid.
25. Ibid., pg. 49.
26. Fullerton, *The Twenty-Sixth Infantry*, pg. 46.
27. *History of the First Division*, pg. 212.
28. Fullerton, *The Twenty-Sixth Infantry*, pg. 47.
29. Frasier, "Operations of the Third Battalion," pg. 49.
30. Fullerton, *The Twenty-Sixth Infantry*, pg. 47.
31. *The Wisconsin Alumni Magazine*, Volume 25, Number 1 (November 1923); Ferritto Collection, LOC.
32. RG 117, letter from Edgarton, June 29, 1926.
33. RG 117, letter from Richards, September 4, 1926.
34. RG 117, letter from Ducket, October 5, 1928.
35. Fullerton, *The Twenty-Sixth Infantry*, pg. 47.
36. *The Story of the Sixteenth Infantry in France* (Frankfurt, Germany: Martin Flock, 1919); Capt. Ben H. Chastaine, *History of the 18th U.S. Infantry, First Division, 1812-1919* (New York: The Hymans Publishing Company, n.d.), pg. 98; *The Story of the Twenty-Eighth Infantry in the Great War* (N.p., n.d., but Germany, 1919), pg. 32.
37. *History of the First Division*, pg. 213.
38. "The Fighting 69th at Landres-et-St. Georges," blog entry for March 9, 2014, in Michael Hanlon's Roads to the Great War, http://roadstothegreatwar-ww1.blogspot.com/.
39. Albert M. Ettinger and A. Churchill Ettinger, *A Doughboy with the Fighting Sixty-Ninth: A Remembrance of World War I* (Shippensburg, PA: White Mane Publishing Company, Inc., 1992, pp. 154-155.
40. Ibid., pg. 156.
41. Nimrod T. Frazer, *Send the Alabamians: World War I Fighters in the Rainbow Division* (Tuscaloosa, AL: The University of Alabama Press, 2014), pg. 177.
42. Fullerton, *The Twenty-Sixth Infantry*, pg. 47; Cornish, "The Twenty-Sixth Infantry," pg. 8.
43. RG 117, letter from Edgarton, June 29, 1926.

Chapter 8:
"Anxious to show their mettle," Relief and Replacements, October 13 through November 5

1. Frasier, "Operations of the Third Battalion," pp. 50-51.
2. Ibid., pg. 41.
3. RG 120, Morning Reports for Company E, 26th Infantry Regiment. For some reason, this notation was repeated on the Morning Report for November 26.
4. Ibid., Morning Reports for Company I, 26th Infantry Regiment.
5. Based on the Roll of Honor in Fullerton, *The Twenty-Sixth Infantry*, combined with additional research, the author believes this to be a fair reckoning of the number of men killed in action or died of wounds received from October 1 through 12 (also included are some men who died between October 13 and October 31). The tally no doubt has some inaccuracies. For example, the regimental history lists Pvt. Joseph W. Boyce of Headquarters Company as being killed in action at Soissons, on July 21, 1918, but Lt. Forster, Boyce's platoon leader, stated that Boyce was killed by machine gun fire on October 5 while firing his 37mm gun at German positions north of Hill 212. Likewise, the author, while examining statement of service cards from some soldiers from Kenosha, Wisconsin, discovered at least three men who were killed in action during this time, but are not listed in the regimental honor roll; the men are, however, listed in the division history honor roll. On the other hand, Pvt. Francesco Muto of Company I was wounded on October 5, but was listed on company morning reports as missing in action since October 10, and the 1st Division history lists him as killed in action. Muto survived and was awarded the Silver Star with one oak leaf cluster (RG 120, Casualty Reports, 26th Infantry Regiment, one undated and one dated November 12, 1918; see also *History of the First Division*).
6. Hall of Valor, Distinguished Service Medal citation for Colonel Erickson.
7. Roosevelt, *Average Americans*, pp. 195-196; "Roosevelt Plans to Attend State Legion Sessions," *The Charleston Gazette*, Charleston, West Virginia, May 10, 1927, page 9, column 2, http://newspaperarchive.com/; letter from Lt. Fullerton to "Louise," October 24, 1918, and letter from Lt. Fullerton to his brother Will, October 26, 1918, used courtesy of Patricia Fullerton Hamman.
8. Charles Pelot Summerall, *The Way of Duty, Honor, Country: The Memoir of General Charles Pelot Summerall* (Lexington, KY: The University of Kentucky Press, 2010), pg. 149; Fullerton, *The Twenty-Sixth Infantry*, pg. 51.
9. Ferritto Collection, LOC; Frasier, "Operations of the Third Battalion," pg. 51; the regimental history states that 1,000 replacements were assigned to the 26th.
10. RG 120, Morning Reports for Company E, 26th Infantry Regiment; Ferritto Collection, LOC.
11. *History of the First Division*, pg. 217.
12. Frasier, "Operations of the Third Battalion," pg. 51.
13. Ibid.

14. Ibid.; Capt. George R. F. Cornish, "The Operations of the First Division (U.S.) in the Third Phase of the Meuse-Argonne" (The Infantry School, Company Officers' Course, Fort Benning, Georgia, 1924-1925), pg. 3.
15. Cornish, "The Operations of the First Division," pg. 10.
16. RG 117, letter from Andrews, August 8, 1926, and letter from Dye, November 14, 1928.
17. Letter from Fullerton to "Louise," October 24, 1918, used courtesy of Patricia Fullerton Hamman.
18. *History of the First Division*, pg. 218; Fullerton, *The Twenty-Sixth Infantry*, pg. 52.
19. Fullerton, *The Twenty-Sixth Infantry*, pg. 53; Table of Organization in Gawne, "The WWI Squad, Section and Platoon," pg. 11; Company rosters, October 31, 1918, courtesy Colonel Robert R. McCormick Research Center, First Division Museum at Cantigny, Wheaton, Illinois. The table reflects only those officers actually on duty in each rifle company; a few officers were detailed to various duties, such as duty with Supply Company or battalion headquarters, and they are not reflected in these totals. On the roster, Lt. Meeker is shown as present for duty with Company B, but he was soon injured and evacuated, and he is not included in Company B's count here. Compare with the table shown in Chapter 2 reflecting the totals at the start of the offensive.
20. This episode is reported in Frasier, "Operations of the Third Battalion," pp. 53-54, and Fullerton, *The Twenty-Sixth Infantry*, pg. 54. The two accounts differ slightly but agree in essentials.
21. *History of the First Division*, pp. 222-223; Frasier, "Operations of the Third Battalion," pg. 53.
22. Fullerton, *The Twenty-Sixth Infantry*, pg. 54.
23. Frasier, "Operations of the Third Battalion," pp. 53-54.
24. Roosevelt, *Average Americans*, pg. 203. Roosevelt gives Card's rank as captain, but I've used his rank as it appears on the October 31, 1918, company roster. Card was assigned to Company A, but was on special duty as 1st Battalion supply officer at the time.
25. Fullerton, *The Twenty-Sixth Infantry*, pg. 54.
26. Frasier, "Operations of the Third Battalion," pg. 54; Frasier puts the incident on November 5.
27. Cornish, "The Operations of the First Division," pg. 9.
28. Fullerton, *The Twenty-Sixth Infantry*, pg. 54.
29. Ibid.
30. *History of the First Division*, pg. 226; Frasier, "Operations of the Third Battalion," pp. 55-56.
31. Roosevelt, *Average Americans*, pg. 206.

Chapter 9:
"A nightmare of marching," November 6 through November 11; Post-War Duties

1. Cornish, "The Operations of the First Division," pg. 12; Fullerton, *The Twenty-Sixth Infantry*, pg. 54; RG 117, undated letter and notes from Cornish, about 1926.
2. Cornish, "The Operations of the First Division," pg. 12.
3. RG 117, letter from Dye, January 15, 1927.
4. Fullerton, *The Twenty-Sixth Infantry*, pg. 54; *History of the First Division*, pg. 227. Frasier, "Operations of the Third Battalion," pg. 55, incorrectly indicates the 2nd Battalion in support.
5. Cornish, "The Operations of the First Division," pg. 13.
6. Fullerton, *The Twenty-Sixth Infantry*, pg. 54; RG 120, "Report on the Operations of the 26th Infantry Oct. 31 to Nov. 8, 1918," November 12, 1918.
7. RG 117, letter from Dye, January 15, 1927.
8. RG 117, letter and annotated map from Dye, January 15, 1927.
9. RG 117, letter from Dye, January 15, 1927.
10. RG 117, letter from Clarkson, July 11, 1927.
11. RG 117, letter from Clarkson, July 11, 1927, and letter from Burrell, March 1, 1929.
12. RG 117, letter from Clarkson, July 11, 1927.
13. Frasier, "Operations of the Third Battalion," pg. 55.
14. Ibid.
15. RG 117, letter from Dye, January 15, 1927.
16. RG 117, letter from Frasier, August 2, 1927.
17. RG 117, letter from Dye, January 15, 1927.
18. Ferritto Collection, LOC; RG 117, letter from Dye, January 15, 1927.
19. RG 120, Field Messages.
20. RG 117, letter from Mulvey, November 13, 1928.
21. Fullerton, *The Twenty-Sixth Infantry*, pg. 55; RG 120, "Report on the Operations of the 26th Infantry Oct. 31 to Nov. 8, 1918," November 12, 1918.
22. Fullerton, *The Twenty-Sixth Infantry*, pg. 55; Roosevelt, *Average Americans*, pg. 211; RG 120, "Report on the Operations of the 26th Infantry Oct. 31 to Nov. 8, 1918," November 12, 1918; RG 117, undated notes from Leck, probably early 1927.
23. *History of the First Division*, pg. 229.
24. RG 117, letter from Dye, January 15, 1927.
25. RG 117, letter from Dye, January 15, 1927, and letter from Clarkson, July 11, 1927; Cornish, "The Operations of the First Division," pg. 14, mentions only one gun.
26. Cornish, "The Operations of the First Division," pg. 14.
27. RG 117, letter from Clarkson, July 11, 1927.
28. RG 117, letter from Clarkson, July 11, 1927, and letter from Dye, January 15, 1927.

29. RG 117, letter from Frasier, August 2, 1927.
30. Arthur Hafner, editor, *Directory of Deceased American Physicians, 1804-1929: a genealogical guide to over 149,000 medical practitioners providing brief biographical sketches drawn from the American Medical Association's Deceased Physician Masterfile* (Chicago: American Medical Association, 1993), excerpt via http://home.ancestry.com/; Fullerton, *The Twenty-Sixth Infantry*, pg. 55; *History of the First Division*, pg. 228; Roosevelt, *Average Americans*, pp. 207-208; RG 117, letter from Clarkson, July 11, 1927; RG 92, John G. Skilling, Burial Information File, testimony of Pvt. Willard Hollat.
31. RG 117, letter from Dye, January 15, 1927.
32. RG 117, letter from Frasier, August 2, 1927.
33. Order quoted in *History of the First Division*, pg. 229.
34. *History of the First Division*, pp. 231-232; Frasier, "Operations of the Third Battalion," pg. 56, erroneously states that there were only four columns.
35. *History of the First Division*, pg. 229; Frasier, "Operations of the Third Battalion," pg. 56.
36.RG 117, letter from Manning, January 19, 1927.
37. RG 117, letter from Dye, January 15, 1927, and letter from Clarkson, July 11, 1927.
38. *History of the First Division*, pg. 232; Roosevelt, *Average Americans*, pg. 212.
39. RG 120, "Report on the Operations of the 26th Infantry Oct. 31 to Nov. 8, 1918," November 12, 1918; RG 117, undated notes from Leck, probably early 1927.
40. Cornish, "The Operations of the First Division," pg. 19.
41. *History of the First Division*, pg. 232; Frasier, "Operations of the Third Battalion," pg. 66.
42. Frasier, "Operations of the Third Battalion," pg. 57.
43. Roosevelt, *Average Americans*, pp. 209; Frasier, "Operations of the Third Battalion," pg. 57.
44. RG 117, letter from Dye, January 15, 1927.
45. Letter from Fullerton to his brother Will, November 28, 1918, courtesy of Patricia Fullerton Hamman.
46. RG 117, letter from Manning, January 19, 1927.
47. RG 117, letter from Mulvey, November 13, 1928.
48. Roosevelt, *Average Americans*, pg. 209; RG 117, letter from Manning, January 19, 1927.
49. RG 117, letter from Manning, January 19, 1927.
50. Frasier, "Operations of the Third Battalion," pg. 57.
51. Frasier, "Operations of the Third Battalion," pp. 57-61; RG 117, letter from Frasier, August 2, 1927. Major Frasier, in his two versions written in the 1926-1927 time frame, at times contradicts himself. Details regarding order of march, meeting French troops, and areas of attack vary among Frasier's two versions, Manning's version, and Cornish's version.
52. RG 117, letter from Frasier, August 2, 1927; Frasier, "Operations of the Third Battalion," pg. 58.

53. RG 117, letter from Manning, January 19, 1927.
54. Ibid.
55. Ibid.
56. Cornish, "The Operations of the First Division," pg. 23.
57. Ibid.
58. Frasier, "Operations of the Third Battalion," pg. 59.
59. Frasier, "Operations of the Third Battalion," pp. 59-60. Major Legge, in a handwritten note in Cornish, "The Twenty-Sixth Infantry," stated that Capt. Walter R. McClure was commanding Company M at this time; McClure would be awarded the Distinguished Service Cross for heroism during the first part of the campaign.
60. Frasier, "Operations of the Third Battalion," pg. 66.
61. Handwritten notes by Maj. Legge, in Cornish, "The Twenty-Sixth Infantry."
62. RG 117, letter from Frasier, August 2, 1927.
63. RG 117, letter from Dye, January 15, 1927.
64. Frasier, "Operations of the Third Battalion," pg. 61; RG 117, undated notes from Cornish.
65. Copy of a letter from Roosevelt to Cornish, May 5, 1931, in Cornish, "The Twenty-Sixth Infantry."
66. Letter from Fullerton to "Mr. Bull," December 29, 1919 [*sic*, 1918], used courtesy of Patricia Fullerton Hamman.
67. Ibid.
68. RG 117, letter from Dye, January 15, 1927.
69. Frasier, "Operations of the Third Battalion," pg. 61; Roosevelt, *Average Americans*, pg. 211; letter from Fullerton to his brother Will, November 28, 1918, used courtesy of Patricia Fullerton Hamman.
70. RG 117, letter from Dye, January 15, 1927.
71. RG 117, letter from Clarkson, July 11, 1927; letter from Fullerton to his brother Will, November 28, 1918, used courtesy of Patricia Fullerton Hamman.
72. Frasier, "Operations of the Third Battalion," pg. 61; Cornish, "The Operations of the First Division," pg. 24.
73. *History of the First Division*, pg. 235.
74. RG 117, letter from Manning, January 19, 1927.
75. RG 117, letter from Frasier, August 2, 1927.
76. RG 117, letter from Manning, January 19, 1927.
77. Frasier, "Operations of the Third Battalion," pp. 66-67.
78. Ibid., pg. 67.
79. RG 117, copy of Parker's Operations Report, November 9, 1918.
80. Ibid.
81. Ibid.
82. Roll of Honor in Fullerton, *The Twenty-Sixth Infantry*.
83. Frasier, "Operations of the Third Battalion," pg. 62; Fullerton, *The Twenty-Sixth Infantry*, pg. 58; RG 117, letter from Dye, November 14, 1928. Fullerton attributed the firing after the armistice to gunners vying to see who could fire the last shot (letter from Fullerton to "Mr. Bull," December 29, 1918).

84. Letter from Fullerton to "Mr. Bull," December 29, 1918, used courtesy of Patricia Fullerton Hamman.
85. Letter from Fullerton to an unidentified recipient, November 18, 1918, used courtesy of Patricia Fullerton Hamman.
86. Ibid.
87. Fullerton, *The Twenty-Sixth Infantry*, pp. 58-62.
88. *History of the First Division*, pp. 248, 255-256.
89. Ibid., pp. 259-260.
90. Frasier, "Operations of the Third Battalion," pg. 62; this paean is even printed on the cover of the 1st Division's official history. For the full text of this unique General Order, see Appendix B.
91. "Popular Elmiran Wounded," *The Telegram*, Elmira, New York, November 10, 1918, http://fultonhistory.com/.
92. Gold Star Veteran Index on COGenWeb (Colorado Genealogy Project), http://www.cogenweb.com/.
93. RG 120, Morning Reports for Company E, 26th Infantry Regiment; "Italian Boy in 26th Infantry Among Missing," *Bridgeport Telegram*, Bridgeport, Connecticut, November 30, 1918, page 1, column 3, http://newspaperarchive.com/.
94. "War Victim's Mother Dies of Grief," *Terre Haute Saturday Spectator*, Terre Haute, Indiana, April 17, 1920, page 6, column 2, http://newspaperarchive.com/; "Indiana's War Mother Expires at Leesville," *The Brownstown Banner*, Brownstown, Indiana, June 14, 1922, page 1, column 2, http://newspaperarchive.com/.
95. RG 92, Gustav A. Erickson, Burial Information File, letter from John Erickson, Emma C. Erickson, and Ellen W. Erickson, January 7, 1921.
96. RG 92, John Skilling, Burial Information File; RG 92, Eric Cummings, Burial Information File.
97. Letter from Fullerton to his brother Will, February 23, 1919, used courtesy of Patricia Fullerton Hamman.
98. Letter from Roosevelt to Fullerton, March 15, 1919; letter from Fullerton to "Uncle B___", February 23, 1919, used courtesy of Patricia Fullerton Hamman.
99. "Says Report of His Death was Mistake," *Reno Evening Gazette*, Reno, Nevada, April 30, 1921, page 9, column 7, http://newspaperarchive.com/.
100. "Shelby and Pentwater Seek Hocking May 30th," *The Ludington Daily News*, Ludington, Michigan, April 20, 1928, page 9, columns 5-6, http://newspaperarchive.com/.
101. "Bought Liberty With Soap," *The Kansas City Star*, Kansas City, Missouri, February 20, 1919, page 12, column 5, http://newspaperarchive.com/.
102. Antonio Giorno, award card, NARA.

Chapter 10: Analysis

1. Frasier, "Operations of the Third Battalion," pp. 62-63.
2. Forster, "37-mm Gun Platoon," pg. 9.

3. Thomas, *History of the AEF*, pg. 317, states that from October 4 through 12 alone the 1st Division "lo st 9,387 officers and men, the heaviest casualties suffered by any American division in the Meuse-Argonne offensive." *History of the First Division*, pp. 213, 229, and 236, however, gives a figure of 7,520 officers and men killed, wounded, and missing for October 4 through 12, and 860 officers and men killed wounded, and missing for November 1 through 11, for a total of 8,380 for the entire campaign. Legge, "The First Division in the Meuse-Argonne," pg. 34; Frasier, "Operations of the Third Battalion," pg. 65; Cornish, "The Twenty-Sixth Infantry," pp. 9-10.
4. Cornish, "The Twenty-Sixth Infantry," pg. 9; Frasier, "Operations of the Third Battalion," pg. 65.
5. Legge, "The First Division in the Meuse-Argonne," pg. 35; Cornish, "The Twenty-Sixth Infantry," pg. 9.
6. RG 120, "Report on the Operations of the 26th Infantry Northeast [*sic*] of Verdun, Sept. 30, 1918 to Oct. 11, 1918," October 18, 1918.
7. Frasier, "Operations of the Third Battalion," pg. 64.
8. *History of the Seventh Field Artillery*, pg. 98.
9. Ferritto Collection, LOC.
10. Frasier, "Operations of the Third Battalion," pp. 64-65; Legge, "The First Division in the Meuse-Argonne," pg. 35.
11. Cochrane, "The 1st Division Along the Meuse," pg. 51.
12. Frasier, "Operations of the Third Battalion," pg. 64.
13. Maj. Oscar I. Gates, "The Operations of the Seventh Field Artillery, First Division, in the Meuse-Argonne Offensive, 1 October - 11 November, 1918" (Command and General Staff School, Fort Leavenworth, Kansas, n.d.), pg. 1.
14. Ibid., pg. 7.
15. Legge, "The First Division in the Meuse-Argonne," pg. 35.
16. Frasier, "Operations of the Third Battalion," pg. 63.
17. Forster, "37-mm Gun Platoon," pg. 23; Frasier, "Operations of the Third Battalion," pg. 64; Legge, "The First Division in the Meuse-Argonne," pg. 35.
18. RG 120, "Report on the Operations of the 26th Infantry Northeast [*sic*] of Verdun, Sept. 30, 1918 to Oct. 11, 1918," October 18, 1918.
19. Helsley, "Operations of the Machine Gun Company, 16th Infantry," pg. 17.
20. For a good discussion of weapons and the idea of "combat physics," see Faulkner, *The School of Hard Knocks*, pp. 233-256.
21. Frasier, "Operations of the Third Battalion," pg. 69.
22. RG 120, "Report on the Operations of the 26th Infantry Northeast [*sic*] of Verdun, Sept. 30, 1918 to Oct. 11, 1918," October 18, 1918.
23. RG 117, letter from Edgarton, June 29, 1926.
24. "Two Battlers are Back From War; Both Wounded," *The Daily Republican-News*, Hamilton, Ohio, February 7, 1919, page 1, column 5, http://newspaperarchive.com/.
25. Field Order quoted in Maj. Henry W. Stiness, "The Evacuation of Prisoners by the First Division in the Meuse Argonne Offensive" (Command and General Staff School, Fort Leavenworth, Kansas, 1932).

26. Quoted in Stiness, "The Evacuation of Prisoners."
27. Letter from Fullerton to "Louise," October 24, 1918, used courtesy of Patricia Fullerton Hamman.
28. Cornish, "The Twenty-Sixth Infantry," pg. 9.
29. Forster, "37-mm Gun Platoon," pg. 22.
30. For Conover, see *NYNG Officer Service Cards prior to 1/1/1930*. Saratoga Springs, New York: New York State Military Museum, http://home.ancestry.com/; for Burrell, see http://www.findagrave.com/index.html; for Fullerton, see "Charles Bushnell Fullerton," a two-page biography, used courtesy of Patricia Fullerton Hamman; for Wortley, Youell, Cornish, Foster, Starlings, and Manning, see National Archives and Records Administration (NARA); Washington, D.C.; *Returns from Regular Army Infantry Regiments, June 1821 - December 1916*; Microfilm Serial: *M665*; Roll: *289*, http://home.ancestry.com/.
31. Legge, "The First Division in the Meuse-Argonne," pg. 36 Cornish, "The Twenty-Sixth Infantry," pg. 9.
32. Frasier, "Operations of the Third Battalion," pg. 64.
33. Forster, "37-mm Gun Platoon," pg. 2.
34. Ibid., pg. 22.
35. Frasier, "Operations of the Third Battalion," pg. 66.
36. Forster, "37-mm Gun Platoon," pg. 21.
37. Cornish, "The Twenty-Sixth Infantry," pg. 9.

Appendix A: Roll of Honor, 26th Infantry Regiment, September 26 to November 30, 1918

1. The term "disease" was used during the war to indicate any kind of illness, most often influenza and its chief complication, pneumonia. Dysentery was also a problem. In general, there are some discrepancies in the data presented in the rosters, casualty lists in the unit histories, and morning reports. The appendix and the two casualty tables in the text are the author's best efforts to determine casualty figures. See Fullerton, *The Twenty-Sixth Infantry*, pp. 78-97; *History of the First Division*, pp. 300-312; Charles A. Gechas, John Lonika, and Martin F. Rawleigh, Statement of Service Cards, Wisconsin, Adjutant General's Office: Regimental Muster and Descriptive Rolls, World War I.

Appendix B: General Headquarters, AEF, General Orders No. 201

1. Thomas, *History of the AEF*, pp. 318-319. See also *History of the First Division*, pp. 366-367.

BIBLIOGRAPHIC ESSAY

Most Great War regimental histories were written in the years immediately following the war by men who were in the regiments. These men could testify to the events they describe, and they had easy access to other eyewitnesses and to official documents. They often wrote at the behest of the regiment, as a keepsake or memento for members of the regiment and their families. Later writers of necessity must rely on these previous works; they must strive also to find other documents that attest to the historical facts of the regiment in question. The starting point for research on the 26th Infantry Regiment during the Great War is the official regimental history written by the regimental adjutant, Capt. Charles Bushnell Fullerton, in Germany in 1919 (*The Twenty-Sixth Infantry in France*, Martin Flock & Co.). The portion of the book covering the Meuse-Argonne Offensive is only seven pages long; Fullerton based much of this on official operations reports written immediately after the battle.

The 1st Division's official history, *History of the First Division During the World War, 1917-1919* (The John C. Winston Company, 1922), is credited to the Society of the First Division; Maj. Gen. Charles P. Summerall, commander of the division during the first part of the Meuse-Argonne Offensive, claimed, in his memoirs (*The Way of Duty, Honor, Country: The Memoir of General Charles Pelot Summerall*, edited and annotated by Timothy K. Nenninger, The University of Kentucky Press, 2010), to have written most of the book. However, Maj. Barnwell R. Legge, commander of the 1st Battalion during the Offensive, later claimed that the history was written by a committee of officers in the months after the war. The various reports from the officers were compiled and circulated among other officers, and "a number of months was spent verifying the detail of each operation by conference with officers and enlisted men of the Division, and the history committee was given a free rein." When the data was compiled, the division commander sent five officers to revisit the battlegrounds to further verify facts. Following this the narrative was completed and circulated among combat officers of the division until 1922 when Gen. Summerall was satisfied as to the book's accuracy and completeness, at which time it was finally published (see Legge, "The First Division in the Meuse Argonne," introduction). In any event, the history is thorough and authoritative; other division officers writing after the war stated that it is accurate in its details. Of tremendous value is the packet of twelve maps accompanying the book. These maps are copies of what must have been the actual tactical maps used by the division and its subordinate units, and they are essential to understanding the terrain confronting the 26th in their zone of operations. Sadly, these maps are now very hard to find.

Another excellent source is the American Battle Monument Commission's *1st Division Summary of Operations in the World War* (United States Government Printing Office, 1944). Part of a series published by the Commission, the *1st Division Summary of Operations* is based upon extensive interviews of participants in the battle. I've also used draft versions that the Commission sent to officers for their input (Record Group 117, National Archives and Records Administration).

Subsequent to these three valuable sources, there are only two other histories covering these units during World War I. Steven Weingartner's *Blue Spaders: The 26th Infantry Regiment, 1917-1967* (Cantigny First Division Foundation, 1996) and James Scott Wheeler's *The Big Red One: America's Legendary 1st Division from World War I to Desert Storm* (University Press of Kansas, 2007) each devotes limited space to the Meuse-Argonne Offensive.

Each of the other three infantry regiments in the division published official histories immediately after the war (*The Story of the Sixteenth Infantry in France*, by the Regimental Chaplain, Martin Flock & Co., 1919; *History of the 18th U.S. Infantry, First Division, 1812-1919*, by Capt. Ben H. Chastaine, The Hymans Publishing Company, no date; *The Story of the Twenty-Eighth Infantry in the Great War*, no author given, 1919). The histories of the 16th, 26th, and 28th regiments were written and published in Germany in 1919; the 18th Infantry's history, published in New York after 1919, is more substantial. Other division units published official histories after the war; these, too, are useful in providing context to what the men of the 26th experienced during the Offensive (see *A History of the 1st US Engineers, 1st US Division*, 1919; *History of the Seventh Field Artillery, First Division, A.E.F., World War, 1917-1919*, 1929). Many of these older books are available on-line through Hathi Trust (www.babel.hathitrust.org) or Google books (www.books.google.com).

James Carl Nelson's *The Remains of Company D: A Story of the Great War* (St. Martin's Griffin, 2010), and *Five Lieutenants: The Heartbreaking Story of Five Harvard Men who Led America to Victory in World War I* (St. Martin's Press, 2012), are excellent recent histories covering the 28th Infantry Regiment, with which the 26th was brigaded.

Of great interest and edification have been the copies of the field messages sent between the regimental, battalion, and company commanders during the actual fighting. Written in the heat and confusion of battle, these messages depict the veritable fog of war and the leaders' almost insatiable thirst for accurate, up to date information. Using them carefully, one can get an almost hour-by-hour account of the battle. Accompanying these are hand-drawn maps, often very cryptic, of the units involved; drawn under combat conditions, these are often remarkably well done. They were a necessity for battalion commanders to try to depict the situation on their front for the benefit of regimental commander.

I've also consulted a few examples of company morning reports and rosters. These date from the days of the battle and were written by harried company clerks not far to the rear, often under shellfire. Any information that made its way back to the clerks under such circumstances was apt to be incomplete and confusing so it's not hard to understand why the reports for Company E, for example, on October 5, 6, 7, 10, and 11 say "no change" at a time when the company was losing men heavily in combat. Understandably, it took time for all that to be straightened out. Sometimes, as noted in this narrative, things wouldn't be straightened out for a long time.

Another early source is the "Report on Operations of the 26th Infantry Northeast [*sic*, Northwest] of VERDUN, Sept. 30, 1918 to Oct. 11, 1918." This official report, dated October 18, 1918, was compiled by Lt. Charles Ridgely, the Acting Operations Officer, by order of Col. Hjalmar Erickson, the regimental commander. It made its way through channels to become the first official, if brief, account of the 26th's part in the battle. A similar report that covered the final phase of the battle was prepared on November 12. The foregoing documents – the field messages, morning reports, rosters, and operations reports – are all part of Record Group 120, Records of the American Expeditionary Forces, 1917-1923, National Archives and Records Administration.

In the two decades following the Great War, many officers who stayed in the Army attended advanced Army schools, notably the Command and General Staff School at Fort Leavenworth, Kansas, and the Infantry School at Fort Benning, Georgia, to further their professional development. As part of the curriculum of these schools, officers were required to write studies on various topics. Many of these papers were written by veterans of the 26th, and some of the papers cover topics associated with the 26th's role in the Meuse-Argonne Offensive.

These papers have been of great value; their authors were participants in the events they describe and critique, and their perspective is therefore of vital importance in forming an idea of what happened on the slopes, ravines, and woods of rural France so many years ago. Digital copies of many of these monographs are available through the website of the Combined Arms Research Library at Fort Leavenworth (http://usacac.army.mil/cac2/cgsc/carl/).

Of particular note are the papers written by Maj. Barnwell Legge, Maj. Lyman S. Frasier, Capt. George R.F. Cornish, and Capt. (then-Lieutenant) George J. Forster. All of these men were wartime members of the 26th Infantry Regiment. Cornish's paper contains an appendix with hand-written notes by Maj. Legge covering daily troop dispositions and decisions during this period. Major Frasier's account of the activities of his 3rd Battalion is by far the most thorough account of the action. His account differs in some aspects, most notably time frames but also in matters of some substance, from other accounts. I've done my best to reconcile the various accounts; major discrepancies are noted in the text or in endnotes. Another important US Army monograph is Rexmond Cochrane's "The 1st Division Along the Meuse, 1-12 October 1918," part of the US Army Chemical Corps Historical Studies series. Cochrane's thorough analysis of the gas used by and against the 1st Division, along with his coverage of German artillery forces opposing the division, is helpful to understanding what the Doughboys of the 26th experienced during the battle.

When evaluating the monographs as source material, it must be borne in mind that they were written, in most cases, at least a decade after the battle. The authors appear to have taken pains to verify their facts against their own records and other sources. Their monographs are not self-serving, but they read as straightforward recitations of the facts combined with honest analysis. That said, it is also true that the authors, of necessity, often had to rely on their memory; thus the use of such other sources as the regimental field messages serves to reconcile all the accounts as far as is possible.

For a thorough, well-written account of the Meuse-Argonne Offensive, Edward G. Lengel's *To Conquer Hell, The Meuse-Argonne, 1918: The Epic Battle That Ended the First World War* (Henry Holt and Company, 2008), cannot be surpassed. The 26th Infantry Regiment came into contact with other American units during the offensive. A perusal of their unit histories can give insight into the terrain over which the 26th fought in addition to giving some idea of the conditions on the 26th's flank. The American Battle Monuments Commission studies include *35th Division Summary of Operations in the World War, 91st Division Summary of Operations in the World War*, and *42nd Division Summary of Operations in the World War* (all Washington, DC: United States Government Printing Office, 1944), all available online at Hathi Trust Digital Library (http://www.hathitrust.org/). The regiments in the 42nd Division in particular have been the subject of unit histories and personal reminiscences; these can serve to give readers more background and another perspective on the fighting in the area associated with the 26th Infantry.

To learn about how Army officers were trained stateside and in the AEF and how they functioned in combat, one can consult Richard S. Faulkner's *The School of Hard Knocks: Combat Leadership in the American Expeditionary Forces* (Texas A&M University Press, 2012). Faulkner goes into great detail on how limitations in training, supply, personnel policies, and other factors adversely impacted performance in combat. His chapter on combat physics is helpful in understanding the challenges faced by battalion, company, and platoon commanders. For a thoughtful critique of AEF tactics, see Mark E. Grotelueschen's *AEF Way of War* (Cambridge University Press, 2010).

BIBLIOGRAPHY

Archival Sources

Carmine Ferritto Collection (AFC/2001/001/49562), Veterans History Project, American Folklife Center, Library of Congress, Washington, D.C.

Colonel Robert R. McCormick Research Center, First Division Museum at Cantigny, Wheaton, Illinois.

New York National Guard Officer Service Cards, New York State Military Museum, Saratoga, New York.

Record Group 92, Records of the Office of the Quartermaster General, National Personnel Records Center, National Archives and Records Administration, St. Louis, Missouri.

Record Group 117, Records of the American Battle Monument Commission, National Archives and Records Administration, College Park, Maryland.

Record Group 120, Records of the American Expeditionary Forces, 1917-1923, National Archives and Records Administration, College Park, Maryland.

Wisconsin Adjutant General's Office: Regimental Muster and Descriptive Rolls, World War I, Wisconsin Veterans Museum, Madison, Wisconsin.

Books

American Battle Monument Commission. *1st Division Summary of Operations in the World War.* Washington, D.C.: United States Government Printing Office, 1944.

Bareither, Terry M., editor. *An Engineer's Diary of the Great War*. West Lafayette, IN: Purdue University Press, 2002.

Borthick, David, and Jack Britton. *Medals, Military and Civilian, of the United States.* Tulsa, OK: Military Collectors' News Press, 1984.

Butler, Capt. Alban B., Jr. *"Happy Days!" A Humorous Narrative in Drawings of the Progress of American Arms, 1917-1919*. Washington, D.C.: Society of the First Division, A.E.F., 1928.

Chastaine, Capt. Ben H. *History of the 18th U.S. Infantry, First Division, 1812-1919.* New York: The Hymans Publishing Company, n.d.

Dooly, William G., Jr. *Great Weapons of World War I.* New York: Walker and Company, 1969.

Ettinger, Albert M., and A. Churchill Ettinger. *A Doughboy with the Fighting Sixty-Ninth: A Remembrance of World War I.* Shippensburg, PA: White Mane Publishing Company, Inc., 1992.

Farwell, Byron. *Over There: The United States in the Great War, 1917-1918.* New York: W. W. Norton & Company, Ltd., 1999.

Faulkner, Richard S. *The School of Hard Knocks: Combat Leadership in the American Expeditionary Forces.* College Station, TX: Texas A&M University Press, 2012.

Frazer, Nimrod T. *Send the Alabamians: World War I Fighters in the Rainbow Division.* Tuscaloosa, AL: The University of Alabama Press, 2014.

Fullerton, Bushnell. *The Twenty-Sixth Infantry in France.* Martin Flock & Co., Frankfort, Germany, 1919. http://webpages.charter.net/gallison2b/History%20of%2026th%20Regiment%20in%20WWI.pdf

Girton, Fred and Myron E. Adams. *The History and Achievements of the Fort Sheridan Officers' Training Camps.* (Chicago?): The Fort Sheridan Association, 1920. http://babel.hathitrust.org.

Grotelueschen, Mark Etan. *The AEF Way of War: The American Army and Combat in World War I.* New York: Cambridge University Press, 2010.

Hafner, Arthur, editor. *Directory of Deceased American Physicians, 1804-1929: a genealogical guide to over 149,000 medical practitioners providing brief biographical sketches drawn from the American Medical Association's Deceased Physician Masterfile.* Chicago: American Medical Association, 1993. Excerpt via http://home.ancestry.com/.

Hallas, James H. *Squandered Victory: The American First Army at St. Mihiel.* Westport, CT: Praeger, 1995.

Hanton, Capt. Carl et al. *The 32nd Division in the World War, 1917-1919.* Madison, WI: Wisconsin War History Commission, 1920.

Hausee, W.M., and A.C. Doyle, compilers. Soldiers in the Great War - Mississippi. N. p., n. d., 1920. http://usgwarchives.net/ms/greatwar.htm.

A History of the 1st US Engineers, 1st US Division, Coblenz, Germany, 1919. http://www.hathitrust.org/.

History of the Seventh Field Artillery (First Division, A.E.F.), World War, 1917-1919. N.p., 1929. http://www.hathitrust.org/.

Infantry in Battle. Washington, DC: The Infantry Journal, Inc., 1939.

Lengel, Edward G. *To Conquer Hell, The Meuse-Argonne, 1918: The Epic Battle That Ended the First World War.* New York: Henry Holt and Company, 2008.

Levere, William C. *The History of Sigma Alpha Epsilon in the World War.* Published by the Fraternity, 1928. http://www.hathitrust.org/.

Maryland in the World War, 1917-1919, Military and Naval Service Records, Volume II. Baltimore: Maryland War Records Commission, 1933. http://babel.hathitrust.org

Pierce County in the World War. Red Wing, MN: Red Wing Publishing Company, 1919. http://books.google.com.

Roosevelt, Lt. Col. Theodore. *Average Americans.* New York: G.P. Putman's Sons, 1920. http://books.google.com.

Sherwood, Elmer W. *The Diary of a Rainbow Veteran, Written at the Front*. Terre Haute, IN: Moore-Langen Company, 1929.

600 Days' Service: A History of the 361st Infantry Regiment of the United States Army. N.p., n.d. (1919).

The Society of the First Division. *History of the First Division During the World War, 1917-1919*. Philadelphia: The John C. Winston Company, 1922.

The Story of the 91st Division. San Francisco: 91st Division Publication Committee, 1919.

The Story of the Sixteenth Infantry in France. By the Regimental Chaplain. Frankfurt, Germany: Martin Flock, 1919.

The Story of the Twenty-Eighth Infantry in the Great War. N.p., n.d., but Germany, 1919.

Summerall, General Charles Pelot. *The Way of Duty, Honor, Country: The Memoir of General Charles Pelot Summerall*. Edited and annotated by Timothy K. Nenninger. Lexington, KY: The University of Kentucky Press, 2010.

Thomas, Capt. Shipley. *The History of the A.E.F.* New York: George H. Doran Company, 1920. https://archive.org/details/historyaef00thomgoog.

—. *S-2 in Action*. Harrisburg, Pennsylvania: The Military Service Publishing Co., 1940. http://www.hathitrust.org/.

Virginia Military Institute. *Record of Service in the World War of V.M.I. Alumni and their Alma Mater*. Richmond, VA: The Richmond Press, 1920. http://www.hathitrust.org/.

Wilson, Capt. Dale E. *Treat 'em Rough! The Birth of American Armor, 1917-20*. Novato, CA: Presidio Press, 1990.

Wrentmore, Ernest L. *America's Youngest Soldier: On the Front Lines in World War One*. Steve W. Chadde, 2014. Originally published as *In Spite of Hell: A Factual Story of Incidents that Occurred During World War I, as Experienced by the Youngest Soldier to Have Seen Combat Duty With the American Expeditionary Forces in France – As a Member of the Famous Company I, 60th Infantry, Fifth (Red Diamond) Division*, New York: Greenwich Book Publishers, 1958.

Internet Sources

Ancestry.com, http://home.ancestry.com/.

Arlington National Cemetery Website, http://arlingtoncemetery.net .

COGenWeb (Colorado Genealogy Project), http://www.cogenweb.com/.

Combined Arms Research Library, United States Army Combined Arms Center, Fort Leavenworth, Kansas, http://usacac.army.mil/cac2/cgsc/carl/.

Find A Grave, http://www.findagrave.com/.

Google Books, http://books.google.com/.

Hathi Trust Digital Library, http://www.hathitrust.org/.

Internet Archive, https://archive.org/.

Michigan Genealogy Trails, http://genealogytrails.com/mich/.

Military Times Hall of Valor, http://projects.militarytimes.com/citations-medals-awards/.

Newspaper Archive, http://newspaperarchive.com/.
Old Fulton Post Cards, http://fultonhistory.com/.
Roads to the Great War, Michael Hanlon, http://roadstothegreatwar-ww1.blogspot.com/.
Tallis, Alan. Tallis Family, http://www.tallisfamily.co.uk/.
USGenWeb Archives, http://usgwarchives.net/
The University of Toledo Library, https://www.utoledo.edu/library/.
Wikipedia, http://en.wikipedia.org/wiki/Main_Page.

Newspapers and Magazines

Bridgeport Telegram, Bridgeport, Connecticut, "Italian Boy in 26th Infantry Among Missing," November 30, 1918.
The Brownstown Banner, Brownstown, Indiana, "Indiana's War Mother Expires at Leesville," June 14, 1922.
The Charleston Gazette, Charleston, West Virginia, "Roosevelt Plans to Attend State Legion Sessions," May 10, 1927.
The Daily Republican-News, Hamilton, Ohio, "Two Battlers are Back From War; Both Wounded,", February 7, 1919.
Fayetteville Democrat, Fayetteville, Arkansas, "University Student Cited For Gallantry," June 26, 1920.
Gawne, Jonathan. "The WWI Squad, Section and Platoon." *The G.I. Journal*, Vol. 1, Number 3, Fall, 1996.
The Kansas City Star, Kansas City, Missouri, "Bought Liberty With Soap," February 20, 1919.
The Ludington Daily News, Ludington, Michigan, "Shelby and Pentwater Seek Hocking May 30th," April 20, 1928.
McKean Democrat, Smethport, Pennsylvania, "Over the Top 17 Times in 6 Months of Action,", May 23, 1919.
The Racine Journal-News, Racine, Wisconsin, "Letter Tells How Soldier Met Death," April 16, 1919.
Reno Evening Gazette, Reno, Nevada, "Says Report of His Death was Mistake," April 30, 1921.
The Telegram, Elmira, New York, "Popular Emiran Wounded," November 10, 1918.
Terre Haute Saturday Spectator, Terre Haute, Indiana, "War Victim's Mother Dies of Grief," April 17, 1920.
The Wisconsin Alumni Magazine, Madison, Wisconsin, November, 1923.
Zanesville Times Recorder, Zanesville, Ohio, "WWI Anniversary Kindles Memories for City's 'Yankee Doodle Dandies,'" June 26, 1977.
U.S. Army Monographs
Boyd, Capt. Leonard R. "The Operations of the 1st Battalion, 16th Infantry, in the Second Phase of the Meuse-Argonne." The Infantry School, Company Officers' Course, Fort Benning, Georgia, 1924-1925.
Cochrane, Rexmond C. "The 1st Division Along the Meuse, 1-12 October 1918."

Gas Warfare in World War I, Study Number 8, US Army Chemical Corps Historical Studies. U.S. Army Chemical Corps Historical Office, Army Chemical Center, Maryland, 1957.

Cornish, Capt. George R. F. "The Operations of the First Division (U.S.) in the Third Phase of the Meuse-Argonne." The Infantry School, Company Officers' Course, Fort Benning, Georgia, 1924-1925.

—. "The Twenty-Sixth Infantry (U.S.) in the Meuse-Argonne Offensive." The Command and General Staff School, Fort Leavenworth, Kansas, 1931.

Forster, Capt. George J. "Operations of the 37-mm Gun Platoon, 26th Infantry, 1st Division, October 1-12, 1918." The Infantry School, Advanced Course, Fort Benning, Georgia, 1931-1932.

Frasier, Capt. Lyman S. "Operations of the Third Battalion, 26th Infantry, First Division, in the Second and Third Phases of the Meuse-Argonne Offensive." The Infantry School, Fort Benning, Georgia, 1926-27.

Gates, Maj. Oscar I. "The Operations of the Seventh Field Artillery, First Division, in the Meuse-Argonne Offensive, 1 October - 11 November, 1918." Command and General Staff School, Fort Leavenworth, Kansas, n.d.

Helsley, Capt. Albert B. "Operations of the Machine Gun Company, 16th Infantry (1st Division), During the Second Phase of the Meuse Argonne Offensive, September 30 - October 12, 1918." The Infantry School, Advanced Course, Fort Benning, Georgia, 1930-1931.

Hodgson, Maj. P. A. "A Critical Analysis of the Infantry Scheme of Maneuver of the 1st Division at the Battle of St. Mihiel." Command and General Staff School, Fort Leavenworth, Kansas, n. d.

Legge, Capt. Barnwell R. "The First Division in the Meuse Argonne. September 26 - October 12, 1918." The Infantry School, Fort Benning, Georgia, 1922-1923.

McClure, Maj. Walter R. "Operations of Company M, 26th Infantry (1st Division) in the St. Mihiel Offensive, September 12 – September 16, 1918." The Infantry School, Advanced Course, 1932-1933, Fort Benning, Georgia.

Stiness, Maj. Henry W. "The Evacuation of Prisoners by the First Division in the Meuse Argonne Offensive." Command and General Staff School, Fort Leavenworth, Kansas, 1932.

INDEX

F

G

H

J

K

L

M

N

O

P

R

S

T

V

W

Y

American Military Units

French Military Units

German Military Units